Ethnographies of Youth and Temporality

In the series *Global Youth*,
edited by Craig Jeffrey and Jane Dyson

Also in this series:

Martin Demant Frederiksen, *Young Men, Time, and Boredom in the Republic of Georgia*

Daniel Mains, *Hope Is Cut: Youth, Unemployment, and the Future in Urban Ethiopia*

Mary E. Thomas, *Multicultural Girlhood: Racism, Sexuality, and the Conflicted Spaces of American Education*

Ethnographies of Youth and Temporality

Time Objectified

Edited by
Anne Line Dalsgård, Martin Demant Frederiksen,
Susanne Højlund, and Lotte Meinert

Afterword by Michael G. Flaherty

TEMPLE UNIVERSITY PRESS   PHILADELPHIA

TEMPLE UNIVERSITY PRESS
Philadelphia, Pennsylvania 19122
www.temple.edu/tempress

Copyright © 2014 by Temple University
All rights reserved
Published 2014

Library of Congress Cataloging-in-Publication Data
Ethnographies of youth and temporality : time objectified / [edited by] Anne Line Dalsgård . . . [et al.].
    pages cm. — (Global youth)
  Includes bibliographical references and index.
  ISBN 978-1-4399-1066-5 (cloth : alk. paper) —
ISBN 978-1-4399-1068-9 (e-book)   1. Youth—Cross-cultural studies.   2. Adolescent psychology—Cross-cultural studies.
3. Time—Cross-cultural studies.   I. Dalsgård, Anne Line, 1960–
  GN483.E75 2014
  305.235—dc23
                                                    2013019895

∞ The paper used in this publication meets the requirements of the American National Standard for Information Sciences—Permanence of Paper for Printed Library Materials, ANSI Z39.48-1992

Printed in the United States of America

2 4 6 8 9 7 5 3 1

Contents

Introduction: Time Objectified
• MARTIN DEMANT FREDERIKSEN AND ANNE LINE DALSGÅRD   1

1. Waiting for the Start: *Flexibility and the Question of Convergence*
• JENNIFER JOHNSON-HANKS   23

2. Stunted Future: Buryong *among Young Men in Manila*
• STEFFEN JENSEN   41

3. Aske's Dead Time: *An Exploration of the Qualities of Time among Left-Radical Activists in Denmark* • STINE KRØIJER   57

4. Heterochronic Atmospheres: *Affect, Materiality, and Youth in Depression* • MARTIN DEMANT FREDERIKSEN   81

5. Standing Apart: *On Time, Affect, and Discernment in Nordeste, Brazil* • ANNE LINE DALSGÅRD   97

6. Certificates for the Future: *Geographical Mobility and Educational Trajectories among Nepalese Youth* • KAREN VALENTIN   117

7. The Normativity of Boredom: *Communication Media Use among Romanian Teenagers* • RĂZVAN NICOLESCU   139

8. Making a Name: *Young Musicians in Uganda Working on the Future*
   • LOTTE MEINERT AND NANNA SCHNEIDERMANN   153

Afterword • MICHAEL G. FLAHERTY   175

Contributors   191

Index   193

Ethnographies of Youth and Temporality

Introduction
Time Objectified

MARTIN DEMANT FREDERIKSEN AND
ANNE LINE DALSGÅRD

This book takes as its point of departure a recognition that time is materialized and social. It seeps into every twist and turn of life and affects the perception of the moment—a phenomenon that, when felt as boring or as not leading in the right direction, may motivate reconsideration and change. People may choose to work on time to change their bleak prospects or the uncertainty of not knowing where to go. They may choose to anchor time in objects that represent the life they wish for themselves, thus turning these objects into affirmations of the realization of their hopes and longings. And they may experience bad times as dreadfully absorbing, not being able to drag themselves out of the depression and lack of possibility that are transmitted.

There are many matters of time: a pomegranate, prison walls, cell phones, a name, an Argentinean football T-shirt, a never-finished building, travel documents, a birth certificate, a novel in a place where literature is rare, a shouting crowd, a dead body, statistics, and a music CD. In this book we argue that such matters of time can be worked with, on, or against to change who and where one is. "The present, not the future, is ours," John Dewey writes (1957: 194), and confusion and uncertainty in relation to present activities are the occasion for deliberate action. The young people whom we focus on are caught up in situations that necessitate either reflection or action, and our interest centers on the temporal aspects of their efforts. Ideas about rational choice have been widely contested in the social sciences, but without disregarding the critique of the notion of the rational agent, we argue that a certain kind of rationality is at play in the lives we describe—rationality in the sense proposed by William James: for the individual actors, their choices and actions provide a feeling of sufficiency in the present and banish uncertainty from the future (cited in Barbalet 1998: 47). At the core of this rationality is the force and logic of emotion and the effects materiality can have. This book is thus an investigation into the experience of time as an often-troubling, external factor in life, as well as the concomitant emotional unrest and the perhaps innovative acts motivated by it. In the following sections we expand further on our focus—time objectified as seen through the prism of youth—and the contributions to anthropological understandings of time that we hope our work will offer. We then provide a short summary of the chapters and a condensation of some of the central themes of the book. We do not offer definite conclusions but do indicate questions for further research.

Time and Youth

Our approach to time breaks with the idea of time as an independently progressing lawfulness. As a heuristic device we bracket Newtonian time and look into the conditions that make the experience of time stand out. We concur with those who see time as a constitutive dimension of social life (Fabian 1983: 24) and an inherent part of practice in the sense that "practice is not in time but makes time" (Bourdieu 2000: 206). But ours is not an interest in time as naturally incorporated in practice as much as it is an attention toward time as a figure standing out in experience. Daylight and darkness, the biological functioning of the body, clock time, institutional schedules, rising and falling levels on the stock market, and public policies all constitute markers of time, informed by social and cultural notions and not necessarily working in harmony (James and Mills 2005: 13). Often they are perceived as natural and social givens that must be adhered to if one wants to survive. But sometimes conformity is not possible.

There are occasions that might make individuals stop, perhaps step back, and realize that something has changed. That the wind is changing, that a bird portends the coming of a new season, that a bodily function is not what it used to be, that a year has suddenly passed or perhaps just an hour. Often such realizations of the presence of time in one's life do not pose a problem; they merely form part of our knowledge that this is the way life is: time passes. But time may pass too slowly or too quickly, or a feeling of temporal discontinuity or exclusion from the time of others may arise. Biological age and social status may diverge, as when grey hair troubles a young man while he is still living with his parents and has no prospects for change. What is at stake when the realization of time becomes troublesome? Finding oneself incapable of following the timing of society may radically challenge one's sense of agency. Feeling passive and receptive opposes the very idea we carry of the beings we wish to be—an inherently modern idea of humans as active and in control (Hansen 2011; Jackson 1998). And feeling time as empty and slow, without attraction of any kind, opposes the expectation of excitement that is inherent in consumer society (Bauman 1998). When it emerges as something in itself time has to be worked on and resisted.

In this book, we probe the question of troublesome time through the prism of youth. Although young people are not the only ones to experience time as a problem, the category of youth offers a particularly sharp lens through which to explore how matters of time affect daily life. "Youth" as a category is often temporally defined as a transitory period between childhood and adulthood, and hence young people are often forced to reckon with the future in relation to their present social positions (cf. Cole and Durham 2008). Ideas of proper and improper transition dominate much thinking about youth, and cultural constructions of social problems, like early school dropouts, teenage pregnancies, and youth gangs, are the result of such thinking. In Recife, where Anne Line Dalsgård has worked, expectations regarding young people's orientation toward the future are influenced by middle-class lifestyles, and consequently, young people from low-income families cannot move forward as expected and are often cast as problematic and at risk. Even better-off young people experience frustration and uncertainty, as they cannot always follow the script of transition mapping out a linear and unbroken movement from private schools to university, job, and family (Dalsgård, Franch, and Scott 2008). Where Victor Turner once looked at initiation rites as sound mechanisms for the incorporation of young people into adult society (1970, 1995), today we may see this transition more as a dominant idea than an actual practice. However, it is an idea that powerfully structures the lives of young people and that carries connotations of control and continuity.

In the context of global social, political, and economic changes, continuity seems to have become an increasing problem for young people all over the world. The United Nations World Youth Report (2005) emphasizes that globalization, the rapid development of information and communication technologies, the HIV/AIDS epidemic, and armed conflicts are factors that increasingly affect young people's lives and create extensive social marginalization. For young people affected by these events, the future is uncertain and not immediately controllable (Bauman 1998; see also Vigh

2006). Nations have particular interests in youths in this category in that they are seen as being threatened by detrimental patterns (Ejrnæs 2006) that could make them potentially dangerous. Simultaneously, somewhere else, a celebration of the playfulness of youth makes labor and responsibility less attractive and, in fact, worrisome for the individual who wishes to uphold a sense of youthfulness or a lack of contamination, as we see among, for instance, left-wing activists in Western societies (see Chapter 3). These tendencies seem to be opposite; however, we may see both as part of a widespread disruption of any naturalness related to the passage to adulthood.

In recent years, a growing body of anthropological literature has explored the relationship between youth and time, mainly with reference to the question of the future (Amit and Dyck 2011; Cole 2010; Cole and Durham 2008; Christiansen, Utas, and Vigh 2006; Frederiksen 2013; Jeffrey 2008; 2010; Jensen 2008; Meinert 2009; Valentin, Dalsgård, and Hansen 2008). In their introduction to *Figuring the Future*, Jennifer Cole and Deborah Durham rightly note that much literature on youth has tended to analytically privilege space over time as space emerges in ideas about "scapes," mobility, global flows, and geographical marginality. Although such foci are not unimportant, they argue, "most current analyses fail to take sufficient account of the temporal nature of youth and childhood" (2008: 5). Taking up the challenge posed by Cole and Durham, we explore time as a troublesome figure in young people's lives, but more than that, we ask what an anthropology of youth has to offer to wider anthropological theorizing on time.

We argue that a focus on how time becomes objectified in the lives of young people allows us to broach the study of time in anthropology in relation to subjects such as boredom, waiting, inactivity, subjunctivity, and inertia on an everyday level. Although a few authors have recently worked on these and related issues (e.g., Jeffrey 2010; Musharbash 2007; Whyte 2002), these are themes that generally remain neglected in anthropological theorizing and have yet to be viewed in a comparative perspective. We provide a cross-cultural comparison of how time emerges in everyday life with contributions from the Philippines, Brazil, Romania, Uganda, Nepal, Denmark, Georgia, Cameroon, and the United States.

Analytical Topics to Be Addressed

The premise that action and experience are intimately connected with questions of time has a long history in the social sciences. From the early years of the twentieth century onward, sociologists, philosophers, and psychologists heatedly debated questions of intentionality and cause and effect in relation to the notion of time. Some of the foremost thinkers of the twentieth century, such as William James (1842–1910), George Herbert Mead (1863–1931), Martin Heidegger (1889–1976), and Alfred Schütz (1899–1959), dealt with this issue in much of their writing (Flaherty 2011). Their thoughts have lately reemerged in several anthropological studies of time. Indeed, time as an object of anthropological analysis has become prominent in recent years. Although it has been an important element in many classic anthropological studies of social change, tradition, and historicity, as well as in the development of praxis theory (Dalsgaard and Nielsen 2013; Hodges 2008b), studies that in various ways make time a constitutive part of analysis have recently multiplied (e.g., Birth 2008; Crapanzano 2004; Das 2007; Gell 1992; Guyer and Lambin 2007; Ingold 2000; James and Mills 2005; Miyazaki 2004; Ssorin-Chaikov 2006). It is widely agreed in these studies that multiple temporalities coexist and that time (or temporalities) frame social life.

As Matt Hodges argues, recent anthropological writings on time have tended to focus on notions of "flow," "flux," "tempo," "rhythm," "process," and "fluidity" (2008b: 400; 2008a). This renders time a constitutive element of social life, but as already pointed out above, it fails to describe situations in which such flows are broken. Ours will be an exploration of the experiences of temporal impasse, where boredom or hopelessness stands out, and the means young people employ to work on it.

Overwhelmed by Time

Pierre Bourdieu put time at the forefront of analysis in his development of practice theory (e.g., 1977, 1990, 2000). Time, he writes, usually passes unnoticed, as people are immersed in the games of the world and their "forth-coming," or things anticipated. However, when there is discrepancy between what is anticipated and the logic of the game, the engagement with the practical sense of the forth-coming of the world gives way to time objectified, and relations to time such as waiting, impatience, regret, nostalgia, boredom, or discontent come into being (Bourdieu 2000: 206). But as Maria Louw rightly notes, despite putting time at the forefront, Bourdieu does not grant these objectified relations to time much attention and therefore does not see their significance as social phenomena (Louw 2007: 141). Louw traces this to a general downplaying of consciousness, abstraction, and reflexivity in Bourdieu's work in the sense that actors are granted little opportunity to reflect on their conditions of existence (192). Because actors for Bourdieu are so deeply immersed in the field, anticipations of and adjustments to the forthcoming are done on the spot, in the twinkle of an eye, in the heat of the moment, "in conditions which exclude distance, perspective, detachment and reflection" (12). Although there is much to be learned from Bourdieu's work on time, his distinction between the real world and the imaginary overlooks the importance of situations in which individuals are forced to reckon with this gap or where the gap, or rather objectified relations to time, is what constitutes everyday life. Although the anthropological toolbox is thus well equipped in terms of describing people's actions, it is less well equipped when it comes to approaching the inaction experienced in troubled times.

Referring also to Bourdieu's work on time, Michael Jackson has described childbirth and death as instances when we are "thrown" in a temporal sense, as nothing seems to exist outside these events as they take place (Jackson 2007: 206). In such instances a feeling of outrage can arise over "the outside world . . . still going about its business, keeping up with schedules and timetables, indifferent to our struggles for life, oblivious to our pain." Yet in the moments following a birth or a death, people will begin to reclaim the autonomy they felt they had lost and return to the world that was momentarily lost (207). However, such returns are not always possible, and at times they are even kept at bay. As the chapters in this book make clear, temporal tension can be a staging ground leading to new forms of creativity and action, but it can just as well involve apathy, inactivity, and passivity.

Figure and Ground: The Case of Boredom

"Everyday life" may be an elusive and diffuse category, as what we label "everyday life" exists only as a background condition against which particular events stand out (Lewis 2000: 539). The same may be said about an objectified relation to time such as boredom. Only because something stands out as interesting do we know that a lack of interest exists. However, boredom may also be the figure (not the ground) we focus on. For many of the young people described in this volume, boredom is one of the most prominent characteristics of their lives. It attracts their thoughts, worries, and self-criticisms, as they know life should be different—exciting and in movement. A leading characteristic of boredom is stillness, problematic stillness, but for stillness to be experienced as problematic, movement has to be expected.

Routines and repetitions are not necessarily boring. People may work on the same assembly line day after day and not find it boring. Observations of people with jobs high in repetitive tasks and low in complexity show that socially fulfilling relationships may prevent the workers from experiencing monotony (Bauman 1998: 40). It could thus be that the experience of boredom is "in the eye of the beholder," as Peter Conrad puts it, because "what may be boring to one person may be fascinating to another. Boredom is not a characteristic of an object, event or person, but exists only in the relationship between individuals and their interpretation of their experience" (1997: 465). But as several of the contributions to this volume show, the eye of the beholder is intersubjectively constituted: all perspectives are informed by culture and social norms, and it may be impossible to keep up the standards of those around one when standards of the good life are set and constantly raised, far away from one and one's companions (see also Bauman 1998: 40; Højlund, Dalsgård, Frederiksen, and Meinert 2011).

If the good life in present-day societies is to a large degree cast in terms of excitement and constant choice and renewal, as Bauman finds, *the quality of time itself*, not the product of its use, becomes the figure to be evaluated. If time is found to be without the appropriate quality, we may wish to make it disappear or quickly pass. Boredom is linked to this way of seeing time as something that has to be passed rather than as a horizon for opportunities (Svendsen 2005: 23). But as Hans-Georg Gadamer asks, "What is actually passed when passing time? Not time, surely, that passes? And yet it is time that is meant, in its empty lastingness, but which as *something* that lasts is too long and assumes the form of painful boredom" (quoted in Svendsen 2005: 23). When foregrounded as *something*, time is problematic, at least if a socially accepted purpose of enduring time is not at hand.

Routine may even be a potential site of meaning and agency, as in tai chi, for instance, in which routine is treated "as the very ground of consciousness and as a technical means to maintain an alert and reflexive orientation towards the world" (Slater 2009: 223). The practice of tai chi involves the repetition of a series of small moves. In the beginning these are mechanically reproduced, but over time they are done with deeper and deeper awareness of the changes that are taking place in the muscles, balance, and breathing. Tai chi may be boring to some; for others its repetition and lastingness is a deeply meaningful practice. The crucial question is whether there is a purpose beyond the actual practice—that is, if through my awareness of the immediate present, I can see a larger whole to which I add my small part. If I am not allowed to contribute to the world around me, repetition means standing still, eternally returning to the now.

Routine may therefore lead to resignation and loss of interest, but if nothing more is expected this can be accepted and compensated for. If, for instance, a repetitive activity leads to a remunerative end (for instance, piecework; see Barbalet 1998: 640), it may be meaningful despite being tedious. Thus, in *Righteous Dopefiend* (2009), Philippe Bourgois and Jeff Schonberg refer to an interview with the young man Carter, a San Francisco drug addict who has just gotten himself a legitimate job after a life of criminal activity. When Carter states that he is "in a way . . . bored," Bourgois asks whether *working as such* is boring, and Carter answers, "No. It's not boring to work, right, but if I had a motherfuckin' dental plan, a benefit package, a credit union, and all of that . . . no motherfucker could pull me from my job. I'd be working twenty-four/seven, with all the overtime I could get" (2009: 163). That Carter does not earn enough to live a decent life makes him bored with his job, whereas the capacity to live with a dental plan and the like would make any toil meaningful to him.

When society changes from being guided by an ethic of work and production to being ruled by the aesthetics of consumption, toiling loses its meaning, as it does not enhance one's capacity to consume (Bauman 1998). It feels as if it is a waste of time, as time was meant for more. *This*, not the hard work itself, may be deeply boring or create a sense of discontent.

Boredom is an active discomfort—that is, an emotion rather than a complex of emotions such as anxiety, anger, disappointment, or hopelessness. When boredom springs forth as the figure, not the ground, it is present as an absence. Indeed, as Conrad notes, "it would be difficult to experience boredom unless we anticipated the possibility of something else" (1997: 468). Boredom is only explicable in terms of the fact that something is "not-yet" (Anderson 2004: 750). This "not-yet" may open up an overwhelming gap of meaninglessness, if whatever is absent is experienced as never coming into being, perhaps because "values and circumstances fail to correspond, when ways of being in the world and the world . . . are coming together in a meaningless fit" (Musharbash 2007: 315). Indeed, as Martin Demant Frederiksen has shown in his study of time and marginality among young men in the Republic of Georgia, such meaningless fits—or objectified relations to time, as we call them here—can come to constitute the very core of individual experience, rather than something that merely stands out momentarily. Sometimes what does not come together may just be the biological aging of one's body and the lack of possible routes to adulthood in one's present situation. Something as simple and concrete as a pair of grey hairs may epitomize the problem—that is, growing old in one sense while remaining young in another (2013).

In different ways the chapters in this book focus on time as a troubling figure and the emotional and often existential effects it has in young people's lives. However, we also claim that the background—the everyday, the easiness and casualness—should be taken into account to fully understand the situations and efforts we describe. It may be that life is difficult for many of the young people we write about, but exactly because life is also more than that, it is possible to work on time.

Acting on Time

The agentic dimension of social action should be seen as a temporally embedded process (see Emirbayer and Mische 1998: 963; Mische 2009). We act on the present while acting on the future, and vice versa, at times even to change the past (see Mattingly 1998). When everything runs smoothly we may dream and imagine a splendid future for ourselves, but only when this imagined self, with its innate promises of agency and rationality, is contested and threatened by the present do we act deliberately (Dewey 1957: 194). But if our experience of time reflects both desires and circumstances (or agency and structure), then how, asks Michael Flaherty (2011: 3), do people try to alter or customize various dimensions of their temporal experience and resist external sources of temporal constraint or structure? How do people themselves make time more concrete? In his work on what he calls "the textures of time," Flaherty describes different forms of "time work"—that is, "the intrapersonal and interpersonal effort directed toward producing or preventing various temporal experiences" (11).

Some individuals or groups find themselves somehow separated from the time of society, but as several chapters in this volume make clear, this does not necessarily mean that they are left in complete passivity. Although, for instance, the future can be a burdensome presence in daily life for some young people, as the horizons ahead cannot necessarily be crossed (see Jackson 2007: xviii; Sneath, Holbraad, and Pedersen 2009: 10), the future can also be an open field of possibilities. The mere fact that it has not happened yet makes it fertile ground for the imagination. As David Sneath, Martin Holbraad, and Morten A. Pedersen write, if we accept that imagination is pervasive in all human apprehension and can be studied empirically as an outcome more than a "holistic backdrop that conditions human activities" (2009: 19), we have a key to an understanding of much of the activity written about in this volume. The outcome of various processes of imagination is, as they write, underdetermined by the environment that brings it about and, hence, playful in character.

When the Romanian teenagers that Răzvan Nicolescu describes send text messages on their mobile phones instead of an instant message on the Internet, they play with the (relative) slowness of the phone system, which extends the waiting for an answer. When the young woman Evinha in Dalsgård's study shows up for a job interview she was never invited for, she plays with the possibility that she will be hired. And when the activists presented in Stine Krøijer's chapter provoke the police by their peaceful demonstration, they play with chance and the likelihood of a violent response to call forth exactly the situation that confirms their picture of the relationship between activists and police. In all three cases, nothing is fully conditioned; it may turn out in one way or another, but the important thing is the open-endedness of the situation, not the secure outcome.

In the chapters of this volume we describe both victories and defeats, but more than anything else, we highlight the indeterminacy of the lives we describe. We, the anthropologists (and markedly within youth studies), tend to become the judges of whether the hopes of our informants should be deemed prospective or deceptive. Or we tend to write analyses that are either too pessimistic or too optimistic, because we wish to determine the future or come to terms with it in a very literal sense (Dalsgård and Frederiksen 2013). We cannot tell how things will turn out. Indeterminacy is therefore also a condition for our writing, a fact that is addressed differently in the chapters constituting this book.

Overview of the Chapters

In Chapter 1, Jennifer Johnson-Hanks explores waiting as a state of "suspended action" that is often experienced by young people who finish school without having any plans or prospects for the future. How, she asks, do young people make a living and make a meaningful life under these conditions? In comparing empirical data from her fieldwork in, respectively, Cameroon and the United States, she shows how the activities, constraints, and aspirations of contemporary, young, college-educated American women have come to resemble those of the Cameroonian elite of a decade ago. Young Americans have begun to objectify and relate to time in the same way as Cameroonians in making uncertainty, flexibility, and the suspension of planning a new normal. This, she argues, is a contrast to the widely held assumption that global convergence will eventually lead young people in poorer countries to lead lives increasingly similar to youth from the richer North.

In Chapter 2, Steffen Jensen describes the confinement of young marginalized members of brotherhoods in the Philippines as even more concrete, as many of them have been imprisoned. In prison one's own time stands still, while the rest of society outside prison moves on. The brotherhoods define the local idiom of *buryong*, which is a particular form of boredom. *Buryong* is a "dark passenger," a despair or sense of aloneness carried on the shoulders that always threatens to take over. *Buryong* or boredom as a way of being in time stands out here almost as a bodily symptom. Once free, outside the prison walls, the young men's *buryong* is even more difficult to handle because they are then surrendered to their own passivity—there is no excuse for not doing something other than that they are not able to. *Buryong*, writes Jensen, becomes a symptom of a present projected hopelessly into the future.

Chapter 3, Stine Krøijer's contribution, illuminates how left radical activists in Scandinavia perceive their own activities and the quality of the time in between large spectacular protest events. She shows how public discourse in Scandinavia tends to classify activists as young, implying that they are not considered to be fully fledged political citizens and leading to their being relegated to a position of waiting until their views and actions in public are taken seriously. Krøijer demonstrates how some activists perceive capitalism as an all-encompassing system with no point of transcendence, leaving little hope for the future. She borrows the phrase "dead time" from an activist protest video to describe the bodily experience of being stuck in somebody else's world.

In Chapter 4, Martin Demant Frederiksen considers governmental material constructions in the Republic of Georgia that are built to signify particular futures. However, as he shows, these objectifications of time often came to signify times other than the ones they were intended to, creating what he terms a "heterochronic atmosphere"—that is, the sensation that multiple and often contradictory temporalities coexist in the urban sphere, making uncertain both what the future was and who was part of it. This was particularly true in the groups of young men Frederiksen conducted fieldwork with, who continually used the notions of boredom and being in depression to depict their situation, despite being surrounded by images of the future. The story of a pomegranate given to Josef Stalin is used to convey the notion of a heterochronic atmosphere.

In Chapter 5, Anne Line Dalsgård looks into specific ways of talking about life perspectives, opportunities, and emotional attitudes toward the future of young people in a low-income neighborhood in northeast Brazil. She discusses time as a flow of events that stir up affects and tends to swallow up subjective hopes and desires in boredom, depression, disillusionment, or anger. However, she argues, the experience of affects may also constitute a potential for change. Thus, the objectification of time is understood here as a distancing (and detachment) from events and dominant affects, where societal time is no longer an active force in the face of which one is a victim. Instead it is an object to be observed and, if an opportunity arises, to be acted on.

In Chapter 6, Karen Valentin examines the role of certificates among young Nepalese migrants. Migration within Nepal and from Nepal to India has been a common practice for young Nepalese males for generations and plays an important role in their transition to adulthood. Through ethnographic insights gained from working with Nepalese people in Nepal, India, and Denmark over the last fifteen years, Valentin sheds light on the relationship between geographical trajectories and ideas of futurity through a specific focus on documents as material manifestations of objectified time, which circumscribe young people's ideas of the possible and the impossible.

In Chapter 7, Razvan Nicolescu explores boredom in relation to communication technologies and practices within a group of Romanian teenagers. Nicolescu shows how, through the use of communication media such as computers and cell phones, teenagers practice their subjectivities inside particular private spaces that are far away from the surveillance of parents or teachers. In doing so, they transform their experiences of boredom from a solitary experience into a social and meaningful practice. This, writes Nicolescu, does not render boredom completely unproblematic. However, it endows time spent alone with a certain social meaning.

In Chapter 8, Lotte Meinert and Nanna Schneidermann examine practices of creating a name among young male artists in Uganda as a specific kind of time work that objectifies and appropriates wished-for personal and social futures. The authors analyze the giving and taking of names as processes of condensing time. By taking artists' names, they argue, the young men break the rule that it is usually others who name a person. In naming themselves, the musicians try to project their own dreams on to the future in a realm of possibility that is defined not by kinship, tribe, or denomination but by popular culture and depends on an audience and fans who make them what they propose themselves to be.

Themes of This Volume

The chapters of the book overlap thematically in their descriptions of objectified time. In this final section, we present some of the themes that emerge when the chapters are viewed in a comparative light. We present our contributions within three overall frameworks: the time of the times, being outside time, and time work as relational.

The Time of the Times

Occurrences, events, and circumstances can be ascribed to the times we live in; they can be said to be symptoms of our times. But what is our time, or rather, what kind of time (or quality of time) is inherent in and constitutes particular societal contexts? Certain ideas of time, shaping both practice and expectation, are historically embedded in specific periods. As several authors have argued, these ideas are not necessarily consistent, in the sense that multiple temporalities can coexist within particular frames (e.g., Gell 1992; Krøijer 2011; Shove, Trentmann, and Wilk 2009; Ssorin-Chaikov 2006). One such frame may be that of modernity. While modernity can be seen (or experienced) as a period that has allowed humanity an increased sense of choice and rationality, it can also be seen (or experienced) as a period in which society has trapped individuals "into an ever-increasing pace of forced routine, that industrial lives are built around the careful choreography of simultaneous rhythms which exhaust and drain us" (Wilk 2009: 146). Although these two situations represent extremes, their coexistence can help explain why modernity allows both boredom and activity.

Qualities of time can be modeled by ideological or religious principles. The former is exemplified in this volume by Krøijer's chapter on young left-wing political activists and the question of capitalism and by Frederiksen's chapter on the ideas of time inherent in the ideological foundations of the Soviet state. Another example of a societal configuration of time is that of living in a post-something context—that is, living in a society that is held to have moved away from something else, be it war or a political regime. Johnson-Hanks takes this up in her chapter on postwar Cameroon. Here crisis has become endemic rather than being an isolated period. Rather than being something people move through, it has become something people move in (see Vigh 2008: 5). As Johnson-Hanks shows, this creates particular ways of relating to the future. In Cameroon, for instance, "flexibility" was widely invoked by her young informants in the 1990s as a result of the uncertain circumstances that surrounded them. Interestingly, as she further shows, the same word gained prominence in the United States in colloquial speech and commercials in post–financial crisis United States. In a Taussigian manner, in both places flexibility has become a mode of "ordering disorder" (Taussig 1992: 17).

Political language in crisis and postcrisis contexts is often infused with temporal metaphors. It is, for instance, no wonder that Barack Obama's rhetoric of hope was so forceful during the U.S. election campaign in 2008 as a counter to the increasing financial crisis. While such political language can be both useful and forceful in specific periods, it being forceful depends on change actually coming into being. In Chapter 4, Frederiksen shows how a political rhetoric of hope in another "post" context, post-Soviet Georgia, has turned into a stalemate. Here, being "post" does not necessarily entail being on the way to somewhere else; for some groups of young people, it is equally likely to entail the experience of being stuck (see Pedersen and Højer 2008). Frederiksen has elsewhere referred to this as being "haunted by time"—that is, being affected by the eerie and stubborn presence of times that were supposed to be past but that somehow remain present (2013: 6). Hence, where in one setting (Cameroon) we see the emergence of the notion of flexibility among young people as a way of experiencing temporal tensions, in another (Georgia) we see the emergence of depression. This highlights the importance of considering context not just as a particular sociohistorical configuration but also as a temporal one where time takes on certain meanings and where the societal construction of time can in various ways become problematic to certain individuals and groups. The question of particular historical times (or moments in time) thus stands out in several chapters as an important aspect of individuals' and groups' perceptions not just *of* time but also of their position *in* time.

The question of youth becomes particularly immanent in this relation. For one thing, societal scripts and dominant ideas of time in understanding, for instance, the passage from youth to adulthood can clash with the actual experience of young people (Dalsgård, Franch, and Scott 2008). For another, the time of the times is not necessarily experienced in the same manner by different generations. As Maurice Merleau-Ponty observes, "What we call disorder and ruin, others who are younger live as the natural order of things; and perhaps with ingenuity they are going to master it precisely because they no longer seek their bearings where we took ours" (Merleau-Ponty 1964: 23). Similarly, in a much quoted article on generations, Karl Mannheim (1972) argues that particular generations interact with their surroundings in particular ways, a younger generation having the opportunity to experience the world anew (what Mannheim calls "fresh contact" [108]). This is not to say that young people have more agency than older generations but rather that they may experience things differently (see Jeffrey 2010: 185; Durham 2008). Hence, "the times we live in" are lived in and within different ways by different generations. For instance, a time representing order for an older generation may be perceived by a younger one as confinement. Conversely, a time can be seen by an older generation as one of chaos and sudden rupture, whereas for younger people it might be seen as a backdrop or a time of possibility. Such differences are not necessarily confined to generations but may also be played out among groups of youth who are each other's contemporaries or, as Krøijer demonstrates in her chapter, even within one person.

Considering time as context raises a series of important questions: How quickly is one's perception of time affected by social circumstances and contexts? How quickly is a crisis forgotten? How does inertia come into being?

How much do former times and narratives of the past that are retold in stories, sayings, and lullabies matter? How are temporal misfits created?

Being outside Time

The question of societal time, or perhaps more precisely, dominant ideas of time in society, raises the question of whether certain groups or individuals believe themselves to be part of these times (see Frederiksen 2013). Being outside time may be a spatial matter. As David Harvey argues in criticizing capitalism's geographical developments of urban space, spatial form controls temporality by building geographical landscapes in its own image only to destroy them later to maintain its own dynamic of endless accumulation (2000: 177).

Constructions of what he calls "spaces of hope" may in unintended ways generate divisions, as this kind of spatial distribution of time inevitably leaves some groups behind as modernity or capitalism continues its push forward. In effect, urban space is actively implicated in creating context-dependent meanings, constituting physical, social, and moral frames that condition young people's opportunities and restrictions (Valentin, Dalsgård, and Hansen 2008). We see this in the Brazilian context described by Dalsgård, where young men from the poorer areas of the city provoke immediate suspicion when they leave their neighborhoods. They are routinely stopped in the street by the police, some people cross the road when they see them, and drivers waiting for a red light may close their windows if they see these young men nearby. In Batumi, Georgia, the young men with whom Frederiksen experienced the town avoided the conspicuous fountains in the city center, perceiving them as false and deceitful depictions of what the city, in their eyes, really was.

But being outside time in a spatial manner may also be more concrete, as described in, for instance, Jensen's chapter on young, imprisoned criminals in the Philippines. In the confines of prison one is removed from the time of the surrounding society. But as Jensen shows through the notion of *buryong*, this is both a spatial *and* a bodily matter, as the experience of being in a different time is something people carry with and even in themselves. Similarly, in Krøijer's chapter on left-wing activists in Denmark, we see how the experience of dead time stands out as a kind of solitude and shows how symptoms of time (whether dead time or *buryong*) hurt when one is alone. Johnson-Hanks describes time as a holding pattern. She distinguishes between the waiting for a beginning and the waiting for an ending and notes how some activities create time, whereas others do not. In Nicolescu's contribution we see how teenagers use technologies such as mobile phones and the Internet to declare publicly to friends that they are bored, hoping that this will lead to an exchange of text messages or chat or a real-life activity. Sending out the message "I am boooored . . . ," they try to overcome the restlessness and isolation associated with the boring situation. A like kind of emotion work takes place among the young men in Dalsgård's study. Living in a low-income neighborhood, where boredom and depression are common responses to the lack of interesting prospects, they keep themselves aloof from the temptation of pessimism by supporting each other and orienting themselves toward the future.

Time Work as Relational

While certainty is often held to be pivotal in terms of planning ahead, knowing the future or at least having a relatively clear idea of it is not necessarily attractive, leading possibly to resignation but also to alternative modes of action (see Lindquist 2005). The young people in Dalsgård's contribution know very well that the day is likely to be one of downswing and disappointment. It is exactly the certainty that nothing will happen that makes them seek to do or to be prepared for something else (see also Dalsgård and Frederiksen 2013). The question of flexibility raised by Johnson-Hanks similarly conveys a situation of actively maintaining the position of availability to chance. Flexibility appears here as a particular management of time or, in other words, a particular attitude toward circumstances. As Jackson notes (2004), one can change the given into the chosen by telling the story about what has happened in a particular way. This becomes evident in Nicolescu's chapter, in which teenagers actively make use of being bored. As Nicolescu argues, by being shared, boredom in itself gains a social ethics and becomes a mode of activity. Here, we see how the introduction of new technologies allows new types of arrangements, potential spaces, and imagined times to become possible—one can, for instance, sit alone with others on the Internet.

In Meinert and Schneidermann's contribution on young musicians in Uganda, naming appears as a kind of time work. Seeking to become famed and respected musicians, the young men create artist names that are both ironic comments on their situation and expressions of who they want to be in the future. By acting as if it were so, the young men in Uganda seek to change the times they live in and become someone else, if only momentarily while they are on stage. This reveals how placing oneself outside the time of society can in some instances be an active position conducive of change. This ethnography points out that time work is often a relational matter.

As is the case with the Romanian teenagers described by Nicolescu, the young Ugandans might work on (and with) time on their own, but for their time work to work, it needs an audience or a form of recognition by others. Hence, overcoming time problems becomes a highly social and intersubjective activity.

Both recognition and trust are central issues in relation to various forms of time work. When several temporalities are at stake, how does one know what or whom to listen to? Does one trust official rhetoric promising a bright future in the long term? Does one trust the immediate signs contradicting these promises? Does one trust passing emotions of despair or the knowledge that in the end everything will be all right? What are the registers (emotional, social, symbolic, material, or technological) through which we can know the future and seek to influence it? These are some of the questions asked by several of the chapters in this volume.

A Challenge

In his book on the philosophy of boredom, Lars Svendsen quotes Georges Bernano's impressionistic lines: "[Boredom] is like some sort of dust. One comes and goes without seeing it, one breathes it, one eats it, one drinks it, and it is so fine that it doesn't even scrunch between one's teeth. But if one stops for a moment, it settles like a blanket over the face and the hands. One has to constantly shake this ash-rain off. That is why people are so restless" (Bernano quoted in Svendsen 2005: 14). Situations in which waiting, boredom, impatience, regret, nostalgia, or discontent is immanent in experience seem to be at stake for a growing number of young people around the world (Jeffrey 2010; Ehn and Löfgren 2000). This book explores such experiences by viewing young people in time and, in several chapters, also over time. The times they are in are social and societal as well as individual and existential, posing problems as well as possibilities, the settling dust creating both inertia and unrest.

Bringing attention to objectified relations to time raises questions as to the working of anthropology. For a discipline that often takes its vantage point in describing what people *do*, describing inactivity and passivity is a challenge. Likewise, for an analytical discipline like ours it may be a remote thought to take informants' insistence on openness and indeterminacy at face value. However, there may be ways of writing the experience of open-endedness or uncertainty into our analyses and allowing inactivity to be present. The chapters that follow take up this challenge, whether in relation to a pomegranate, a prison wall, cell phones, a name, or other matters of time, and while some show that creativity, agency, and action may be embedded in, for instance, ways of waiting or being bored, others present more sinister aspects of the role of time in the lives of global youth.

ACKNOWLEDGMENTS: *We thank our coeditors, Susanne Højlund and Lotte Meinert, for their input in writing this Introduction and the participants at the workshop Time Objectified, held in Aarhus in 2011. We are particularly grateful to Susanne Dybbroe, who provided vital criticisms, reflections, and suggestions for carving out the general themes of the book. We also extend a sincere thank-you to Michael Flaherty for agreeing to write the Afterword. The book is the result of a research project funded by the Danish Independent Research Council, Humanities.*

REFERENCES

Amit, Vered, and Noel Dyck. 2011. *Young Men in Times of Uncertainty*. London: Berghahn Books.

Anderson, Ben. 2004. "Time-Stilled Space Slowed: How Boredom Matters." *Geoforum* 35:739–754.

Barbalet, Jack. 1998. *Emotion, Social Theory, and Social Structure*. Cambridge: Cambridge University Press.

Bauman, Zygmunt. 1998. *Work, Consumerism and the New Poor*. Buckingham, UK: Open University Press.

Birth, Kevin. 2008. "The Creation of Coevalness and the Danger of Homochronism." *Journal of the Royal Anthropological Institute* 14 (1): 3–20.

Bourdieu, Pierre. 1977. *Outline of a Theory of Practice*. Cambridge: Cambridge University Press.

———. 1990. *The Logic of Practice*. Cambridge: Polity Press.

———. 2000. *Pascalian Meditations*. Cambridge: Polity Press.

Bourgois, Philippe, and Jeff Schonberg. 2009. *Righteous Dopefiend*. Berkeley: University of California Press.

Christiansen, Catrine, Mats Utas, and Henrik Vigh. 2006. *Navigating Youth, Generating Adulthood: Social Becoming in an African Context*. Uppsala, Sweden: Nordic Africa Institute.

Cole, Jennifer. 2010. *Sex and Salvation: Imagining the Future in Madagascar*. Chicago: University of Chicago Press.

Cole, Jennifer, and Deborah Durham. 2008. "Introduction." In *Figuring the Future: Globalization and the Temporalities of Children and Youth*, edited by Jennifer Cole and Deborah Durham, 3–23. Santa Fe, NM: School for Advanced Research Press.

Conrad, Peter. 1997. "It's Boring: Notes on the Meaning of Boredom in Everyday Life." *Qualitative Sociology* 20 (4): 465–475.

Crapanzano, Vincent. 2004. *Imaginative Horizons: An Essay in Literary-Philosophical Anthropology*. Chicago: University of Chicago Press.

Dalsgård, Anne Line, Monica Franch, and Russell Parry Scott. 2008. "Dominant Ideas, Uncertain Lives: The Meaning of Youth in Recife." In *Youth and the City in the Global South*, edited by Karen Tranberg Hansen, with Anne Line Dalsgård, Katherine Gough, Ulla M. Madsen, Karen Valentin, and Norbert Wildermuth, 49–73. Bloomington: Indiana University Press.

Dalsgård, Anne Line, and Martin Demant Frederiksen. 2013. "Out of Conclusion: On Recurrence and Open-Endedness in Life and Analysis." *Social Analysis* 57 (1): 50–63.

Dalsgaard, Steffen, and Morten Nielsen. 2013. "Introduction: Time and the Field." *Social Analysis* 57 (1): 1–19.

Das, Veena. 2007. *Life and Words: Violence and the Descent into the Ordinary*. Berkeley: University of California Press.

Dewey, John. 1957. *Human Nature and Conduct: An Introduction to Social Psychology*. New York: Modern Library.

Durham, Deborah. 2008. "Apathy and Agency: The Romance of Youth and Agency in Botswana." In *Figuring the Future: Globalization and the Temporalities of Children and Youth*, edited by Jennifer Cole and Deborah Durham, 151–178. Santa Fe, NM: School for Advanced Research Press.

Ehn, Billy, and Orvar Löfgren. 2000. *The Secret World of Doing Nothing*. Berkeley: University of California Press.

Ejrnæs, Morten. 2006. "Forskningperspektiver uden pointer: En kritisk vurdering af forskningsprogrammet om social arv." *Dansk Pædagogisk Tidsskrift* 1:28–65.

Emirbayer, Mustafa, and Ann Mische. 1998. "What Is Agency?" *American Journal of Sociology* 103 (4): 962–1023.

Fabian, Johannes. 1983. *Time and the Other: How Anthropology Makes Its Object*. New York: Columbia University Press.

Flaherty, Michael G. 2011. *The Textures of Time: Agency and Temporal Experience*. Philadelphia: Temple University Press.

Frederiksen, Martin Demant. 2013. *Young Men, Time, and Boredom in the Republic of Georgia*. Philadelphia: Temple University Press.

Gell, Alfred. 1992. *The Anthropology of Time*. Oxford: Berg.

Guyer, Jane, and Eric Lambin. 2007. "Time and African Land Use: Ethnography and Remote Sensing." Special issue, *Human Ecology* 35 (1).

Hansen, Thomas Blom. 2011. "Self Possessed: On the Unhomeliness of Modern Convictions." Paper presented at the conference "Futures in the Making: Youth, Conflict and Potentiality," Copenhagen, January 20–21.

Harvey, David. 2000. *Spaces of Hope*. Edinburgh: Edinburgh University Press.

Hodges, Matt. 2008a. *The Ethnography of Time: Living with History in Modern Rural France*. Queenston, Ontario: Mellen Press.

———. 2008b. "Rethinking Time's Arrow: Bergson, Deleuze and the Anthropology of Time." *Anthropological Theory* 8 (4): 399–429.

Højlund, Susanne, Anne Line Dalsgård, Martin Demant Frederiksen, and Lotte Meinert. 2011. "Well-Faring towards Uncertain Futures: A Comparative Perspective on Youth in Marginalised Positions." *Anthropology in Action* 18 (3): 45–56.

Ingold, Tim. 2000. *The Perception of the Environment*. London: Routledge.

Jackson, Michael. 1998. *Minima Ethnographica: Intersubjectivity and the Anthropological Project*. Chicago: University of Chicago Press.

———. 2004. *The Politics of Storytelling: Violence, Transgression, and Subjectivity*. Copenhagen: Museum Tusculanum Press.

———. 2007. *Excursions*. Durham, NC: Duke University Press.
James, Wendy, and David Mills. 2005. Introduction: From Representation to Action in the Flow of Time. In *The Qualities of Time: Anthropological Approaches*, edited by Wendy James and David Mills, 1–18. Oxford: Berg.
Jeffrey, Craig. 2008. "Waiting." *Environment and Planning* 26 (6): 954–958.
———. 2010. *Timepass: Youth, Class, and the Politics of Waiting in India*. Stanford, CA: Stanford University Press.
Jensen, Steffen. 2008. *Gangs, Politics, and Dignity in Cape Town*. Chicago: University of Chicago Press.
Krøijer, Stine. 2011. "Figurations of the Future: Forms and Temporalities of Left Radical Politics in Northern Europe." Ph.D. diss., University of Copenhagen.
Lewis, J. Lowell. 2000. "Sex and Violence in Brazil: *Carnaval, Capoeira*, and the Problem of Everyday Life. *American Ethnologist* 26 (3): 539–557.
Lindquist, Galina. 2005. *Conjuring Hope: Healing and Magic in Contemporary Russia*. London: Berghahn Books.
Louw, Maria. 2007. *Everyday Islam in Post-Soviet Central Asia*. London: Routledge.
Mannheim, Karl. 1972. "The Problem of Generations." In *The New Pilgrims: Youth Protest in Transition*, edited by P. Altbach and R. Laufer, 101–138. New York: David McKay.
Mattingly, Cheryl F. 1998. *Healing Dramas and Clinical Plots: The Narrative Structure of Experience*. Cambridge: Cambridge University Press.
Meinert, Lotte. 2009. *Hopes in Friction: Schooling, Health and Everyday Life in Uganda*. Charlotte, NC: Information Age.
Merleau-Ponty, Maurice. 1964. *Signs*. Evanston, IL: Northwestern University Press.
Mische, Ann. 2009. "Projects and Possibilities. Researching Futures in Action. *Sociological Forum* 24 (3): 694–704.
Miyazaki, Hirokazu. 2004. *The Method of Hope: Anthropology, Philosophy, and Fijian Knowledge*. Stanford, CA: Stanford University Press.
Musharbash, Yasmine. 2007. "Boredom, Time, and Modernity: An Example from Aboriginal Australia. *American Anthropologist* 109 (2): 307–317.
Pedersen, Morten Axel, and Lars Højer. 2008. "Lost in Transition: Fuzzy Property and Leaky Selves in Ulaanbaatar." *Ethnos* 73 (1): 73–96.
Shove, Elisabeth, Frank Trentmann, and Richard Wilk. 2009. "Introduction." In *Time, Consumption and Everyday Life: Practice, Materiality and Culture*, edited by Elisabeth Shove, Frank Trentman, and Richard Wilk, 1–13. Oxford: Berg.
Slater, Don. 2009. "The Ethics of Routine: Consciousness, Tedium and Value." In *Time, Consumption and Everyday Life: Practice, Materiality and Culture*, edited by Elisabeth Shove, Frank Trentman, and Richard Wilk, 217–230. Oxford: Berg.
Sneath, David, Martin Holbraad, and Morten Axel Pedersen. 2008. "Technologies of the Imagination: An Introduction." *Ethnos* 74 (1): 5–30.
Ssorin-Chaikov, Nikolai. 2006. "On Heterochrony: Birthday Gifts to Stalin, 1946." *Journal of the Royal Anthropological Institute* 12:355–375.
Svendsen, Lars. 2005. *A Philosophy of Boredom*. Chicago: University of Chicago Press.
Taussig, Michael. 1992. *The Nervous System*. New York: Routledge.
Turner, Victor. 1970. *The Forest of Symbols*. Ithaca, NY: Cornell University Press.
———. 1995. *The Ritual Process*. London: Aldine Transaction.

United Nations. 2005. *World Youth Report 2005: Young People Today, and in 2015.* Available at http://www.un.org/esa/socdev/unyin/documents/wyr05book.pdf.

Valentin, Karen, Anne Line Dalsgård, and Karen Tranberg Hansen. 2008. "Finding a Place for Youth: Comparative Perspectives on Urban Space and Citizenship." In *Global Urban South: Setting the Agenda*, edited by Allison Garland, Mejgan Massoumi, and Blair Ruble, 36–56. Washington, DC: Woodrow Wilson International Center for Scholars and USAID.

Vigh, Henrik. 2006. *Navigating Terrains of War: Youth and Soldiering in Guinea-Bissau*. Oxford: Berghahn Books.

———. 2008. "Crisis and Chronicity: Anthropological Perspectives on Continuous Conflict and Decline." *Ethnos* 73 (1): 5–24.

Whyte, Susan Reynolds. 2002. "Subjectivity and Subjunctivity: Hoping for Health in Eastern Uganda." In *Postcolonial Subjectivities in Africa*, edited by Richard Werbner, 171–190. London: Zed Books.

Wilk, Richard. 2009. "The Edge of Agency: Routines, Habits and Volition." In *Time, Consumption and Everyday Life: Practice, Materiality and Culture*, edited by Elisabeth Shove, Frank Trentman, and Richard Wilk, 143–157. Oxford: Berg.

1
Waiting for the Start
Flexibility and the Question of Convergence

JENNIFER JOHNSON-HANKS

Most grand narratives of modernity assume an eventual global convergence—that people from diverse backgrounds and cultures lead lives that are increasingly similar in structure, content, and experience over time. In demography, the convergence is expected to come about in terms of family size and composition, with two-child nuclear families all around the world (e.g., Bongaarts 2001). In American sociology, most interest has focused on the apparent increase in cross-national similarities in educational systems, cultural norms, and political organization, as well as on the processes of diffusion that are its presumed causes (e.g., Bonikowski 2010; Dorius and Firebaugh 2010; Meyer, Boli, Thomas, and Ramirez 1997). Even though anthropologists have rejected the cross-national comparisons on which claims of convergence are generally made, stressing instead detailed case studies embedded in the idea that there are "multiple modernities," a term coined by Shmuel Eisenstadt (2000: 1), we have often tacitly assumed its inevitability in the large number of anthropological studies of global media, transnational migration, multiple citizenships, and global neoliberalism. In particular, scholars have assumed that people from around the world will come to relate to time in the same way, seeing it as a valued commodity to be saved or spent. And indeed, in at least some domains, important global convergences are taking place. However, this chapter argues that the new normal on which we are collectively converging is not a pattern from the rich West but rather one from the global

South. Perhaps the best examples of this appear in the lives of young people and concern time and the ways it is objectified.

By convergence, I mean that modes of life or modes of action in diverse locales become increasingly similar over time. This is more specific than the mid-twentieth-century concern with cross-cultural structural-functional similarities, for example, in the Human Relations Area Files project (see Naroll, Michik, and Naroll 1976), though it can be related to it. Assuming that it is not the result of random chance, *similarity* can arise through three processes: shared origins, diffusion, and structural necessity. Convergence can also arise through all three processes, although the sequence of events from shared origins to social convergence is less straightforward than through the others. Diffusion occurs when a mode of life or mode of action that is common in one area spreads to others through some combination of imitation, habituation, or coercion: it is historically particular. Most of the work on globalization describes this kind of process, and the concept of diffusion has become central in contemporary studies of demographic change (see, for example, Bongaarts and Watkins 1996; Montgomery and Casterline 1996). Structural necessity obtains if specific socioeconomic forms necessarily lead to given modes of life or modes of action; an increase in the prevalence of these structural forms will lead to an increase in the respective modes of life or action. This is the sort of explanation that Jack Goody (1990) offered—rightly or wrongly—for the relationships between modes of production and kinship systems. The term "shared origins" here refers to any situation in which two distinct social units share traits because both inherited them independently from a shared set of social ancestors: similarities in the political culture of the United States and Australia, for example, would fit here. Note that these kinds of shared origins can, in some instances, be interpreted as the result of diffusion in the second degree—that is, diffusion processes that occurred a very long time ago. Note too that they are immediately available to explain similarity rather than convergence. However, under some conditions, I suggest, historically shared repertoires of value can lead to the convergence of ways of life when conditions suddenly become more similar.

My topic in this chapter is the convergence in modes of life and modes of action between American youth of today and African youth of a decade ago. This modality can be described as waiting in a state of suspended action, of interstitial pause, of persistent temporariness. For example, when young people finish school with no plans or prospects for the future and simply wait, they are in the kind of suspension that interests me here. At its core this mode of being is a way of relating to time or to "the experience of time as an often-troubling, external factor in life," as Martin Demant Frederiksen and Anne Line Dalsgård note in the Introduction. A number of authors have described contemporary life in Africa and elsewhere as marked by a sense that everything is temporary and provisional, involving the dissolution of long-term stability or coherent long-term trajectories as an option, the delay in achieving full adulthood, and the ongoing curating of multiple possible futures, wealth in prospects replacing the wealth in people that classically defined African social aspirations (on wealth in people, see Guyer 1993; on contemporary uncertainty, especially in Africa, see Berner and Trulsson 2000; Bledsoe 2002; Ferguson 1999; Johnson-Hanks 2006).

How do young people make a living and make a meaningful life under these conditions? In particular, how do they relate to time as an object? Comparing educated young women in Yaoundé (Cameroon) in 1998 and 2001 with educated young women in the San Francisco Bay Area in 2010 in this chapter, I pay particular attention to their understandings of two major life-course transitions: finishing school and starting work. I make three related claims. First, the activities, constraints, and even aspirations of young college-educated American women have come to resemble those of the Cameroonian elite of a decade ago. Second, their stance toward (some of) these activities offers a somewhat different, more optimistic lens through which to view the situation of Cameroonian women than has been commonly used in the Africanist literature. Third, these convergences arise out of a combination of structural necessity and shared historical origins, not out of recent diffusion. This is not a case of the McDonaldization of the world. In particular, I suggest that the repertoire of cultural schemas that certain American and African youth have deployed in responding to changed resource structures has a common history in the post–World War II period and a shared Christian orientation.

Cast of Characters

We turn to four vignettes involving Sandrine and Adele in Yaoundé and Sarah and Kelsey in San Francisco. The names are, of course, pseudonyms. Where necessary, I have changed minor details to protect the anonymity of my interlocutors. The quotes from Sandrine and Adele come from tape-recorded and transcribed interviews, for which I obtained standard informed consent. Sarah and Kelsey were my students, and I have asked them for permission to include their stories here. However, our conversations were never formal interviews and were originally conducted for pedagogical, not research, reasons. In these cases, I paraphrase from memory and some notes.

The young woman I call Sarah graduated from the University of California, Berkeley, with a degree in anthropology in 2010. She excelled as a student, winning prizes for her undergraduate research and collaborating with senior professors. From a conservative Asian American family, Sarah had to defend her decision to study anthropology to her parents, who wanted her to do something practical. Her parents were even more distraught when graduation day approached and Sarah had not started to think about finding a job. "Something will come along," she insisted to them, explaining that the worst job market in fifty years meant that there was little point in setting your sights on anything specific. Instead, it was important to keep her eyes and ears open and wait for the right opportunity to present itself. She had planned to go to graduate school eventually, but not right away, and wanted to get some real-world experience first. After graduation, through a friend of a friend, she was offered a contract position with Apple. The work is exciting, demanding, and decidedly short term. Her contract is for fifteen months, and from the beginning it has been clear that it would not be extended. Nor would she want it to be, as fifteen months seems like a pretty long time to her. What will she do next? She does not know. Graduate school is still an option but so is further contract work. She likes, she explained, the flexibility.

Kelsey also graduated from Berkeley in 2010. She continues to work part-time in the record store that had employed her as a student. She is looking for something more permanent, or at least with more hours, since she is now spending more money than she earns, and her parents are not willing to subsidize her over the long term. She was thinking of taking some evening classes to get a sense of what she might want to do next but hesitates to spend even more, and so for now she is "kind of in a holding pattern," as she described it. She has a lot of time she does not know what to do with, she explained; she hangs out with friends from school, but none of them have the money to do many of the things they would like to. Her job search takes only a couple of hours a week, since there are not many jobs to apply for. She described herself as overall "pretty smart, but lacking focus," without direction or a sense of what to do. She came to see me to inquire about graduate school but hesitated when I noted that a master of arts degree takes two years. "That's too long," she said. "I need more flexibility."

Two things about Kelsey's self-description are particularly important for present purposes. First is the metaphor of a holding pattern, or the way an airplane circles above an airport before it is cleared to land. The metaphor is both apt and inapt. It is apt because it stresses her boredom and her feeling that she is just waiting, with no control over her future and no sense of the timeline on which things might change. But airplanes that come in to land *complete* something, whereas whatever it is that Kelsey is waiting for is not a completion but a start. The second thing about Kelsey's narrative that merits our attention is the importance she places on flexibility, which here seems to mean not being tied to a specific commitment for too long. For Kelsey, flexibility is mostly about the management of time and her relationship to time. In its dictionary definition, "flexible" refers first to things that can be bent or changed easily and without harm—a rubber band, say. But here, "flexible" means not so much something that can be changed easily but rather time that is open, not fully accounted for, and therefore adaptable in a variety of directions. It is a term that Sarah uses too, and in a very similar way. This understanding of flexibility contrasts with an older view of strategic action in which you forgo short-term benefits in exchange for greater long-term gains. Instead, Sarah and Kelsey emphasize the importance of keeping their options open, of not foreclosing alternative possible futures too quickly. In a similar vein, a recent article in the *New York Times* has the title "A Major in Engineering, with a Minor in 'Keeping an Open Mind'" (Tamir 2010).

Flexibility and the withdrawal of a potential future also show up clearly in the stories of the Cameroonian women Sandrine and Adele, both of whom I knew reasonably well when they were students in 1998. I visited both of them again in the summer of 2001 and of course asked what they had been doing in the meantime. With Sandrine, the conversation went as follows:

> JJH: When you left school, then what did you do?
> Sandrine: Nothing.
> JJH: Nothing?
> Sandrine: Really nothing. I just stayed at home all the time.
> JJH: Didn't you work at home?
> Sandrine: No, no. I just cooked manioc and things like that. I didn't even do anything. At home, there is nothing to do. Not even a market. Nothing. So I did nothing.

Of course, she did not do "nothing." She had full days of heavy labor: weeding fields, pounding manioc, hauling water, and washing clothes. But nothing she did had an intrinsic implied trajectory; nothing had a built-in future orientation. The labor each day was much like the labor of every other day, with no prospect for improvement or even change. The framing is important here. "Nothing" in Sandrine's accounting means "nothing with a narrative," nothing that constitutes a project. This "nothing," therefore, only makes sense in the context of narrative alternatives, other ways of spending time that *do* imply trajectories, that *do* have implicit futures. School is the most obvious and compelling of these, but many forms of paid work too are activities that suggest transit, change, and most of all improvement. And so the "nothing" that Sandrine insists on is a massively modern one. Before the break that we call modernity, a life of washing clothes, feeding babies, and weeding manioc would have been called life, not nothing. It becomes nothing only in contrast to a hypothetical something that is more than its own present. We can think productively about Sandrine's nothing through Jane Guyer's reflections on the "evacuation of the temporal frame of the 'near future'" in millennial Christianity. She describes this near future as "the reach of thought and imagination, of planning and hoping, of tracing out mutual influences, of engaging in struggles for specific goals, in short, of the process of implicating oneself in the ongoing life of the social and material world" (2007: 409). Sandrine sees her life as lacking this "near future," making her activities worth nothing.

Sandrine's domestic labor in her parents' compound is more productive than Kelsey's part-time work at the music store. Although neither was paying her own way in the cash economy, Sandrine is a hard worker, who almost certainly pulled more than her own weight at home. And both (although not in these passages) talked about their status as one of waiting: waiting for some unspecified future, waiting for something to open up for them to do, waiting for things to begin. Talk of waiting was also central to Adele's self-description in 1998:

> JJH: What do you want to do after the *bac* (high school diploma)?
> Adele: We'll see. Perhaps we'll see after the *bac*.
> JJH: You don't have any general ideas?
> Adele: I do not yet have a precise idea, you see. I'm waiting. If I succeed, if the exams turn out successfully, then tomorrow I will tell you what's what.
> JJH: But in order to decide tomorrow, don't you have to have some ideas today?
> Adele: Your vocation is not like that. It comes from the Holy Spirit.
> JJH: Yes, yes. I understand that, but don't you like something?
> Adele: Today, is it necessary to like something? Whatever presents itself in front of you, you do.

Three years later, Adele had indeed found something that had been presented in front of her. She began her studies in communication at a private college in Yaoundé. It was expensive, and so meant searching every semester for help with the fees, but better in her view than the public university because of the resources that were available. Why communication? Well, for the flexibility, she explained. "This way, even though I don't know where the opportunities are going to open up for me, with this I will be sure to have something, because everything is about communication nowadays." This last phrase is particularly evocative: it is good to study communication not only because communication is implicated in everything (and its study thus maintains flexibility) but also because flexibility is more important than ever as a result of everything being about communication. Communication, after all, is itself deeply about adaptability and the potential for change. Adele was living in a small room in a cement-block building with other students, and we talked at the somewhat makeshift café at the nearby intersection. She was excited about the enormous new possibilities being brought by the Internet, by global exchange, and laughed about how she would like to meet me at a café in Berkeley one day and to talk in English. "Flexibility" for Adele means keeping her options open so that the most promising are not overlooked. It is, in a certain sense, the overvaluation of the possible over the feasible.

Convergence on the African Model

Adele, Sandrine, and others like them were foremost in my mind as I developed the idea of "judicious opportunism" (Johnson-Hanks 2006: 194), a mode of action "in the subjunctive mood" (after Wagner-Pacifici 2000: 3) that stands in contrast to conventional means-ends rational action. It is focused on keeping options open, maintaining possibilities, keeping flexible, and then being ready to pounce when a promising chance comes along: wealth in prospects. Again and again during my fieldwork in Cameroon, people emphasized how their present condition made planning impossible. They could not imagine a particular future or make specific plans. Uncertainty was so normal that many people found assertions about certain futures absurd. Knowing that I was interested in young women's marital, fertility, and professional intentions, people sometimes asked me these same questions. How many children would I like to have? What job would I like to do? What would I do if my husband took a second wife? These conversations came to have a familiar rhythm. I would say I wanted two children, and my interlocutor would ask what I would do if I had five instead. I would say that I would not have five; I will stop when I have two. Then my interlocutor and any bystanders would laugh uproariously and tell me that it is God who gives children, which "one cannot refuse!" Similarly, if I said that I wanted to be a professor, I would be asked what I would do if I had to work in the fields instead. When I asserted the impossibility of my being forced to work in the fields in the United States, my conversational partner would laugh and remind me that no one can know the future and that anything is possible in this world. As I, along with many others, have argued, in many poor countries people are habituated into agnosticism about the future: life is so uncertain that plans are always tenuous, partial, more hope than conviction.

What is important in the stories of Kelsey and Sarah is the degree to which they too describe their present modes of action "in the subjunctive mood," stressing the importance of maintaining flexibility, seeing where promising options open up, and waiting. Flexibility is therefore a regime of temporality in which the dominant mode is waiting. The waiting can have more positive (as for Adele and Sarah) or more negative (for Sandrine and Kelsey) valences, but either way it stands in dramatic contrast to the view of means-ends rationality that has been taken for granted since Max Weber. Whereas means-ends rationality posits action in which the actor selects a specific desired end and then uses the available means as efficiently as possible to achieve it, this judicious opportunism is a mode of action in which no specific ends can be formulated, only, perhaps, vague notions of what constitutes a good life or what would be a promising chance, and in which the primary activity is apparent inaction. Time loses its sense of before and after because intentional projects are impossible.

If it is clear that there has been a convergence between American and Cameroonian youth in this relationship to time and the future, it is far less clear how it happened. Did Cameroonian ideas and practices somehow diffuse to the United States? No, I think not. Rather, I suggest that the convergence of modes of life between American and Cameroonian youth is from a combination of structural overdetermination and shared history. Central among the structural forces involved is economic crisis, which had gripped Cameroon for a decade by the time I conducted my fieldwork there in 1998 and is now highly salient in the United States. In both countries, the economic crisis was severe—in Cameroon, a decline in global commodity prices led to the value of exports falling by half, setting off an extended and painful period of economic stagnation. People often called it "la crise morale" because of the significant social consequences of the economic downturn. No, others insisted, this is rather "la crise totale." But whatever its name, the Cameroonian economic crisis is now echoed in the United States. Kelsey and Sarah graduated from college during the worst economic downturn in the United States since the 1930s: the overall unemployment rate was 9.5 percent and not coming down, institutions from households to the U.S.

government were deeply in debt, and uncertainty was ubiquitous. At some level, Kelsey and Sarah's agnosticism toward the future and their unwillingness to make specific plans represent an inevitable retreat into the subjunctive mood that is appropriate to an economic crisis.

Robert Reich (2010) argues that, over decades of stagnating wages, the lifestyle of the American middle class—and with it, American optimism about the future—was maintained through the sequential deployment of women's increased labor-force participation, then longer hours of work for both spouses, and finally, borrowing against the inflated prices of homes. But people can only work so many hours and borrow so much. When the last available trick ran out, economic crisis was inevitable. Indeed, it had been inevitable for decades, merely postponed. From an economic perspective, surely, Reich is right. But experientially, the Great Recession has meant something radically different in the sense that people may have known that they were working longer or borrowing more, but did not see it as a systemic problem beyond themselves. It is one thing to be nervous about your own ability to fulfill the American dream, but the Great Recession made it clear to people that it was the dream itself, not their own place in relation to it, that was in disarray. Conjoined with the threat of terrorism since September 2001, the doomsday financial news since 2007 in the United States represents a significant historical rupture.

When I say rupture, what I mean is that the direction of change has been reversed. For decades, as a rule, life in most domains in the United States was getting more stable and more predictable. Life expectancy rose, and the range of ages at death shrank. Contraception became more and more available, increasing certainty over fertility numbers and timing. Because of the actions of the Federal Reserve banking system, the business cycle flattened out, and recessions became shallower. Residential mobility led to increasingly homogenous neighborhoods and within them increases in educational and political homogamy. Credit markets were stabilized, making liquidity constraints less severe..And so on and so on. Perhaps most importantly, people came to assume that predictability was good, even that it was natural. But no longer. The change has come in two major ways: first, uncertainties large and small have grown in some important domains of life, and second, perhaps paradoxically people have come to put much greater positive value on spontaneity and flexibility. When Kelsey and Sarah reject professional or educational commitments that would limit their flexibility, this reflects both a negative reaction to the contemporary American economic and social crises and a positive valuation placed on flexibility, one that relates to the crisis in nuanced and complicated ways.

To think about the positive value placed on flexibility in relation to the crises, we turn first to a series of articles that have appeared in the *New York Times* over the past year and explored the changing nature of work in the United States. In these articles, the most often cited change is the rise of flexible or contingent labor, or short-term contracts, often without benefits. Here again, we see the term "flexible" being used in a specific relationship to temporality. "Flexible" labor is contracted over brief time horizons, without long-term commitment on the part of the employer. This is the category of work that Sarah is doing, although the category includes a wide range of arrangements. It is therefore hard to count, and most of the evidence of its considerable increase over the last three years is anecdotal. Still, the *Times* correspondent notes:

> In just one snapshot of what is going on, the number of people who describe themselves as self-employed but working less than 35 hours a week because they cannot find full-time work has more than doubled since the recession began, reaching 1.2 million in December 2009, according to the [U.S.] Bureau of Labor Statistics. . . . Many people are apparently looking at *multiple temporary jobs as the equivalent of a diversified investment portfolio.* (Luo 2010: A14; emphasis added)

The phrase "diversified investment portfolio" is particularly interesting for us. It closely resembles a common image used by many of my interlocutors in Cameroon to talk about why one should have multiple boyfriends (in case of a problem with one, it is good to have "various businesses"). Indeed, the value of diversification in the face of uncertainty is one of the key reasons that action in the subjunctive mood has many of the characteristics that it has. Still, contingent work being somehow safer than the long-term, stable employment on which middle-class lives have depended for decades does seem rather ironic. But that is the sense of the times. The same article included an interview with a man who explained that "he actually prefers his life as an independent contractor—constantly being laid off and rehired, sometimes juggling multiple jobs—to his old corporate position. 'I think it's far less risky than being in a full-time job somewhere and cut at will and left with nothing'" (Luo 2010: A14).

This perspective is certainly convenient, given that some 26 percent of the jobs created in the U.S. private sector since December 2009 have been temporary or contingent positions (Bureau of Labor Statistics, cited in Rich 2010). Indeed, most of the benefits of a flexible workforce would seem to accrue to employers—who do not have to pay benefits and who can easily adjust their workforce to suit the work available—rather than to the employee. For decades, unions and other prolabor groups prevented American businesses from expanding temporary work too much. But this recession comes after the 1990s, during which *workers* insisted on flexible hours and telecommuting, leaving traditional corporations to work in new, uncertain companies (especially dot-com start-ups) with a much more flexible, temporary, spontaneous form. We return to this dream of the 1990s below. Employers are now insisting on that same kind of flexibility: this is the new normal. Mokoto Rich writes that "the whole notion of what constitutes a permanent job may simply be changing. Workers 'need to expect that their lives and jobs will change much more often than they have in the past'" (2010: A1).

The Dream of the '90s

The celebration of flexibility and spontaneity evident in the changing shape of American work echoes a far more exuberant celebration of the flexibility and spontaneity in nonwork life that have been made possible by technological innovation over the past couple of decades. Two that are salient to Sarah and Kelsey are cell phones (and with them, texting and the mobile web) and the computation-intensive matching algorithms behind programs like Pandora, Match.com, and even Amazon's recommendations. Over several generations, major U.S. corporations offered the consumer reliability, predictability, security, and uniformity (think of General Electric, Ma Bell, Ford, or McDonalds). The hip companies of the new economy, however, offer almost the inverse: individuation, flexibility, and autonomy. That is, they market a limited kind of uncertainty.

In poor countries, where telecom infrastructure is limited and few people have access to landlines, cell phones have meant a massive increase in efficiency and productivity. In many villages, the only communication alternative to cell phones (or now texting) is a physical relocation. Without a private vehicle, this can mean a full day of uncomfortable transit to travel fifty kilometers. In the United States also, cell phones have increased efficiency to a limited extent. However, their most prominent effect in the lives of young people has been a reorganization of social life. Instead of "Let's meet at six on Friday at the restaurant," American twenty-year-olds increasingly use "Call me Friday afternoon and we'll see what we feel like doing." Canceling plans ("flaking" in common parlance) has also become more acceptable, given that it no longer necessarily means that the person you would have met is waiting alone outside some restaurant, cold and uncomfortable. The pattern of last-minute canceling is so common that its etiquette and social implications have become major topics on online forums, from Experience Project ("Life experiences from people like you") to Mamapedia ("The wisdom of moms") to Fluther.com ("Tap the collective"). In other words, technology has made plans *more* provisional, *more* temporary, *more* explicitly in the subjunctive mood. That is, since cell phones became ubiquitous, social plans in the United States have become more like everyday plans in Yaoundé in the late 1990s.

The social effects of computation-intensive matching algorithms, such as those used by Pandora and Match.com, are less concrete but no less interesting. Pandora is a website that allows users to enter the name of a song they like, and Pandora then plays a stream of songs that resemble the selected song. Users are therefore introduced to a variety of new music that they are likely to like. The online matchmaking service Match.com takes a similar approach to dating, using an elaborate and proprietary matching algorithm to offer users introductions only to "good" potential matches. In both cases, users receive suggestions for music or people that they might like, based on what they say they do like. In one reading, this service has no generative content, since all it does is offer people more of what they already like. But in another reading it introduces a considerable new element of randomness, of spontaneous chances, into the sets of options that people face. That is, it increases a limited and desirable form of everyday uncertainty.

Historically, people in the United States found their spouses and information about new jobs, desirable neighborhoods to live in, books, movies, and music, and so on, through the networks of people they knew. (This phenomenon has been expanded, but at some level remains essentially unchanged, through the explosion of social networking sites like Facebook.) Mark Granovetter's classic article on the strength of weak ties argues that these networks function in a specific way, using the example of people looking for work (1973). Such people, Granovetter argues, receive little benefit from those with whom their social links are strongest, since the latter are embedded in the same social networks as the job seeker and therefore have little information that the job seeker does not already have. Instead, it is through contacts with whom the job seeker has weak ties—people whose primary affiliations are in other social networks—that the job seeker can gain new information and therefore new opportunities. Paradoxically, weak social ties therefore have a greater effect on outcomes than do strong ones. In the decades since its publication, hundreds of papers have shown the (sometimes partial) application of Granovetter's insight to domains as wide as partner search, political affiliation, and even cultural tastes. What Match

.com, Pandora, and similar services do is massively increase everyone's access to weak ties—albeit now in the form of an algorithm!—thus making the structure of their social network less important and increasing the possibilities of a promising chance falling their way. Match.com is the new weak tie in everybody's network.

Keeping yourself and your options open to the possibility of unpredictable, promising chances lies at the heart of the mode of action I call judicious opportunism. And in many ways, sites like Pandora and Match.com offer exquisite examples of how this modality of action stresses coincidence and happenstance without dissolving into paralysis. You have to register with these sites, engage with them, and actively maintain a space of possibility for chance to strike. The time costs and potential gains are lower with Pandora than with Match.com, but both—and indeed dozens of similar algorithm-based services—habituate their users to the experience of promising chances coming along, as well as to the practice of cultivating the opportunity for that to happen.

Two aspects regarding the social effects of cell phones and algorithm-driven matching programs are interesting for our purposes. First, they increase the ways life for young Americans is organized around spontaneity, flexibility, and maintaining openness to interesting potential chances. That is, they make the texture of nonwork life much more similar to the "permanent temporariness" that the *New York Times* writer Rich (2010) suggests is the present—and will be the future—of American work. In that regard they normalize uncertainty and with it a stance of open-minded waiting. Second, they make this stance attractive. Whereas most of the writing about the rise of a flexible workforce emphasizes that temporary contracts are an inferior alternative to the model of permanent corporate employment that has prevailed for the last fifty years, no one is arguing that Pandora or the iPhone represent the end of the American middle class as we know it. Indeed, the changes in social life made possible by cellular technology, the Internet, and matching algorithms are sources of pleasure: people want them, actively seek them out, and encourage others to do so as well.

Let us look at the TV series *Portlandia*, which offers a comic depiction of life in Portland, Oregon, a midsized city "where young people go to retire." The premise is that the dream of the 1990s never died in Portland, where young people spend their days happily unoccupied and aimless. In the 1990s in the United States, educated young people did in fact leave traditional corporate America in some numbers, opting for flexible contracts at start-up dot-coms with no revenue and sometimes no business model. In the new economy of the 1990s bubble, old rules of thrift and hard work were said to no longer apply; businesses with in-house trampolines and masseuses and come-to-work-in-your-pajamas policies might have been mostly urban legends, but they were powerful and persistent ones. What is interesting about *Portlandia* for our purposes is that young people with part-time coffee-shop jobs—young people who might otherwise be seen as trapped in grave underemployment by the economic crisis—are instead depicted as having happily chosen a lifestyle defined as a celebration of individuality, free spiritedness, and weirdness. This is made more explicit by this lifestyle being characterized in *Portlandia* as distinctly of the 1990s—that is, of an era of massive economic prosperity and well being. Unlike the articles in the *New York Times* in 2012 that describe the rise of the flexible labor force as a problem related to the Great Recession that began in 2007, in this popular-culture reflection, college graduates who work as part-time baristas are voluntarily retro, choosing freedom and flexibility instead of seeking full-time work commitments that could lead to more lucrative careers.

So far, I have argued, first, that much about the modes of life and modes of action that characterize recent college graduates in the San Francisco Bay Area resemble modes of life and modes of action that characterized high school graduates in and around Yaoundé a decade ago and, second, that in the United States these modes of life are chosen and celebrated in ways that are quite different from their counterparts in Cameroon. The most important similarities focus on time and timing. In both places, young women explain that the future is unknowable and therefore cannot be planned for. They do not see their current situations as permanent but, at best, as activities to keep doors open in order not to miss promising chances or, at worst, as a time of undefined waiting, which may be boring but about which little can be done. They thus stress flexibility rather than strategy, openness rather than forethought. Social actors seek to keep doors open, rather than work diligently in pursuit of a single goal. However, contemporary young Americans celebrate this mode of life in a way that Cameroonians in the late 1990s did not. Some see flexible labor contracts not only as the sole option available under the current conditions of economic crisis but also as more commensurate with their values and ideals than old-fashioned corporate work would be. Flexibility is not only a necessary skill to cultivate in the face of systemic uncertainty but also an important and desirable aspect of late modernity made possible by cell phones, the mobile web, and a variety of web-based services. Underemployment and lack of direction are celebrated on TV and normalized in the newspapers. Judicious opportunism is not, for many young American women today, the best of a bad set of options but rather a particularly contemporary and fashionable modality of action.

Some college-educated young people in the United States have come to consider detachment, dwelling in uncertainty, and withdrawal from concrete plans about the future as positive markers of identity. Giving up flexibility would be naïve; working for one company your whole life would be grim. Keeping options open means being part of the network, in the moment, aware of the times. In other words, a stance toward the future serves to construct—or at least represent—the self in the present. Stances toward the future may be particularly apt for constructing the self in the present, as several authors have argued (for example, in anthropology, see Cole 2010; in psychology, see Markus and Nurius 1986: 962). For example, Margaret Frye argues that many young people in Malawi seek to cultivate the identity of "one who aspires," devoting themselves exclusively to their studies despite low chances of academic success and even lower chances of translating their education into lucrative careers. As she explains, "Future goals in this context are not selected through comparing benefits and likelihoods of different outcomes. Instead, by striving for such ambitious goals, these women are asserting themselves as forward thinking and morally worthy" (2012: 1608). The young women I discuss here position themselves in a radically different way to their own futures, but in both cases—those of the women I studied and of Frye's young people in Malawi—they are making present selves out of their stance toward the future.

Sources of the Stance

Why should the lifeways pursued by young American women in 2010 resemble those of urban Cameroonian women in 1998? In thinking about this question, I return to the issue of causes that I raise at the beginning of the chapter and suggest that the recent convergence of modes of life and modes of action between young people in the contemporary United States and Cameroon of a decade ago is the consequence of a combination of structural necessity and shared historical origins. The shared historical origins notably provide a set of cultural schemas for understanding and responding to changing material conditions: what the United States and Cameroon share is a sense that the future is behind us (see Ferguson 1999). Note that this explanation implies that the convergence of interest is not from processes of globalization and diffusion, except in the second-order sense of diffusion many decades in the past.

We have already noted the similarities of structure between the United States and Cameroon: economic crisis; large-scale unemployment and underemployment, particularly for young people; and significant realignments of expectations and possibilities that make long-term planning or investment difficult. To some degree, waiting in a holding pattern, maintaining flexibility, and seizing promising opportunities wherever and whenever they arise might all seem to be straightforward reactions to the structural incentives applicable in Cameroon in the late 1990s and in the United States in 2010. However, the similarities are not entirely attributable to structural necessity, since other potential reactions to these structural patterns are possible. Young people could redouble their efforts to succeed in school and at work, or they could switch their devotion to another sphere, such as the church, family, or social activism. An economic crisis does not necessarily produce a stance of detachment, flexibility, or waiting and seeing.

What does produce this stance, I suggest, is the combination of these economic circumstances contrasted to a collective self-representation of optimism, individualism, and progress. Cameroon and the United States share a set of historical references in the narratives of modernity, progress, and individualism as these were articulated by the United States, its World War II allies, and their soon-to-be-former colonies in the immediate postwar period. "We shall overcome," sang Martin Luther King Jr., and the sentiment resonated with white Americans because they had indeed just overcome and saw themselves as fundamentally a people overcoming. While Frederick Turner's frontier hypothesis, first presented in 1893, identifies American cultural identity in our lengthy relationship with the frontier, the can-do-ism of the postwar era is arguably more important as a moment in which a collective sense of who we are was forged. Cameroonian independence and unification in 1960 and 1961 are very much of a piece with the exuberant optimism of the United States of the same time, and the practical social theory that gave society its feel was largely shared. In both cases, the dominant narratives are ones in which the present is only a staging ground for a more optimistic future. Today's efforts will lead to tomorrow's progress. Creativity, ingenuity, and individuality are the keys to making that effort productive. And each individual indeed has a special calling—a divine vocation—that may for a time be hidden but is nonetheless real.

These are cultural schemas forged in good times, and in such times—in Cameroon in the early 1980s, for example, and in the United States in the late 1990s—they give meaning and form to hard work with individual, yet divinely inspired, aspirations in view. But under conditions of crisis, these Christian-inflected, modernist schemas of progress become a problem of their own. How do you make sense of a present without apparent prospects in a cultural framework that stresses that the present is first and foremost a preparation for a better future, particularly a future that God has designed for you in a particular way? One way is to treat the present as a time of pause, a "holding pattern" in Kelsey's language, of "nothing happening" in the words of Sandrine, of waiting until your vocation "comes from the Holy Spirit," as Adele said. Instead of treating the present as being just itself—just the present—all the young women discussed here hold on to a modernist notion that the future will bring something better. But without an economic structure through which to work systematically toward achieving it, they wait for their futures, holding various prospects open until their providential fates are revealed to them. Being flexible with their time allows these young women to hold true to their individual futures, waiting rather than embarking on some other, perhaps lesser path. That is, flexibility is what one uses to mediate between a cultural schema of progress and individual (often Christian) destiny and a structural reality that makes progress and the fulfillment of destiny impossible, at least as they have been canonically understood. Living in the subjunctive mood is not a rejection of the rationality of the near future but paradoxically a sign of its central cultural importance, despite times of crisis.

As missionaries introduced the church, the school, and the clock tower throughout Africa, they imagined a future in which people of all nations would share a single orientation to knowledge, God, and time. For the better part of a century, Western scholars too have predicted how societies in the underdeveloped South would come to resemble the rich North over time. One important axis on which convergence has been expected concerns how people orient themselves to time in general and to the future in particular. In the last decade, I argue, some important similarities in how young people think of and relate to time have emerged between urban Cameroon and the San Francisco Bay Area. However, they are converging on the Cameroonian pattern. Uncertainty, flexibility, and the suspension of planning have become the new normal.

REFERENCES

Berner, Boel, and Per Trulsson. 2000. *Manoeuvring in an Environment of Uncertainty*. Aldershot, UK: Ashgate.

Bledsoe, Caroline. 2002. *Contingent Lives: Fertility, Time and Aging in West Africa*. Chicago: University of Chicago Press.

Bongaarts, John. 2001. "Household Size and Composition in the Developing World in the 1990s." *Population Studies* 55 (3): 263–279.

Bongaarts, John, and Susan Cotts Watkins. 1996. "Social Interactions and Contemporary Fertility Transitions." *Population and Development Review* 22:639–683.

Bonikowski, Bart. 2010. "Cross-National Interaction and Cultural Similarity: A Relational Analysis." *International Journal of Comparative Sociology* 51 (5): 315–348.

Cole, Jennifer. 2010. *Sex and Salvation: Imagining the Future in Madagascar.* Chicago: University of Chicago Press.

Dorius, Shawn, and Glenn Firebaugh. 2010. "Trends in Global Gender Inequality." *Social Forces* 88 (5): 1941–1968.

Eisenstadt, Shmuel. 2000. "Multiple Modernities." *Daedalus* 129 (1): 1–29.

Ferguson, James. 1999. *Expectations of Modernity: Myths and Meanings of Urban Life on the Zambian Copperbelt.* Berkeley: University of California Press.

Frye, Margaret. 2012. "Bright Futures in Malawi's New Dawn." *American Journal of Sociology* 117 (6): 1565–1624.

Goody, Jack. 1990. *The Oriental, the Ancient and the Primitive: Systems of Marriage and the Family in the Pre-industrial Societies of Eurasia.* Cambridge: Cambridge University Press.

Granovetter, Mark. 1973. "The Strength of Weak Ties." *American Journal of Sociology* 73 (6): 1360–1380.

Guyer, Jane. 1993. "Wealth in People and Self-Realization in Equatorial Africa." *Man* 28:243–265.

———. 2007. "Prophecy and the Near Future." *American Ethnologist* 34 (3): 409–421.

Johnson-Hanks, Jennifer. 2006. *Uncertain Honor: Modern Motherhood in an African Crisis.* Chicago: University of Chicago Press.

Lesthaeghe, Ron J. 1989. *Reproduction and Social Organization in Sub-Saharan Africa.* Berkeley: University of California Press.

Luo, Michael. 2010. "Recession Adds to Appeal of Short-Term Jobs." *New York Times Business Day*, April 19, p. A14.

Markus, Hazel, and Paula Nurius. 1986. "Possible Selves." *American Psychologist* 41 (9): 954–969.

Meyer, Ohn W., John Boli, George M. Thomas, and Francisco O. Ramirez. 1997. "World Society and the Nation-State." *American Journal of Sociology* 103 (1): 144–181.

Montgomery, Mark, and John Casterline. 1996. "Social Learning, Social Influence and New Models of Fertility." *Population and Development Review* 22:151–175.

Naroll, Raoul, Gary L Michik, and Frada Naroll. 1976. *Worldwide Theory Testing.* New Haven, CT: Human Relations Area Files.

Reich, Robert. 2010. *Aftershock.* New York: Knopf.

Rich, Mokoto. 2010. "Weighing Costs, Companies Favor Temporary Help." *New York Times Business Day*, December 19, p. A1.

Tamir, Uyanga. 2010. "A Major in Engineering, with a Minor in 'Keeping an Open Mind.'" *New York Times Education Supplement*, December 30.

Turner, Frederick Jackson. 1893. "The Significance of the Frontier in American History." Paper presented at the American Historical Association conference, Chicago, IL, December 27–30.

Wagner-Pacifici, Robin. 2000. *Theorizing the Standoff: Contingency in Action.* Cambridge: Cambridge University Press.

2

Stunted Future

Buryong *among Young Men in Manila*

STEFFEN JENSEN

> Employment . . . creates time and indeed is time itself. . . . Below a certain level . . . aspirations burgeon, detached from reality and sometimes a little crazy, as if, when nothing was possible, everything became possible, as if all discourses about the future—prophecies, divinations, predictions, millenarian announcements—had no other purpose than to fill what is no doubt one of the most painful of wants: the lack of a future. (Bourdieu 2000: 222–226)

In *Pascalian Meditations*, from which this passage is taken, Pierre Bourdieu discusses the relationship between expectations of the future and the possibilities of fulfilling them. He suggests that most people align expectations and possibilities in ways that powerfully reproduce social structure. To talk of the practical anticipation that mediates between hope and possibility, Bourdieu introduces the term "forth-coming" (*à venir*)—things we unconsciously anticipate encountering. Time, argues Bourdieu, flows, and we really experience "what we call time [only] when the quasi-automatic coincidence between expectations and chances . . . is broken" (208). For Bourdieu, "real" time is intimately related to employment or participation in the labor market, as suggested in the first quotation above. Employment as time presents those Bourdieu calls the "subproletarians" (the chronically unemployed and the marginalized) with a particular conundrum. As they find it hard to access the labor market, they suffer the fate of living in a sort of "non-time of life" (222), a broken time marked by the horrifying lack of an acceptable future.

Taking my cue from Bourdieu, I explore how young men—whom Bourdieu might term subproletarian—in a Manila resettlement site called Bagong Silang understand and cope with broken time. It is in relation to the notion of broken time that the emic term *buryong* is relevant. While it directly translates as either "boredom" or "a form of insanity," it captures the idea of the cognition of broken time and of coping with it. It signifies the fear that nothing will ever change. Thus, it denotes a kind of desperation or, as some drug addicts express it, a "waiting for nothing" (Professor Mike Tan, University of the Philippines, personal communication, May 11, 2011). However, my young male interlocutors are not just "waiting for nothing." I argue that membership in male peer groups (brotherhoods) and employment are ultimately unsuccessful ways of coping with the sense of *buryong* that always threatens to overwhelm people on the margins of possibilities. I investigate the question "How do young men cope with *buryong*, and how does it relate to their image of possible futures?" While *buryong* is specific to the Philippines, this analysis might help us understand broader processes of marginalization and the responses from those caught in broken time.

Concepts like *buryong*, with respect to forthcoming and possible futures, rely on temporal modalities. As stressed in the Introduction, anthropology is often better equipped to discuss spatiality than temporality (see also Cole and Durham 2008). However, looking at the practices of young men in Manila, it is evident that the spatial and the temporal are articulated through each other. To see this it suffices to take a trip north from Manila's administrative center to Bagong Silang, where I conducted ethnographic fieldwork for seven months in 2009 and 2010. The trip could take up to two hours. One needs to travel north on the incredibly busy Commonwealth Avenue to Fairview and then follow the winding and narrow passage of Maligaya Road until reaching the bridge over a little creek that marks the entrance into Bagong Silang. Thus, the spatial marginalization of Bagong Silang is expressed in the time it takes to get there. Bagong Silang is a densely populated resettlement site. People have (been) moved here in successive waves since the mid-1980s as the capital region of the Philippines, Manila, became overpopulated. Slum areas were cleared, roads widened, and development zones constructed (Tadiar 2004). Bagong Silang (and similar areas across the metropolitan area) grew. Today it is the home of approximately 250,000 inhabitants. Unemployment rates run at around 45 percent; 66 percent of households live on an income that is below the national poverty line, and almost 70 percent receive support from members of the household living elsewhere. Despite its density and poverty, Bagong Silang is also for the most part a government-managed space with sanitation, water, and electricity and roads or paths separating the resettlement site from the slum it grew out of. In the beginning Bagong Silang was referred to as *la kubeta* (the toilet), because of all the toilets that could be seen from the air before the actual houses were built around the toilets. This is quite appropriate, as Bagong Silang was where the poor and the unwanted were flushed, taken out of the public eye to live or die. Hence, the spatial sites of marginalization render life itself as *buryong*, and the sense of marginalization and confinement is given urgency because it might never end.

While *buryong* is often loosely translated as "boredom," it bears no relation to the implied inactivity of boredom. Rather, it resembles the notion of "waiting" as introduced by, among others, Craig Jeffrey (2008, 2010), Ghassan Hage (2009), and the editors of this volume. In Jeffrey's account, waiting is not characterized by inactivity. On the contrary, for his young unemployed but educated Indian men (Jeffrey 2010), those structurally confined to waiting, this is an active process of positioning, coping, and wheeling and dealing. The same is true of the young men in Bagong Silang, as they cope with *buryong* in ways I explore here. On the one hand *buryong* designates their feeling of desperation; on the other it propels them into activity. Unpacking Bourdieu's concept of structural domination, Jeffrey identifies three interrelated processes that structure practices of waiting: the liberalization of the national economies of the global South, new forms of organized waiting in detention centers and other "spaces of exception," and the proliferation of linear time that posits that certain steps must be in place before one can move on—for example, a job before marriage—which Flaherty refers to as "time work" (2011: 135). The young men's involvement in the brotherhood, or *kapatiran*, is useful to look at as time work; also useful is considering how the young men relate to employment. I begin this chapter by exploring the concept of *buryong* in more detail. In the second and third parts, respectively, I investigate issues of brotherhood and employment as ways of coping with *buryong* because these two domains are repeatedly mentioned by the young men in relation to their future aspirations. I show that neither the complex identity practices of brotherhood nor the young men's often haphazard participation in the labor market manage to overcome the structural barriers that produce *buryong*. In fact, I conclude that *buryong* might best be understood as an integral part of the subjectivity and ongoing subjectification of people who stay in places like prison and resettlement sites.

Buryong in Prison and Resettlement Sites

The term *buryong* originates from prison and is not an ordinary Tagalog word, though it can be found in the *Tagalog Slang Dictionary*, edited by David Zorc and Rachel San Miguel (1991: 26). It is drawn from prison slang to describe the desperate, the hopeless, and the deranged or insane. Other words to describe its meaning are "weary," "annoyed," and "vexed." Tagalog synonyms suggested by Zorc and San Miguel are *aburido* ("annoyed," "confused"), *magulo ang isip* (literally "thinking badly"), *desperado* ("desperate"), *sira ulo* ("insane," literally "destroyed head"), and *baliw* ("insane"). Although it is an adjective, it also exists in verb form, as when Kay, one of the members of the brotherhood called a *brod*, compares the present tense of "to *buryong*" (*nabu-buryong*) with "to badtrip" (*naba-badtripping*).

Hence, *buryong* is something that one falls prey to, as well as something one does. In most descriptions of the term, including those most clearly expressed by ex-political prisoners, *buryong* is always there, as inescapable as the conditions that produce the emotion. Ka Cesar, who was released in 2010 after serving eighteen years in prison on a politically motivated murder charge, explains, "You cannot avoid *buryong*. It is always with you. When it is coming you have to do something to avoid it. Sometimes it is bad and you get aggressive. Some inmates even hurt themselves; you know, they cut themselves in the arm. Some of them even become suicidal." *Buryong* is thus almost material. He says, "Your *buryong* is always with you." Ka Francisco, still in prison, noted, "You can never escape *buryong*; it is there all the time." One can perhaps liken it to a dark companion whose existence one must learn to accept but that must not be allowed to take over. Ka Francisco, being an artist, paints whenever he feels it coming: "I paint, so when there is *buryong* I will paint the same thing again and again." In this way, *buryong* achieves material reality or expression through the multiple (hidden) layers of paint on a canvas.

Like Ka Francisco, Ka Cesar stresses the creative and productive side of *buryong*. It might end in violence, "but it does not have to result in something bad. When it came I just had to do something. Like I would work out for maybe three hours, so I would stay healthy and strong. Even being involved in the steering committee [in the prison] is a way to avoid your *buryong*." Again, *buryong* creates a material trace across the muscular toning of the imprisoned body and in the administrative practices of the prison. But sometimes it would be bad: "Maybe my daughter visited me, and it was nice, but then she left, and I felt very depressed. So then the *buryong* is coming, and you cannot do so much about it." Ka Cesar's mention of his daughter illustrates the intertwined spatial and temporal dimensions of *buryong*: it was the spatial confinement that prevented him from partaking in his daughter's life. *Buryong* then becomes a vast temporal emptiness where the fear is that the present will perpetuate itself eternally into the future, and hence that the waiting will prove to have been for nothing.

Buryong is intimately connected to prison life but not confined to it. As Ka Cesar says, "It seems that it has been transported out of the jail. You know, many of the people in jail, they are common criminals, so they take the idea of *buryong* with them to describe also what they experience outside." Ka Cesar refers here both to the spatial circulation of bodies between prisons and marginalized communities that produce inmates and to the experiential similarities between ghetto life and prison life that are rendered intelligible through the concept of *buryong*. Arguably, and following Bourdieu (1999), people are also confined to marginal spaces in the ghetto that are hard to escape. I return below to young men's relationship to the labor market, where structural marginalization, poverty, and social and physical distance from centers of production and the global world of capitalism have reconfigured gender relations and the possible futures that might be imagined (Cole 2004; Tacoli 1999; Tadiar 2004; Mahler and Pessar 2006). It is these connections that Kay makes when he tries to explain *buryong* to me:

> For me it is to be irritated and feeling uncomfortable. If, for instance, there is someone who is noisy, I'll say, "Don't be too noisy. I am *buryong*." I am in bad mood, and I don't like to hear people arguing in front of me. I get easily irritated, since my father and mother used to be like that. I also feel *buryong* with my life because I don't have work. I don't have any source of money; my everyday life became routine. I feel annoyed with the situation of being *buryong*, but more than that I am annoyed with myself. I am annoyed with myself because even though I already graduated in high school, I am still here.

Several issues here are important for my purpose. *Buryong* is a feeling of uneasiness and irritability; it reminds Kay of his parents and ongoing struggles, it relates to a lack of options and to the sense of confinement ("I am still here"), and finally it implicates Kay himself. Consequently, Kay was constantly looking for work, talking about it, and being depressed that all his efforts led to nothing. It is in these situations that the *kapatiran* becomes important. Kay says, "Yet I never lose hope. I am not all the time like that. Especially when I am with my brothers in the frat [fraternity, *kapatiran*], I am comforted and find something to be busy about. My focus is diverted with them." However, even the *kapatiran* cannot help for long, and soon *buryong* returns, especially when he is alone: "When serious matters arise, and when I am alone and *buryong*, I really think of many things. I contemplate about things, and most of the time I do things like looking for job."

Combating *Buryong*

In Kay's account, then, *buryong* is intimately related to structural marginalization and the threat of confinement in a present tense being perpetuated into the future. *Buryong* can never be completely escaped but is inscribed on the bodies of people and in their actions, like Ka Francisco's painting or, as we see below, in ritual practices of the brotherhood and in job-seeking trajectories across urban space. At the same time, it marks the absence of time and empty time and can mostly be gauged in terms of its negativity. However, as Ka Cesar stresses, *buryong* is also productive; it drives people toward action because not moving and being alone are unbearable. Only by acting can different futures emerge as possibilities. Kay mentions two activities specifically: looking for work and being with *brods* in the *kapatiran*. In the remainder of the chapter, I explore the dynamics of *kapatiran* and employment, respectively, to understand how the young men cope with *buryong*.

Brotherhood and Buryong

Brotherhoods and secret societies have a long history in the Philippines, from bands of robbers during the Spanish period (Bankoff 1996) through the revolutionary *Katipunan* movement of the war of independence in the mid-1890s (Ileto 1979) to a range of Masonic movements and brotherhoods in the last century that have penetrated even the highest echelons of society: universities, political parties, and the supreme court (Vitug 2010). In this way, brotherhoods and secret societies have been a staple of Philippine male political culture and the reproduction of its elite. Tau Gamma Phi, to which Kay and the other young men belonged, emerges from the same tradition. Greek letter fraternities (and sororities) in the Philippines most likely emerged from the American university fraternity tradition in existence across the United States since the early nineteenth century (Syrett 2009). When the University of the Philippines (UP) was established by the American colonial administration in 1908, fraternities were quick to follow (Zarco 2000). They were and are confined to universities for the most part. This is especially true for elite fraternities, whose alumni have peopled the court system and the offices of political power for most of Philippine independence.

However, a few fraternities, like Tau Gamma Phi, spread outside the universities. Tau Gamma Phi was set up at UP in 1968 by four young men studying social sciences during the tumultuous times leading up to the state of emergency in 1972. Already by 1971 the Triskelion Youth Movement had been established as a community-based wing of Tau Gamma Phi.

To understand how the young men use the brotherhood to cope with *buryong*, it is not necessary to explore the fraternity system in great detail. Suffice it to say that from 2005, and especially after 2008, Tau Gamma Phi began to grow rapidly in poor neighborhoods like Bagong Silang, allegedly claiming up to two million members nationwide. From fewer than ten chapters across Bagong Silang in 2005, by 2010 this number had grown to about sixty chapters, each organizing up to a hundred members. Between 2008 and 2010 Tau Gamma Phi became visible in almost every area through tags on houses and *tambayan* (hangouts), frat shirts with the golden hand on black cloth (the sign of Tau Gamma Phi), and the frequent and loud initiations that could be heard throughout the area on many Sundays. I argue that one of the reasons why Tau Gamma Phi became so popular was that the brotherhood provided a means to cope with the structural forms of marginalization and the problem of stunted time that I have talked about as *buryong*. Initiation rituals play a central role in how young men cope with *buryong* because it creates a transcendent mythical path into adulthood that is often denied to young men on the resettlement site.

The bulk of the new members of Tau Gamma Phi are young men who came from loosely organized peer groups called "tribes." Whereas tribes are not considered a serious business and have few rules (a kids' game), the brotherhood is for men, strictly disciplined, and renowned and respected across the country. To join the brotherhood, the newcomers (or neophytes) need orientation. Orientation concerns the codes, the proper understanding of history, and the moral comportment expected of members. Initiation is an important part of the orientation, being heavily ritualized and quite violent.

With the rise in membership, many chapters frequently initiate neophytes. The neophytes are identified through peer networks, often tribes, in the local neighborhood or through the schools. In the days leading up to the actual initiation, the neophytes must subordinate themselves to effeminizing humiliation like cleaning, washing, and cooking for the initiated *brods*. On the day of the initiation, *brods* from the local chapter and guests from other chapters congregate in a designated house. As violent initiation in the form of hazing is prohibited by law (Republic of the Philippines 1995) and because initiation is supposedly only for the initiates, *brods* try to keep the uninitiated out. However, local residents wander in and out of the "hallowed grounds," and I was invited to attend and film the initiation, and thus the secret is more akin to a "public secret" "that vibrates with sacred light" only on the surface (Taussig 1999: 58). Hence, the secrets of the brotherhood are effective only if people know that the *brods* have them.

Because of the secrecy and illegality of the initiation, the brotherhood often conducts it in local homes or empty lots within the maze of small roads that make up Bagong Silang. On this particular Sunday, six neophytes are to be initiated. The small, dingy house is full to capacity and exceedingly hot under the tropical sun. *Brods* and neophytes line three walls. The last wall is decorated with a tarpaulin exhibiting a large lion-man (the symbol of Tau Gamma Phi) holding the initiation whip (looking like a cricket bat). The whip, also called *lolo* (grandfather), is covered in blood for dramatic effect. Above the lion-man, the name of the visiting chapter is marked in golden Gothic letters. Both tarpaulin and whip are central, sacred objects of the brotherhood, and the individual chapters spend much time in choosing or making the right whip and in designing the tarpaulin.

The initiation begins with a prayer said in a read-and-reply style:

> Almighty God, bless this brotherhood of ours that we may succeed in all our endeavors. Enlighten and strengthen our premier secretary general, governor general, municipal chairmen, and chapter grand Triskelions and so for them to maintain the highest standard of decision making for a better and more successful Tau Gamma Phi, Triskelion's grand fraternity. Amen.

After the prayer, two *brods* hold the arms of the neophyte, who faces a wall blindfolded, standing in a crucifixion-style posture. The master of initiation (MI), asks what the fraternity name of the neophyte will be. Taking turns, the other *brods* hit the neophyte across the upper thighs. At each stroke, the MI reads from the codes and tenets, beginning with the founding fathers: "I love lord high Vedastro 'Tito' Venida, November 17, 1949, A.B. political science. Accept?" The neophyte then receives the blow while responding, "Accept." All the founding fathers must be accepted along with the codes and tenets before the initiation is finished. Strict rules govern the initiation, in relation to both the violence, which needs to be measured and ordered rather than ruthless, and the dress code, under which the initiate and those wielding the whip must wear long trousers and no accessories. After the initiation the newborn *brod* will be welcomed by his new brothers, who will honor him with a drinking session while he recovers.

Performing the initiation is talked about as "giving," whereas the initiate "receives," orientation, discipline, and brotherhood, and the initiate is ultimately transformed by the initiation. Hence, giver and receiver enter into a relationship in which both access a different temporality of the timeless brotherhood. The initiation becomes a stage for the performance of masculinity for both those who give and those who receive, although in different ways. For those who give, it is about the benevolent administration of violence and knowledge about the rules, discipline, and restraint. For those who receive, it is about being able to stomach the pain. However, the drama of initiation also draws on cultural-religious registers specific to Southeast Asia, where self-inflicted pain is central to piety and religious practices (Tiatco and Bonifacio-Ramolete 2008), as well as on more general notions of ritual and sacrifice. For example, in *Prey into Hunter*, Maurice Bloch (1992) explores rituals of initiation in a way that is useful in understanding Tau Gamma Phi's rites of initiation. Bloch suggests that the initiate is taken out of his normal context and ritually sacrificed in ways that endanger him physically. This is similar to Tau Gamma Phi's initiation, in which the initiate enters a different temporal space, marked by a tarpaulin, decoration, dress code, guards at the door, the sound of the whip, and the moans of the initiate, as he performs knee-bending exercises to help blood circulate between each swing. Furthermore, initiation often leads to death-threatening situations as the blood in the thighs clots and prevents circulation. Hence, although initiation has been relaxed, especially after an antihazing law was passed (Republic of the Philippines 1995), initiation must include a level of danger.

Transformation (accessing the transcendental) is accomplished exactly through the violence that the initiate accepts being subjected to. This happens when the initiate "accepts" the next blow that will gain him access to another secret—another part of the transcendental. That the initiate is blindfolded suggests, echoing Bloch's analysis, that he is still not able to face the transcendental but must be left in the "dark" until he is ready—that is, until the initiation is over.

As the initiate returns from the world of the transcendental, the temporal space of the initiation, he brings back some of the transcendental (i.e., the brotherhood's secrets, discipline, and codes and tenets) with which he can "dominate the here and now of which he previously was a part" (Bloch 1992: 5). In this way, the return of the initiate, armed with the vitality of the transcendental, is for Bloch what constitutes the political moment of ritual, the point at which the ritual allows individuals to transcend the everyday life from which they come. Entering the brotherhood means entering a world of order, sacrifice, and meaning, which because of the secret nature of the brotherhood is inaccessible to anyone on the outside. As one *brod* responded to my incessant questioning, "If you are so curious, why don't you join?" This ability to transcend the space of the present is arguably one of the reasons why the *kapatiran* can be used to combat *buryong*. To be faced with *buryong* is to be caught in an ever-perpetuated present located in marginal space. However, through the articulations of identity that relate to an ordered, disciplined, and transcendental masculinity, entering Tau Gamma Phi in Bagong Silang opens another, almost magical, temporal dimension that harks back to the millenarian brotherhoods of the *Katipunan* (the independence movement). Furthermore, through the brotherhood, which was originally based in the university and had members high up in elite society, *brods* can gain access to a fellowship that reaches far beyond the marginalized space of Bagong Silang. These connections virtually materialized in the form of pictures of Tau Gamma celebrities, including senators, TV personalities, and sports stars, which most *brods* had on their phones and proudly displayed to me.

These connections to power were seemingly made real when a leading local politician promised the brotherhood privileged access to resources if they provided the electoral muscle for his political machine. This promise was made on an evening when Tau Gamma Phi in Bagong Silang received recognition in the form of a signed certificate from one of the fraternity's four founding fathers. Assassin, one of the *brods*, said, "This is what we have been waiting for all these years. This is what is making it all worthwhile. I am so proud. One of the people that I respect most in the world actually signed this certificate." In this way, the *kapatiran* at universities, the real *kapatiran*, had recognized the value, equal status, and legitimacy of the *brod* in the resettlement area in a way that is not often experienced by the young men who are confined spatially and temporally in *buryong*.

However, this inclusion into another space and temporality never succeeds in permanently combating *buryong*. To repeat Bourdieu's words at the beginning of the chapter, "Prophecies, divinations, predictions, millenarian announcements had no other purpose than to fill what is no doubt one of the most painful of wants: the lack of a future," something that the brotherhood and its rituals do not really achieve. For instance, although local politicians woo the *kapatiran* with promises of money and recognition, *brods* are realistic about the promises of the powerful. Although Mike Defensor, a politician running for office in the largest city in Metro Manila, is a *brod*, as is the famous TV personality and politician Vic Sotto, few *brods* would assume that his life was in any significant way linked to the life of the celebrities. Furthermore, when Assassin celebrated the recognition, it was already the day after the ceremony where only the (symbolic and actual) hangovers of inclusion remained at a drinking session that looked no different from the many that had gone before and the many that were sure to follow. Although the *brods* taste the transcendental through their initiation or through the letter from the founding father, transcendence is not permanent. Hence, rituals do not express or reproduce structure, as Victor Turner argues (1969); rather, as Judith Butler (1993) and Catherine Bell (1992) claim, rituals are all there is, and they need to be performed over and over again. Hence, although the brotherhood promises symbolic inclusion into different spaces and temporalities, it never really manages to combat *buryong*. In fact, like Ka Francisco's paintings and Ka Cesar's body toning, the rituals constitute the material trace of *buryong* as stunted future rather than its solution.

Employment and Buryong

Although much less spectacular than the initiation rituals, employment and access to the labor market seem to be a different and more effective way of combating *buryong*. As Kay said, when *buryong* in the form of a fear that the present will be perpetuated into the future overwhelms him, he goes and looks for a job. The ordering of employment above the *kapatiran*, which is not surprising, rests on a temporal logic as well, fraternity member Tayo said: "I don't have time for the brotherhood now. I have a family that I need to provide for." He told me this after I had met him again in May 2011. The year before, he had been very active in the brotherhood, but since his girlfriend had given birth to a child, he had been working as a sales representative for a furniture company. Hence, the brotherhood was posited as an organization whose activities one engaged in during one's coming of age. After this time, members would either leave the brotherhood altogether or literally graduate into becoming an elder or an alumnus. Drawing on ideas of generational authority, both terms were used in Bagong Silang to signify that one's identity changed once one became older and assumed different responsibilities, like providing for a family and advising the young. This logic was based on a notion that transformation into adulthood was possible and would not be impeded by structural barriers. Although the transformation is possible to a greater extent than Bourdieu's account seems to allow, Tayo's case illustrates some of the difficulties, as well as the possibilities.

In many ways Tayo was lucky. He had managed to secure a reasonable job not too far away. It was commission based, but he had a basic salary of 2,000 Philippine pesos (P 100 is roughly US$2) a month. With his commissions, and in a good month, he could land as much as P 5,000. This is an average salary for many men in Bagong Silang working in construction or as tricycle drivers, although it is well short of the national minimum salary of about P 9,000 a month, which is almost entirely for graduates from tertiary education. Those in cleaning jobs and caretaker jobs, baggers and security guards in supermarkets, and stay-in workers (that is, living in their place of employment) often earn well below this, sometimes no more than P 2,000 a month. Tayo is also lucky that he does not have to commute, which in Manila is a true nightmare because of cost and wasted hours. Assassin, mentioned previously, works a factory job some ten kilometers away, but because of traffic it takes three hours to get to work and up to three hours for the return. Hence, with an eight-hour shift he will be gone from Bagong Silang for almost fourteen hours a day. Like Assassin, Mariza earns a minimum salary in her job as a cashier in a restaurant. Her commute also lasts for three hours. Some days, she will leave at 9:00 A.M. and return at 1:00 A.M. She must change public transport lines three times between her home in Bagong Silang and her work in up-market Ortigas some thirty kilometers away. Commuting is also expensive, and Mariza spends up to a third of her salary commuting back and forth (P 150 out of P 426). The commute is problematic in other ways for Mariza. The lonely hours in the noisy bus have become her personal entry into a state of *buryong*. She explains:

> I don't experience *buryong* when I am at work. I am so busy, and when I get back home, it's okay too because I am so tired. But in the bus I have so much time, and I am alone. So I sit and think about the future. What will I do for my kids? How will we survive? And I think that I am thirty-five years old. Have I come far enough? No! And then I panic. Once I had a real attack, and I couldn't move. Now I always carry a paper bag that I do like this with [*shows how she inhales and exhales into the bag*]. It's always in my bag.

Jojo and Dennis both left Bagong Silang to take up positions as stay-in workers elsewhere in the urban economy. To stay in is often the solution to the prohibitive cost of transport. When I met him, Jojo was working with Tayo (before Tayo landed his sales job) delivering purified water to householders. One day, Jojo told me that he had managed to find a job in Makati, the Manila business district and a place of money and opportunity. One of his relatives knew someone there, and they had promised him a stay-in job. The Monday after he was supposed to have gone, I found him back in the neighborhood. When I asked what had happened, he gestured that he did not want to talk about it. It turned out that the conditions had been so bad and the salary so low that he would rather face another round of waiting in Bagong Silang. Dennis, another *brod*, returned to Bagong Silang two months into my fieldwork. He had been working in Manila and only rarely made it back to Bagong Silang because of the cost of transport. I asked him why he came back, and he spoke of constant humiliations, accusations of drug use and drug peddling, low pay (P 2,000 a month), and twelve to fourteen hours under the blazing sun selling goods for a Chinese boss who despised him and served him half-rotten food. He too preferred to wait it out in Bagong Silang, even if that meant making a humiliating peace with his stepfather.

Both Dennis and Jojo were faced with global changes in production (Jeffrey 2010) that meant that it was difficult to find jobs, and when they did the jobs were so bad that staying in Bagong Silang was to be preferred, even if the resettlement site, like other marginalized spaces across the world, seemed to form the end station of ambitions and hope. However, as Mariza's paper bag illustrates, working is not always the solution to the problem of *buryong*. What is more, neither Jojo nor Dennis gave in to *buryong* in Bagong Silang. In fact, while Bagong Silang represented the boundaries of possibility, it also made it possible for them to survive through their networks. When Jojo and Tayo delivered water, for instance, their profit was only marginal (Guyer 2004), at around P 10 per delivery. They delivered water to twenty-odd people a day, but because of their *diskarte*—that is, their ability to get along and survive—they managed to earn a little extra by cheating the supplier. *Diskarte*, the ability to make something out of even the tiniest possibility, is a recognized art form in areas like Bagong Silang, and it relates precisely to the ability to read social maps and act on them. This might not represent much of a future, but it gets the young men through the day.

In many ways, the case of Kay, whom we met above, illustrates the dilemmas and barriers involved in escaping the resettlement site and the ever-looming threat of *buryong* through employment. Kay is constantly looking for a job but without success, despite his having finished high school and being generally intelligent and sensitive. However, Kay's problems go deeper than simply the lack of work. The family of a girl he once dated claimed that he fathered her child. In the meantime, the girl married a Korean and now lives in Saigon with the child. Kay says the first time we meet, "Maybe it's mine, I don't know," and later on, asserting greater certainty of his fatherhood with respect to the little girl he has never seen, "I miss her so much." "I will save money, and I will go to her," he tells me rather sadly at the end of my fieldwork. In a way, Kay lives the symptoms of the crisis of masculinity in all its aspects: at the bottom of the global sexual food chain and with very few options but to wait while his time is invested in the brotherhood, which only promises temporary respite for young men—no future for a man. However, like the others, Kay not only waits. Although he identifies *buryong* as a central feature of his life, he tries to react. He decided to fix his half-rotten teeth, which prevented him from smiling in public. He also struggled hard to get his "requirements," the papers necessary to work, study, go abroad, and vote. Fixing his teeth and getting his requirements were material articulations of *buryong* and clearly did not spell certainty of success. Like the teeth fixing there is just no guarantee of success, and his and his fellow *brods*' endeavors are fundamentally marked by uncertainty. Maybe, just maybe, what is here now is what will be forever. Maybe the future, as anything but this present, will inevitably recede before them, accompanied by the ever-looming specter of *buryong*.

Conclusion: *Buryong* and the Future

In this chapter I show how people in prison and ghettos employ the concept of *buryong* to describe the presence—almost materially as objectified time—of a dark companion, desperation, loneliness, and insanity. *Buryong* represents the fear that present-day predicaments will be perpetuated into a future temporal and spatial wasteland where all remains frightfully similar. However, *buryong* also prompts activity. I therefore argue that *buryong* constitutes a central element in the subjectivity of people in Bagong Silang. I show how young men in fraternities use these organizations as ways of coping with the structural forms of marginalization that produce *buryong* by constructing meaningful relations transcending temporal and spatial forms of marginalization. The ritualized initiation into the brotherhood opened up symbolic connections with powerful people in the history of the Philippines and with people in power outside the resettlement site. Thus, the brotherhood enabled recognition of sorts. However, ultimately the brotherhood failed to provide a permanent respite because inclusion was undermined by structural barriers and because the *brods* saw the brotherhood as part of reaching adulthood, indeed manhood (through its focus on disciplining and ordering), without it being central to an accomplished manhood. That demanded gaining employment and assuming responsibility. However, in line with both Bourdieu (2000) and Jeffrey (2010), employment is equally precarious as a way of coping with *buryong*. There is often very little work to be found, as unemployment rates testify. When there is work, it is far away, pays little, and is never short on humiliation. For these reasons, the young men in the brotherhood get by through their *diskarte*, their ability to survive using networking and social skills, which often depend on their staying in Bagong Silang. Hence, Bagong Silang is central simultaneously to temporal and spatial marginalization and to coping with the structures that produce *buryong* as a central element in the subjectivity of people there. While this might not represent a future in Bourdieu's understanding, it does help the young men get by and survive—at least for another day.

REFERENCES

Bankoff, Greg. 1996. *Crime, Society and the State in Nineteenth Century Philippines.* Manila: Ateneo University Press.
Bell, Catherine. 1992. *Ritual Theory, Ritual Practice.* Oxford: Oxford University Press.
Bloch, Maurice. 1992. *Prey into Hunter: The Politics of Religious Experience.* Cambridge: Cambridge University Press.
Bourdieu, Pierre. 1999. *The Weight of the World: Social Suffering in Contemporary Society.* Oxford: Polity Press.
———. 2000. *Pascalian Meditations.* Stanford, CA: Stanford University Press.
Butler, Judith. 1993. *Bodies That Matter.* London: Routledge.
Cole, Jennifer. 2004. "Fresh Contact in Tamatave, Madagascar: Sex, Money, and Intergenerational Transformation." *American Ethnologist* 31 (4): 573–588.
Cole, Jennifer, and Deborah Durham. 2008. *Generations and Globalization: Youth, Age, and Family in the New World Economy.* Gary: University of Indiana Press.
Flaherty, Michael. 2011. *The Textures of Time: Agency and Temporal Experience.* Philadelphia: Temple University Press.
Guyer, Jane I. 2004. *Marginal Gains: Monetary Transactions in Atlantic Africa.* Chicago: University of Chicago Press.
Hage, Ghassan. 2009. *Waiting.* Carlton, Australia: Melbourne University Publishing.
Ileto, Reynaldo. 1979. *Pasyon and Revolution: Popular Movements in the Philippines, 1840–1910.* Manila: Ateneo University Press.
Jeffrey, Craig. 2008. "Waiting." *Environment and Planning D: Society and Space* 26 (6): 954–958.
———. 2010. *Timepass: Youth, Class, and the Politics of Waiting in India.* Stanford, CA: Stanford University Press.
Mahler, Sarah, and Patricia R. Pessar. 2006. "Gender Matters: Ethnographers Bring Gender from the Periphery toward the Core of Migration Studies." *International Migration Review* 40 (1): 27–63.
Republic of the Philippines. 1995. Republic Act No. 8049, "An Act Regulating Hazing and Other Forms of Initiation Rites in Fraternities, Sororities and Organizations and Providing Penalties Therefore." Available at http://ofyourdream.com/anti-hazing-law.htm.
Syrett, Nicholas. 2009. *The Company He Keeps: A History of White College Fraternities.* Chapel Hill: University of North Carolina Press.
Tacoli, Cecilia. 1999. "International Migration and the Restructuring of Gender Asymmetries: Continuity and Change among Filipino Labor Migrants in Rome." *International Migration Review* 33 (3): 658–682.

Tadiar, Neferti. 2004. *Fantasy-Production: Sexual Economies and Other Philippine Consequences for the New World Order.* Manila: Ateneo de Manila University Press.

Taussig, Michael. 1999. *Defacement: Public Secrecy and the Labor of the Negative.* Stanford, CA: Stanford University Press.

Tiatco, Sir Anril Pineda, and Amihan Bonifacio-Ramolete. 2008. "Cutud's Ritual of Nailing on the Cross: Performance of Pain and Suffering." *Asian Theatre Journal* 25 (1): 58–76.

Turner, Victor. 1969. *The Ritual Process: Structure and Anti-structure.* New York: Aldine de Gruyter.

Vitug, Marites Dañguilan. 2010. *Shadow of Doubt: Probing the Supreme Court.* Manila: Newsbreak.

Zarco, Ricardo. 2000. "Report on Student Organization Conflicts, University of the Philippines, Diliman, 1991–1998." Unpublished paper, University of the Philippines.

Zorc, David, and Rachel San Miguel. 1991. *Tagalog Slang Dictionary.* Manila: De La Salle University Press.

3
Aske's Dead Time

An Exploration of the Qualities of Time among Left-Radical Activists in Denmark

Stine Krøijer

It is early evening. Aske, a twenty-four-year-old activist from Copenhagen, and I are walking along a snowy street in Copenhagen looking for a pub. "Argh! I need a beer—that meeting just went on forever," says Aske, sighing deeply. For the past three hours we have been sitting together with some two hundred climate activists on a cold floor in an abandoned municipal building to evaluate Reclaim Power, a spectacular confrontation between activists and police during the UN climate summit of 2009. Most people, including Aske and me, had left the meeting when the agenda changed from shared reflections on the successes and failures of the action to "future movement building."

We have fallen behind a group of fellow activists from Climate Justice Action, a network of activists committed to taking action on climate change. Aske shivers slightly in his big coat and confesses to having been "kind of depressed" for the past few months, ever since the eviction and deportation of a group of Iraqi refugees from a squatted church in the neighborhood. Aske had been involved in this action for several months as an organizer, after which he disappeared, claiming he was depressed and "burned out." He reappeared a few weeks before the climate summit to participate in Reclaim Power. "It was nice to be back on the streets," he says now with a boyish smile.

This chapter explores the qualities that time assumes among left-radical activists through Aske's experiences as an activist. I address what it entails to be depressed and burned out and illuminate the relationship of this to being active and on the streets. In recent years, several anthropologists have analyzed the moments in time when apparently nothing happens and have conceptualized these as situations of waiting (Hage 2009; Jeffrey 2010), boredom (Svendsen 2005), or doing nothing in particular (Ehn and Löfgren 2010). According to the Introduction, it is during these particular moments that time presents itself to consciousness and becomes an object of concern and deliberate action. Youth is considered a phase in life when this is most acutely troublesome. I add to this line of thinking about time by building on Brian Massumi's concept of affect (Massumi 1987, 2002) to cast light on the various ways the (activist) body engenders time. Following Massumi's thinking, affects are understood as prepersonal and nonconscious experiences of bodily intensity (Massumi 1987: xvi). For Aske and other activists activism plays itself out as two qualities of time: a bodily sense of dead time, characterized by apathy, burnout, and a sense of singularity, and active time, experienced as moments of heightened vitality and bodily strength. In this chapter I am concerned particularly with dead time, not as an alternative to the concepts of waiting or boredom but as a "native" concept (Holbraad 2012, xvii) that in this context illuminates the particular relationship between body and time.

Even through radical activists like Aske have received a lot of political attention in Denmark because of their spectacular protests, and hence sometimes find themselves taking center stage, they are often placed in a condition of waiting. In my exploration of Aske's sense of dead time, I show how activists are relegated to an "imaginary waiting room of history" (Povinelli 2011: 77) in at least two ways. First, I show how the discourse about youth in Scandinavia as a period of finding themselves and their place in society (Gullestad 2006; Anderson 2008) considers young people as politically immature and as having to wait to fully participate in political life. Second, I find that Aske's dead time is not simply an effect of youth or of finding oneself in a transitory period in life but ties into activists' bleak views of the possibilities of radical change. I explore activist perceptions of the chances of overcoming capitalism, and I argue that these perceptions give rise to a sense of temporal discontinuity between the present and the future. These factors contribute to a sense of waiting, or of dead time, to be more precise, but never fully determine the way things are. Instead of sinking into a permanent state of apathy and inaction, activists begin to experiment with ways of doing politics, which in practice plays out as apathy and burnout and, in other moments, as bodily vitality and strength.

Spoiled Middle-Class Kids

To the Danish public, left-radical activists are known for their recurrent and spectacular confrontations with the police during summits, against austerity measures of the European Union, and during conflicts over the eviction of squatters from houses and self-managed social centers, which are social centers organized by activists themselves and, at least in their view, outside the control of the authorities. "Left radical" is an umbrella term used by activists in northern Europe to refer to people on the extraparliamentarian left of anarchist, autonomist, and anticapitalist persuasions. In Denmark they were previously referred to as squatters (*BZ'ere*) or autonomous activists (*autonome*) because of their focus on establishing and running self-managed social centers. After the protests against the World Trade Organization in Seattle in 1999, they were characterized as the radical strain of the global justice movement (see Graeber 2002, 2009; Juris 2008; Maeckelbergh 2009; Sullivan 2005). In later years they have appeared as the Indignados in Spain and the Occupy movement on Wall Street and elsewhere (Razsa and Kurnik 2012). "Radical" in the emic sense refers to someone who advocates radical change from the roots of capitalist society. Yet how this is envisioned and practiced is, as I show below, strikingly different from other revolutionary movements.

I first met Aske in 2007, about six months after the eviction and demolition of a social center known as Ungdomshuset (Youth House). Aske is a graduate student of history and is living temporarily in a co-op house on the outskirts of Copenhagen, which was rented by a group of activist friends of his a few years back. Even though he has been politically active on the left-radical scene in Copenhagen for only a few years, he has become a central figure in the sense that he is someone to call when direct actions are being planned. He is smiling and outgoing, with a rare mixture of macho recklessness and theoretical self-reflection, and he almost always seems prepared to engage in a variety of practical tasks.

Aske is of middle-class background, and his parents are left wing. Before starting university, Aske was a student at the Free Gymnasium, an alternative secondary school that stresses direct consensus democracy among students and faculty and is often talked of as a stepping stone to the left-radical milieu in Copenhagen. Aske did not "get engaged" in activism right away but turned up at Ungdomshuset for parties and to hang out with friends. During an interview in the garden of the co-op, we talk about how he first became involved:

My political interest started though reading texts, even classical Marxism and critiques of political economy. I was very negative and quite apathetic at the time. I was not engaged in anything specific. When I began university I teamed up with some people from the Front of Socialist Youth [a youth political party], but that was too much organization. . . . Direct action is more my kind of thing. [*Lights a cigarette*] Sometimes problems just become too big, too structural: it is like hitting a cushion [with no effect]—climate issues, for example. That is probably why I started with Ungdomshuset.

During the interview Aske describes the way many activists sometimes feel, that changing or even influencing the way things are is impossible, making it seem not worthwhile to even try. Aske's explanation of his thinking proved to be key in my understanding activist perceptions of the near and distant future and of dead time and how it can be overcome. He describes this sense of being unable to influence things using a bodily idiom, an apathy healed by neither reading political theory nor becoming a member of the formal youth organization of a leftist party but only by engaging in direct action with others.

The term "direct action" refers to forms of action that engage a problem in such a way that the acts themselves simultaneously embody a solution to the problem (see Graeber 2009; Maeckelbergh 2009). For example, instead of organizing a demonstration against racism in front of the town hall, which according to activists leaves action on the problem to others (i.e., elected politicians), direct action would involve cutting down the fence around a refugee detention center, producing simultaneity of action and effect. In the interview Aske mentions the defense of Ungdomshuset as a way to get involved in direct action.

Six months before our first conversation, in March 2007, dramatic clashes took place in the district of Nørrebro in Copenhagen over the ownership of Ungdomshuset, established by activists twenty-five years ago (Hansen 2008; Karker 2007; Karpantschof and Mikkelsen 2009). Ungdomshuset was the backbone of the squatter's movement in the 1980s, and over the years the building served as an alternative scene for punk music, street theater, and circus. It had a weekly vegan soup kitchen, a café, a bookshop and printing workshop, and a weekly cinema. The municipality owned the buildings but had delegated the running of the house to the users since 1982. After a fire in the building in 1999, the municipality decided to put the house up for sale, which was bought by the Christian sect Faderhuset (Father House) (see Krøijer and Sjørslev 2011 for a more detailed analysis).

Most activists, including Aske, describe how they started frequenting Ungdomshuset by hanging around the place with friends, drinking, and going to concerts. Several people have described how at some point they became "absorbed by" (*optaget af*) activities there: vegan cooking for the weekly soup kitchen, concert or action planning, bartending, or guerrilla gardening in the small backyard of the house. These activities were described as being as imminently meaningful and as political as the long theoretical discussions that were said to characterize the youth parties or as the actions to influence global structural issues such as climate change.

Aske became involved in the fight against the eviction of Ungdomshuset, which hitherto had mostly been a social base for him. Like many other left-radical activists, he has had a short-lived attachment to more traditional left organizations, but as already noted he experienced these as having "too much organization," a common criticism by activists of what are seen as the more hierarchically organized political parties, nongovernment organizations, and labor unions. Aske and many other activists instead took an intense interest in the effects and tactics of direct action, the detailed procedures of decision making within social centers, and mundane activities such as food provision and eating, which in a Billy Ehn and Orvar Löfgren (2010) perspective could have been considered utterly unimportant or even boring.

How these mundane activities became positive, political actions can be illustrated by describing Aske's friend Sara (see also Krøijer and Sjørslev 2011). A twenty-six-year-old artist who lives in a small one-room apartment only a few blocks from Ungdomshuset, Sara has for almost ten years participated in different activities at the house, both inside and outside. She started out by playing music in a punk band and hanging around the house with friends. Later, she helped run the soup kitchen. She soon came to see the house as point of departure for activities in public space, such as the People's Park Initiative to restore, run, and defend a park and playground for locals. For Sara, being an activist was a matter of constant labor: "Obviously, walking through the door to Ungdomshuset was not like taking a shower that would wash away all the norms, values and hierarchies of the surrounding society, but we did work hard to *do* things differently," she explained on one occasion (Krøijer and Sjørslev 2011: 89).

Sara told of her involvement in setting up a printing workshop to describe the activities in the house. She had the idea of building a movable printing machine to print flyers, posters, and artwork. She said she carried out the idea together with a couple of fellow activists and with materials they "picked up for free" around town. To Sara, Ungdomshuset was a place where you were allowed to "take initiatives on your own and create something concrete" (Krøijer and Sjørslev 2011: 89), the concreteness of political action being thought of as particularly positive. Making politics concrete, however, required persistence and things being done in specific ways: materials for the machine had to be stolen or retrieved from garbage bins to "liberate" the action from the market economy, and considerable time had to be put into organizing people to take part and do things for free in order to build new social norms and alternative economies. Sara managed to get her printing machine running for several months, after which she went traveling. When she returned, the machine and its room at Ungdomshuset had been taken over for other purposes.

Sara found it difficult to abandon something she had created, but at the same time she was happy that people had found a new use for the machine, and she soon found herself involved in a new project. Later, she recalled feeling that in Ungdomshuset, at its best, "Everything fitted together from the cleaning and bar jobs in Ungeren [Ungdomshuset], the vegan cooking and dumpster diving, to the meetings and demos." She described this as a positive experience of "becoming engaged in" (*blive engageret*) or "becoming absorbed by" (*blive optaget af*) something (Krøijer and Sjørslev 2011: 89).

Aske had the same kind of willingness to engage in practical, routine tasks but never found the activities concerned with the running of the house sufficiently interesting. His engagement as an activist started when Ungdomshuset was threatened with eviction, and he mostly focused his efforts on organizing spectacular protests and actions, which nevertheless also involved many routine tasks.

Right-wing politicians and respectable citizens had for years called the house's inhabitants and frequent visitors "spoiled middle-class kids" who had not been properly educated by their parents. In addition, the kids were renowned "troublemakers" who displayed undemocratic behavior in their recurrent clashes with the police after the house had been put up for sale (Krøijer and Sjørslev 2011: 91). Ungdomshuset was described as a filthy, inhospitable, and somewhat conspicuous place without contact with the surrounding world. In the debates in the municipal council over the sale, several politicians said that it had been their desire to erase this black spot from the map of Copenhagen all along. In one council meeting in 1999, a council member put it in plain words:

> I agree with Enhedslisten's [the Red-Green Party's] statement that young people are the gold nugget of our society. We need to protect them and give them the best conditions possible. But not that pile of rotten stones at Jagtvej 69 [the address of Ungdomshuset]. Tear

the shit down. Period! Let's get all the blather over and done with. (Borgerrepræsentationen 1999)

As this quotation indicates, the view, held by some of my informants, that the young users of Ungdomshuset were "unruly children" and "spoiled kids" who should be taught to stop making a nuisance of themselves in public is one in which young people are politically immature and hence in need of protection while they learn how to play a full part in public politics.

As the names Ungdomshuset (Youth House) and Faderhuset (Father House) only too ironically illustrate, the "Ungdomshus problem" was understood from a generational perspective and associated with young people's finding themselves (*finde sig selv*) and finding their place (*finde deres plads*) in adult society (Gullestad 2002: 255–257; 2006: 82–88; Krøijer and Sjørslev 2011). To find themselves, people are expected to become aware of their individual identities and potential. As part of this process, young adults are expected to venture increasingly into public space, but following the Danish thinker Hal Koch's ideas about democracy and citizenship, a widespread perception prevails that only grown-ups are fully fledged citizens, and young people must wait and learn and wait some more before participating in public political affairs (see Korsgaard 2001: 73–76; Anderson 2008).

Politicians had differing views as to whether Ungdomshuset was what Karen Olwig and Eva Gulløv have called a "proper place for children" (2003: 2–3). Apart from the belief that Ungdomshuset was an improper place for children because of its lack of hygiene and adult supervision, other politicians and public commentators argued that it was a "growth-layer for talented young people" (Borgerrepræsentationen 1999). Using "growth" to describe the process of generational succession suggests that, to find themselves, young adults must refashion the values transmitted by the family, which implies that a certain level of resistance and rebelliousness is desirable. It was therefore necessary to give the young activists some freedom and "a space of their own" (Krøijer and Sjørslev 2011: 92).

In other words, defining the activists in and around Ungdomshuset as young was a way for politicians and political commentators to abandon them to a position of waiting because only time, or more precisely their coming of age, was thought able to resolve their undesirable behavior. Nevertheless, this discourse cannot be assumed to fully condition how activists perceive themselves and their own actions. Interestingly enough, Ungdomshuset—which in this light can be thought of as a waiting room for immature political subjects—was characterized by not just apathy and hanging around but also frenzied activity and absorption in myriad concrete activities. As Elisabeth

Povinelli put it in *Economies of Abandonment*, in which she explores the alternative social worlds that sometimes open up as a consequence of abandonment, people tend not to be waiting in the "imaginary waiting rooms" they are confined to (2011: 77). Instead, people like Sara start experimenting with forms of being together and render as meaningful the mundane activities that other young Danes would consider boring or meaningless. Yet how can this activism as absorption be explained, and how does it relate to Aske's sense of apathy? In the following I return to Aske, particularly to his and other activists' outlook on the near and distant future, to approach waiting and the qualities of time from a slightly different angle.

Having a Sense of Dead Time

During my conversation with Aske in the garden of his co-op, he tells me about participating in the protests against the G8 summit in Heiligendamm, Germany, in 2007. In Heiligendamm, protesters had blocked the summit venue by inventing a new form of action that entailed a choreography of color-coded blocs. Aske showed me a promotional trailer on YouTube, unimaginatively titled "G8 2007 Protest-Trailer." In watching it I was struck by how it reiterated two key perceptions of capitalism and the future held by many activists: capitalism is an all-encompassing system, with no point of transcendence, but one should avoid painting pictures of utopian alternatives.

Before large-scale actions and protest events, European activists distribute promotional videos on the Internet to induce fellow activists to join them. These trailers are one of the few media means activists use for a kind of public exegesis over the status of capitalism, and the trailers usually follow a similar script. They often begin by displaying the evils and injustices of capitalism: war and starvation, exploitation and global inequality, and the devastation of the planet. These are depicted as effects of corporations' insatiable appetite for profit and political leaders' desire for power, which join forces to keep the world under control. Whether promoting protests against NATO, the G8, or a UN climate summit, the trailers convey the message that capitalism is the underlying force. The second parts of the trailers usually turn to scenes of rioting, burning barricades, and not least moments when activists have defeated or tricked police officers during confrontations in the streets.

This particular promotional trailer for the G8 protests in Heiligendamm in 2007 is saturated with imagery of the apocalypse. In the opening it states that "one demonstration will change the course of earths history" and shows us that something new and better might emerge. We hear the apocalyptic statement that "beneath the ruins of this world lies the world of our dreams" while viewing a city of rubble. Throughout the trailer a short sequence in is repeated: a man and a woman slowly approach each other to kiss. What the scene means is open to interpretation, but it definitely suggests that a better world can be associated with the return of intimacy, freedom of association, and the experience of love between humans. Apart from this, what characterizes "the world of our dreams" is left open and undetermined. In this trailer a future other world is represented by glimmering sunlight in the shields held by a line of riot police, while a subtitle lets us know that we "probably experience powerlessness and apathy in the present world" and have "a sense of dead time." That said, it also imparts a view that taking action will reveal something about the world to come.

These promotional trailers describe being stuck in a world characterized by extreme individuality and greed and also by lurking indifference, apathy, and resignation. While Aske mostly associates apathy with his situation before engaging in activism, others associate it with periods in which they disengage and are caught by "a sense of dead time." The promotional trailer also contains an interesting reference to a different world that hides below the surface of the present. Despite the apocalyptic tone of the trailer, it is not revolutionary in a conventional sense; it does not point to world revolution but to a particular demonstration as the solution. The trailer reflects a sense of a temporal discontinuity between the present and what we normally think of as the distant future, which is bridged through direct action. As I have argued elsewhere this is a key difference between classic Marxist-oriented organizations and anarchist-inspired activist networks (Krøijer 2011a; see also Graeber 2002; Maeckelbergh 2009). There are two elements to this difference: In the first, dead time describes a sense of a temporal discontinuity, of being stuck in somebody else's world and time, but instead of a glorious future on the other side of the revolution, the alternative future is the present as space of action. The future is left as an open question, as an acquaintance of mine once phrased it. In the second element of difference, apathy is the bodily sense of inaction and exhaustion that Aske associated with his situation before he became an activist, when he still accepted climate change's cushion-like qualities, but it may also emerge in the wake of large actions.

Anthropologists often assume that the ontology of time is linear flowing time, a shared astronomical time, which we perceive and experience differently (for a critique of this, see Hodges 2008; Robbins 2001, 2007b). In other words, there is an underlying assumption that time has a direction and flows from the past to the present and the future. Dead time clearly implies an absence of this sense of connection to a distant future, but what, then, about the near future?

In a provocative contribution to *American Ethnologist*, "Prophecy and the Near Future: Thoughts on Macroeconomic, Evangelical and Punctuated Time" (2007), Jane Guyer explores what she sees as a strange emptying of the temporal frame of the near future in the Western world. She argues that the near future has been replaced by a combination of "enforced presentism" and "fantasy futurism" (Guyer 2007: 409–410). This tendency, she argues, is most evident in monetary (read, neoliberal) economic theory and in evangelical ideas about time in that both work with an infinite horizon. In monetarism the emptying of the near future and the emergence of fantasy futurism result from using abstract mathematical models to analyze long-term market developments, whereas evangelicals see themselves as existing within an apocalyptic horizon (see Robbins 2001, 2007a). According to Guyer, the near future has no interim stages to reach for, and no organizational or midterm reasoning prevail (2007: 416). Simultaneously, the midterm is seen as morally dangerous and filled with punctuated time or, in other words, dates and ruptures.

In light of Guyer's analysis, what we might suggest is not that left-radical activism is characterized by fantasy futurism, which left radicals seem to abstain from, but that it abandons midterm organizing. This does not mean that activists do not plan for dated protest events—coordination meetings are many and detailed—but they often do not build enduring movements. As I mention in the chapter's opening, most activists left the evaluation meeting on the Copenhagen climate summit protests when the agenda turned to future movement building and creating an enduring radical climate movement. Most activists, like Aske, do not see the building of movements and traditional goal-oriented policy making as crucially important. But apart from interpreting this as anarchist aversion to leaders and formal organization, I believe it can also be understood as a particular temporal template: organization implies mobilizing and slow movement building to act at a later stage. Whereas revolutionary Marxist movements have historically been based on a strategy of linear mobilization of the masses and the accumulation of revolutionary force en masse, left-radical activists are preoccupied by revolts and direct action in relation to a diversity of issues, as well as with the details of decision making within social centers, the politicization of daily-life routines such as eating and dwelling, and so-called do-it-yourself practices (see Clark 2004; Jordan 2005; Krogstad 1986; Krøijer 2011b, forthcoming; McKay 1998). Direct action does not require a linear foreclosure of the future; instead, the change one vaguely dreams of is, as previously mentioned, supposed to be inherent in the action.

Massimo De Angelis, an intellectual involved in the global justice movement, argues that since the fall of the Berlin Wall the European Left has been suffering from a TINA syndrome: there is no alternative to capitalism (De Angelis 2006). According to my interlocutors, capitalism is in what you eat, how you travel, the goals you set for your life, the way you relate to other people, and how you fall in love (see also Povinelli 2006). Capitalism is depicted as having nothing else outside it or after it; even though the YouTube trailer draws on apocalyptic imagery, no immediate transcendence seems possible. Instead, theorists close to the movement argue, there is only immanent labor of transformation (Hardt and Negri 2000: 396; Gibson-Graham [1996] 2006), as in transforming the form and content of the social relations that activists are immersed in. In sum, for activists there is no, so to speak, Archimedean point from which capitalism can be perceived and attacked in its totality, and this gives activism a particular temporality.

Left-radical activists do not simply operate with the same kind of linear foreclosure of the future that planning entails. Instead all activities are placed on a horizontal plane and potentially ascribed equal political importance. The near future is, as Guyer puts it, "punctuated with dates" (2007: 416) of protest events, such as summit protests, which they must mobilize around. As these dates draw closer, intensity increases and days are filled with coordination meetings, mobilization activities, organization of protest logistics, and so on. These activities are not planning in a conventional sense because they offer equal possibilities of performing politics in a new and meaningful way (such as consensus decision making versus voting in meetings).

To explore the quality of dead time at greater length, I take a "binary license" (Strathern 2011) and describe the Reclaim Power action—the direct action during the climate summit in Copenhagen whose shadow opened this chapter—at some length. The aim is to elucidate the particular connection between activity and apathy or, more precisely, between active and dead time, which is created through their divergence.

Reclaim Power

As of 2013 Reclaim Power still represents the culmination of Danish attempts to renew and adapt forms of mass civil disobedience found on European soil since the Prague World Bank summit in 2000 (Krøijer 2008, 2011a; see also Juris 2005, 2008). Since then, actions have typically been organized in blocs that are color coded to represent a certain form of action and mode of conflict with police. At the G8 summit in Heiligendamm in

2007, blocs with different tactical preferences came together in a choreography of action to block the summit. Since participating at Heiligendamm, Aske had in one way or another been involved in all major Danish mass actions, such as G13, in which protestors attempted to squat a new social center in the wake of the eviction of Ungdomshuset; Shut Down the Camp, which aimed to close a refugee detention center; and Reclaim Power.

The choreography of action is hammered out at large activist gatherings before a protest event. In the case of Reclaim Power, international planning meetings were organized by Danish activists through international networks and electronic mailing lists about one and a half years before the event. At these meetings it was decided that Reclaim Power would consist of three blocs, each following a different route and employing "a variety of tactics" to reach and cross the fence around the summit venue at Bella Center in Copenhagen.

The intent was to push through a fence and lines of riot police around the official summit venue to hold a people's assembly on climate issues in an in-between space (a third space). This formulation of action was inspired by the mass actions of Tute Bianche (White Overalls) from the Italian Ya Basta network (Bui 2001; Juris 2008) at a European Union summit held in Copenhagen back in 2002. At Reclaim Power a blue bloc of participants would collectively push their bodies against the police line—without hitting and kicking or throwing objects—and help each other climb or tear down the fence. A green bloc consisting of small groups of activists deploying a swarming tactic modeled on bee swarms was to move in concert but without a central leader and converge on the same target. Finally, a newly invented bike bloc of activists who had transformed some of the many discarded bikes found all over Copenhagen into machines of resistance, such as two-deck bicycles making it possible to jump the fence, bicycles with loudspeakers that would give the impression of an approaching crowd, and bicycles welded together so they could block a two-lane road. The following description (also recounted in Krøijer 2013) provides an impression of the action and the bodily intensity it produced.

On the morning of the action, the blue bloc left Tårnby train station close to the summit venue at 9:00 A.M. accompanied by a sound truck to provide speeches, chants, music, and not least, guidance on how to proceed. The bloc counted some four thousand participants at most, far fewer than the hundred thousand people who had turned out four days earlier in a joint demonstration to call on politicians to take action on climate change. It was a cold morning with a hint of snow in the air, but even though the Bella Centre was nearby, the participants were able only to walk slowly because of the police vans on their flanks, which steadily moved in on the demonstration. During the walk I caught a glimpse of Aske, who was standing at the sound truck in deep conversation with one of the spokespersons of the Climate Justice Action network, which had organized the action. Well before we reached our goal, everybody was walking in a tight bloc formation with their arms locked together.

There was a moment of hesitation as the blue bloc reached the perimeter of the Bella Centre. Nobody took immediate initiative to storm the police line that had formed in front of a row of vans and a tall fence. People were urged to move left of the sound truck, which was decorated with an oversize bolt cutter. Immediately before the activists' collective push against the police line, Iza, an experienced activist trainer standing on the sound truck, made everybody repeat her words:

Iza: First we will take three steps to the left.
Activists: First we will take three steps to the left.
Iza: Then we will count down from ten.
Activists: Then we will count down from ten.
Iza: Then we will push and push until we get over the fence.
Activists: Then we will push and push until we get over the fence.

During the Reclaim Power action, activists proceeded in accordance with Iza's, or rather their own, words. From the sound truck there was a countdown: "10, 9, 8 . . . Push! Push!" everybody screamed. But the police stood their ground, and in not managing to cross the fence, a tight pack of Ya Basta activists from Italy; British climate campers; and Swedish, German, and Danish left-radical activists was produced between the sound truck, the police, and the fence. There was some serious chaos, screaming, and pushing for around twenty minutes. Several participants had padded themselves up to resist the beatings of the riot police who had formed a ring around the fence. Many were squashed while trying to squeeze through the police line, and meanwhile others were pulled out of the crowd to receive treatment for pepper spray. Movement was disorderly, and simultaneously the collective body of people began to roll in waves, with the movement of one part instantly impinging on the rest. Some people later reported that they had been unable to breathe or began "joint breathing," because their movements and breathing had become indiscernible from those of the people around them.

Only a few activists from the bike bloc made it across a muddy stream into the summit area on air mattresses, where they were quickly arrested. Riot police moved in from behind and managed to get through to the sound truck, where the two Danish spokespersons were arrested; they were ultimately charged for inciting to violence. Aske later explained how he and Iza had managed to escape down the side of the truck with a megaphone. In the end, when it proved impossible to plank the fence and meet the group of delegates coming from the inside, they had called on protesters to settle for holding the planned Peoples' Assembly on Climate Change right there in the snowy street.

A few days later, when Aske and I were leaving the long evaluation meeting, as described at the beginning of this chapter, he vividly recalled the situation. From his position on the sound truck he had watched the fence pushing and commented:

> It was actually amazing how close we were. They [the police] were overwhelmed by that first push, and we were so close to getting through. I could see it from the truck: it was just like one big body acting together. All this talk about forming a new movement: in these situations you *are* the movement.

Becoming a collective body, one big body acting in concert, as Aske experienced it, is frequent at protests and can take a variety of forms. Iza's call and the activists' response generated a sense of bodily synchronicity, or a bodily belonging to the same time.

Moreover, the compression of bodies produced by the intense pushing in front of the fence around the summit area implied an experience of being one big body. To Aske, this compression is paradoxically associated with movement, a contrast to the formal movement that some organizers were talking about at the evaluation meeting. Other activists have also described how "walking in chains together" and "sticking together" during a demonstration or action gives "an enormous strength and feeling of 'setting the agenda'" (Krøijer 2008: 61). This strength is in short an experience of bodily intensity and force associated with being part of a collective body of protesters. In contrast to the apathy and inaction characteristic of the situations that the promotional trailer for the G8 summit in Heiligendamm described as "dead time," this can be thought of as "active time" engendered by the state of collective bodily strength.

In his translator notes to *A Thousand Plateaus*, Brian Massumi explains the concept of affect, which I have found productive for grasping this experience. He argues that affect is "prepersonal intensity corresponding to the passage from one experiential state of the body to another and implying an augmentation or diminution of the body's capacity to act" (Massumi 1987:

xvi). Affect is in other words an experience of intensity, a moment of unformed potentiality that cannot be captured in language (Massumi 2002: 30). In my view, the concept of affect enables us to understand the contradiction between the immobility caused by the compression of bodies during the collective push against the police line and the increased sense of power and strength associated with it, as well as the particular relationship between body and time that is involved in these situations. The moment of the confrontation with the police and the intense pushing entailed a change in the experiential state of the body; it was simultaneously a change in bodily form and its state of vitality (Krøijer 2013: 50–51).

The collective body that emerged during the pushing in front of the fence is an expression of a momentary coexistence of what we normally think of as opposites: action and inaction (or motion and motionlessness), the individual and the collective, and something that might best be expressed as the determinate (crowd) and the indeterminate (future). What I mean by the latter is that the momentary emergence of a collective body figures the future (Krøijer 2011a). Instead of talking about the future, left-radical activists' theory of change is to "build the new within the shell of the old" (Graeber 2009: 203), as an anarchist catchphrase goes. According to my findings this endeavor always takes a bodily and material form in the here and now of everyday life. The body becomes a figure of the future whereby the otherwise ungraspable and verbally undercommunicated hope for a better future becomes, for a moment, the material reality of the body. For a short while taking action can therefore help overcome the present/future discontinuity and reveal something about "the world of our dreams," as the YouTube video phrased it.

In light of this, it would be easy to put forward the simple argument that young activists protest to find a way out of apathy and dead time. This, I believe, is nevertheless not entirely the case, because in left-radical activism there is no simple opposition between everyday life and extraordinary protest events or between dead time and active time. As Sara's story of her engagement in activities in Ungdomshuset illustrates, the place was regarded by activists as a place of action—that is, as a place for common activities opposed to the resignation, apathy, loneliness, and greed thought to be characteristic of the surrounding society. Activism in Ungdomshuset, in other words, implied the same kind of vital common activity as Reclaim Power did in following certain decision-making procedures, cooking a vegan meal, or organizing an action, activities in which a new world can come into view, what Sara referred to in talking about everything "fitting together" (Krøijer and Sjørslev 2011: 89). Being absorbed by common activity—whether in a collective body, in collective chanting, or in a kiss, as hinted at in the

YouTube trailer—has the effect of making the future, which is otherwise left indeterminate, become a state of present bodily affect seen as strength and freedom of action and movement. In sum, what characterizes dead time and active time is not that they are antithetical but that they are different temporal ontologies that both hinge on the body. What interests me in the following is what happens in the aftermath of large actions like Reclaim Power and when people fail to be engaged or even drop out of activism. Dead time is, as I suggest below, the silent follower of frenzied activity—that is, connected to but qualitatively different from active time.

Dead Time as a Temporal Figure

In understanding activism as absorption in a common state of active time, we might also be able to come closer to an understanding of dead time, which, like active time, is talked of in a bodily idiom. Dead time is described by activists as apathy and burnout, but the two terms are used for slightly different situations.

Dead time is when one is not engaged in anything particular. Aske characterized his situation before he became involved in political activism as a time of apathy. Apathy is also used to describe the state of mind of the majority of the population who sink into the sofa and watch TV, eat industrially prepared food without caring about how it is produced or processed, and refrain from questioning the right of politicians and corporations to decide how one should live one's life. As Sara's activities show, it is understood as demanding a lot of work to wrench free from this kind of dead time and as almost impossible to be political in all aspects of life such as one ideally should be when trying to build "a new society within the shell of the old" (Graeber 2009: 203).

For stretches of time activists inevitably fail to be engaged in political action with others and in one way or another come to act with self-interest. While people in their thirties and forties are not a rare sight in social centers, their rhythm of engagement in activism changes; maybe they have become parents or have a more demanding professional job. The reason for dropping out of activism is almost never a change of political views but is often an experience of inadequacy. As a consequence of life changes, activists no longer have available the excessive time demanded by meetings or they drop out of the social contexts in which ideas for actions are generated.

In Denmark many activists are students and are able to find sufficient time for intensive periods of action planning by, for example, drawing out their studies until their late twenties. Others find flexible jobs that allow them sufficient free time or that give them some say in the planning of their work hours. Work is often an issue of concern to activists, not least because it is seen as a waste of valuable time but also because one has to take orders from others and subject oneself to boredom and stress. Many activists have difficulty imagining what job they would like to hold when they finish their studies, as few jobs are considered politically correct in the sense of having an anticapitalist perspective. Taking a job is necessary to making a living, but many young activists constantly attempt to free up time for activism.

As a consequence, the kind of activism associated with actions like Reclaim Power is mostly a youth phenomenon but for reasons different from the rebelliousness associated with finding oneself that is ingrained in Danish perceptions of youth. Only while young are people able to find the time required to practice politics in this particular way, and when activists realize that they are unable to perform politically in the way expected by themselves and their surroundings, this often leads to an acute sense of inadequacy, apathy, and loneliness. The dead time of not being engaged in anything particular is in other words surrounded by significant self-criticism and shame. Choosing to live life differently—when establishing a family or taking a more demanding professional job—also entails abandonment not only of one's social network but also of the "native" concept (Holbraad 2012, xvii) of social change described previously. Curiously, the relationship to the future that can be associated with apathy is not anticipatory waiting for a better future to materialize (see Day, Papataxiarches, and Steward 1999: 2, 10; Robbins 2007a: 434); it manifests itself in the form of time as a continuous flow that sneaks back into the life of activists. Simultaneously, the gap between what is and what will be opens up again insofar as the future no longer erupts unexpectedly from the present (see Grosz 2005: 110).

What I, inspired by the YouTube protest trailer, have described as dead time corresponds to the period before one is engaged in activism or certain turning points in one's life—for example, when an activist drops out of activism altogether; it may also take place proximate to active time. Many activists have explained how they sometimes go through difficult times after major actions or suffer from what is referred to as burnout. Aske was burned out after the violent eviction of a group of Iraqi refugees from a church in Nørrebro in Copenhagen, which led to their subsequent forced repatriation. This action, known as Kirkeasyl (Church Asylum), was unusual in a Danish context, since it aimed at placing the right to political asylum on the political agenda by squatting a church together with sixty refugees who had been denied asylum. The internal organization in the church was a major challenge, particularly with increased pressure on the Iraqi refugees, which was only reinforced by the critical media coverage aimed at criminalizing individual refugees and activists and by the squatting lasting almost two months. Aske found the process very demanding:

> The idea of Kirkeasyl was not very radical—quite the contrary, actually; we made a lot of compromises. It [the action] failed to expose the racism of Danish legislation and instead appealed to people's compassion and generosity. Therefore, it was even more depressing when they were finally evicted. Also because we had got to know them really well by then, and we all worked so hard at making it happen. I felt really angry and depressed and kept to myself for a long time. Sometimes engaging in activism can actually make you feel lonesome and weak, and I have been burned out for several months since then.

This condition was not thought of as peculiar to Aske: most other activists reported the experience of going through difficult times, of being burned out after large actions, Suddenly, days are no longer filled with activity; both the togetherness of camps, meetings, and actions and the pressure from police surveillance and fears of arrest are over. This loneliness, fatigue, and absence of activity are thought to sometimes result in self-destructive behavior such as self-harm and sustained drinking. Fellow activists would often express their understanding, but little is jointly done to cope with the individual experience of burnout, as it is often associated with a shameful weakness.

After the Ungdomshuset eviction and closure, however, a group called Parents against Police Brutality was formed to monitor the behavior of police during riots and demonstrations tied to the conflict over Ungdomshuset. The group later formed Gadeterapeuterne (Street Therapists), consisting of several psychologists whose aim it is to lessen the effects of traumatizing experiences and offer help when activists run into the kind of existential crisis that Aske was talking about. The therapists understand the anger and depression and burnout as "an individual political rebellion against prevailing ideas of normality" (Villemoes 2011: 5). This is also seen as emerging when one puts the cause ahead of individual well-being. The concept of dead time offers a slightly different way of conceptualizing the same existential experiences.

As mentioned previously, I see activism as absorption in common activities, which is epitomized in the experience of becoming a collective body during actions or protests. In these situations the collective body engenders a time that is of the future, so to speak, and that is characterized by bodily strength and freedom of movement. This appreciation of activity, of organizing and being physically active together, has a long historical tradition in northern Europe that ties together the ideals of the civil (civilized and civic minded), physically fit, educated person (Frykman 1993: 170–173; Anderson 2008). Since the beginning of the twentieth century, physical training has been tied to the process of civilization and the reinterpretation of *folkelighed* (popular character) and nationality. According to Jonas Frykman, physical exercises were a way to discipline people to become active citizens and had an emancipatory potential in that they allowed otherwise invisible groups to make their bodies visible in public space (Frykman 1993: 163, 167). In the left-radical scene in Copenhagen this tradition has been extended, but with the significant addition that the stress is on more the joint activity than the formation of individual civic-minded persons, and politics is perceived, rather, as immanent in joint action.

Dead time, on the other hand, is associated with bodily weakness, passivity, and being physically pressed down, as the word "depression" also implies etymologically. What I am suggesting is that, instead of understanding burnout as the rebellion of an individual subject, left-radical activism is challenging the particular way that young people are turned into individuals. To activists, burnout and apathy imply a negative experience of being singled out as individual persons, being alone and cut off from the politics embedded in joint action. Dead time, engendered by apathy and burnout, implies that one is stuck in a world and time where one becomes an individual, and continuous time sneaks back into everyday life.

Conclusion

I argue that it is necessary to take the nature of time into account, and particularly activists' ways of relating to and engendering the future, to understand the raison d'être of left-radical activism. The actions of young activists are tied to a perception of youth as a period of waiting and learning before becoming fully fledged political subjects and to activists' own experiences of a fundamental temporal discontinuity between the present and the future. Yet what characterizes activists' ways of waiting for the future is primarily frenzied activity around dated events interrupted by periodic exhaustion, apathy, and burnout.

The life of an activist thus oscillates between multiple temporal modes of being—namely, between what activists characterize respectively as dead time and active time, which both hinge on the body. Active time entails feelings of solidarity, equality, strength, and freedom, which pertain to a process of absorption in joint activity. These moments of active time are epitomized in the emergence of a collective body during protest actions, but these can be contrasted with several other situations described in this chapter—namely, the moments and periods of dead time. Dead time is associated with being alone, apathetic, and burned out and with slow continuous time, which hold little promise of change. There is not a neat division between the mundane and the extraordinary, and my argument does not imply that political activism can be perceived as a way out of boredom or as an outlet for frustration. Rather, dead time is also inevitably tied to, and even emerging from, active time.

The collective body of protesters, which Aske described as movement, implies a change in the experiential state of the body and that an otherwise indeterminate future momentarily gains determinate form. Elsewhere I have conceptualized this as a figuration of the future (Krøijer 2011a). Both dead time and active time are talked of in a bodily idiom. And maybe this is the principal contribution of this chapter, drawing attention to the particular way boredom and waiting among activists form a temporal figure describing a slow continuous time with no future in store.

Time is, in other words, objectified—as material entity and matter of concern—both in active and dead time, as collective and individual bodies, respectively. Building the future in the body requires constant and ongoing labor to fend off one's absorption into dead time. In this light, bodily control, discipline, and endurance are important political qualities of activists. In sum, the political practices of young left-radical activists must be understood in light of the particular relationship to the future that the forms of actions and bodies entail.

REFERENCES

Anderson, Sally. 2008. *Civil Sociality: Children, Sport and Cultural Policy in Denmark*. Charlotte, NC: Information Age.
Borgerrepræsentationen. 1999. *Københavns Borgerrepræsentations forhandlinger*. May 6. Available at http://subsite.kk.dk/PolitikOgIndflydelse/Moedemateriale/Referater/~/media/AE2F7F1E4D454AA18CA3C443DA47538E.ashx.
Bui, Roberto [Wu Ming 1]. 2001. "Tute Bianche: The Practical Side of Myth Making (in Catastrophic Times)." Available at http://www.wumingfoundation.com/english/giap/giapdigest11.html.
Clark, Dylan. 2004. "The Raw and the Rotten: Punk Cuisine." *Ethnology* 43 (1): 19–31.
Day, Sophie, Evthymios Papataxiarches, and Michael Steward. 1999. "Consider the Lilies of the Field." In *Lilies of the Field: Marginal People Who Live for the Moment*,

edited by Sophie Day, Evthymios Papataxiarches, and Michael Steward, 1–24. Boulder, CO: Westview Press.

De Angelis, Massimo. 2006. "Book Review. The World Social Forum: Challenging Empires." *Development* 49 (2): 125–128.

Ehn, Billy, and Orvar Löfgren. 2010. *The Secret World of Doing Nothing*. Berkeley: University of California Press.

Frykman, Jonas. 1993. "Nationella ord och handlingar." In *Försvenskningen av Sverige: det nationellas förvandlingar*, 120–203. Stockholm: Bokförlaget Natur och Kultur.

"G8 2007 Protest-Trailer." *YouTube*, December 9, 2006. Available at http://www.youtube.com/watch?v=Uk-MBWp4vh8.

Gibson-Graham, J. K. (1996) 2006. *The End of Capitalism (As We Knew It): A Feminist Critique of Political Economy*. Minneapolis: University of Minnesota Press.

Graeber, David. 2002. "The New Anarchists." *New Left Review* 13:61–73.

———. 2009. *Direct Action: An Ethnography*. Edinburgh: AK Press.

Grosz, Elisabeth. 2005. *Time Travels: Feminism, Nature, Power*. Durham, NC: Duke University Press.

Gullestad, Marianne. 2002. *Det norske sett med nye øyne*. Oslo: Universitetsforlaget and Scandinavian University Press.

———. 2006. *Plausible Prejudice: Everyday Experiences and Social Images of Nation, Culture and Race*. Oslo: Universitetsforlaget and Scandinavian University Press.

Guyer, Jane I. 2007. "Prophecy and the Near Future: Thoughts on Macroeconomic, Evangelical, and Punctuated Time." *American Ethnologist* 34 (3): 409–421.

Hansen, Helle. 2008. *69*. Copenhagen: Bastard Books.

Hage, Ghassan. 2009. *Waiting*. Carlton, Australia: Melbourne University Press

Hardt, Michael, and Antonio Negri. 2000. *Empire*. Cambridge, MA: Harvard University Press.

Hodges, Matt. 2008. "Rethinking Time's Arrow: Bergson, Deleuze and the Anthropology of Time." *Anthropological Theory* 8 (4): 399–429.

Holbraad, Martin. 2012. *Truth in Motion: The Recursive Anthropology of Cuban Divination*. Chicago: University of Chicago Press.

Jeffrey, Craig. 2010. *Timepass: Youth, Class and the Politics of Waiting*. Stanford, CA: Stanford University Press.

Jordan, John. 2005. "Notes whilst Walking on 'How to Break the Heart of Empire.'" European Institute for Progressive Cultural Policies, August. Available at http://eipcp.net/transversal/1007/jordan/en.

Juris, Jeffrey S. 2005. "Violence Performed and Imagined: Militant Action, the Black Bloc and the Mass Media in Genoa." *Critique of Anthropology* 25 (4): 413–432.

———. 2008. *Networking Futures: The Movements against Corporate Globalization*. Durham, NC: Duke University Press.

Karker, Andreas. 2007. *Jagtvej 69: Historien om et hus*. Copenhagen: Lindhardt and Ringhof.

Karpantschof, René, and Flemming Mikkelsen. 2009. "Kampen om byens rum: Ungdomshuset, Christiania og husbesættelser i København 1965–2008." In *Kampen om Ungdomshuset: Studier i et oprør*, edited by René Karpantschof and Martin Lindblom, 19–40. Copenhagen: Frydlund og Monsun.

---. 2009. "Ungdomshusoprøret 2006–2008." In *Kampen om Ungdomshuset: Studier i et oprør*, edited by René Karpantschof and Martin Lindblom, 41–102. Copenhagen: Frydlund og Monsun.
Korsgaard, Ove. 2001. *Poetisk demokrati: Om personlig dannelse og samfundsdannelse*. Copenhagen: Gads Forlag.
Krogstad, Anne. 1986. "Punk Symbols on a Concrete Background: From External Provocation to Internal Moralism." *Tidsskrift for samfunnsforskning* 27:499–527.
Krøijer, Stine. 2008. "Direkte aktion: Utopisk nutid blandt venstre-radikale unge." *Jordens Folk* 4:56–62.
---. 2011a. "Figurations of the Future: Forms and Temporality of Left Radical Politics in Northern Europe." Ph.D. diss., University of Copenhagen.
---. 2011b. "Fremtiden i skraldespanden: Temporær perspektivisme blandt venstre-radikale aktivister" [The future in the dumpster: Temporary perspectivism among left radical activists]. *Tidsskriftet Antropologi*, no. 63: 49–67.
---. 2013. "Security Is a Collective Body: Intersecting Temporalities of Security around the Climate Summit in Copenhagen." In *Times of Security: Ethnographies of Fear, Protest and the Future*, edited by Martin Holbraad and Morten Axel Pedersen, 33–56. London: Routledge.
---. Forthcoming. "Revolution Is the Way You Eat: Exemplification among Left Radical Activists and in Anthropology." In *The Power of Example*, edited by Andreas Bandak and Lars Højer. Special issue, *Journal of the Royal Anthropological Institute*.
Krøijer, Stine, and Inger Sjørslev. 2011. "Autonomy and the Spaciousness of the Social in Denmark: The Conflict between Ungdomshuset and Faderhuset in Denmark." *Social Analysis* 55 (2): 84–105.
Maeckelbergh, Marianne. 2009. *The Will of the Many: How the Alterglobalization Movement Is Changing the Face of Democracy*. New York: Pluto Press.
Massumi, Brian. 1987. "Notes on the Translation and Acknowledgments." In *A Thousand Plateaus: Capitalism and Schizophrenia*, by Gilles Deleuze and Félix Guattari, xvi–xx. Minneapolis: University of Minnesota Press.
---. 2002. *Parables of the Virtual: Movement, Affect, Sensation*. Durham, NC: Duke University Press.
McKay, George. 1998. *DIY Culture: Party and Protest in Nineties Britain*. London: Verso.
Olwig, Karen, and Eva Gulløv. 2003. *Children's Places: Cross-Cultural Perspectives*. London: Routledge.
Povinelli, Elizabeth. 2006. *Empire of Love: Toward a Theory of Intimacy, Genealogy and Carnality*. Durham, NC: Duke University Press.
---. 2011. *The Economies of Abandonment: Social Belonging and Endurance in Late Liberalism*. Durham, NC: Duke University Press.
Razsa, Maple, and Andrej Kurnik. 2012. "The Occupy Movement in Zizek's Hometown: Direct Democracy and a Politics of Becoming." *American Ethnologist* 39 (2): 238–258.
Robbins, Joel. 2001. "Secrecy and the Sense of an Ending: Narrative, Time and Everyday Millenarianism in Papua New Guinea and in Christian Fundamentalism." *Comparative Studies in Society and History* 43 (3): 525–551.

———. 2007a. "Causality, Ethics and the Near Future: Commentary." *American Ethnologist* 34 (3): 433–436.

———. 2007b. "Continuity Thinking and the Problem of Christian Culture: Belief, Time, and the Anthropology of Christianity." *Current Anthropology* 48 (1): 5–38.

Strathern, Marilyn. 2011. "Binary License." *Common Knowledge* 17 (1): 87–103.

Sullivan, Sian. 2005. "'We Are Heartbroken and Furious!' Violence and the (Anti-) Globalisation Movement(s)." In *Critical Theories, International Relations and "the Anti-Globalisation Movement": The Politics of Global Resistance*, edited by Catherine Eschle and Bice Maiguashca, 174–194. London: Routledge.

Svendsen, Lars. 2005. *A Philosophy of Boredom*. Chicago: University of Chicago Press.

Villemoes, Søren K. 2011. "Gadeterapeuterne." *Weekendavisen*, December 9.

4

Heterochronic Atmospheres

Affect, Materiality, and Youth in Depression

MARTIN DEMANT FREDERIKSEN

What can a pomegranate given to Stalin on his seventieth birthday in 1949 tell us about young people's experiences of boredom and depression in contemporary Georgia? This is the question I explore here.

During my fieldwork among a group of under- and unemployed young men in the coastal city of Batumi in western Georgia, I found that one of the most common tropes they used for describing their situation was being bored (*mots'qenilobis*) and in depression (*depresia-shi*), a state shared by many young people. These two factors reflected a situation of not having anything to do in the present and having few if any prospects for the future. Such negative depictions of the situation were in stark contrast to the highly optimistic statements made by the Georgian government concerning the future of the nation. Batumi had in fact been chosen as a site to show how Georgia as a country had finally been freed from the political turmoil and social instability that had marked everyday life since the breakup of the Soviet Union in 1991. One of the main ways of doing this was through a massive state-sponsored reconstruction of urban space that was meant to revive Batumi as a resort town by the Black Sea.

My interest in what follows resides in how time was objectified in urban space in these reconstruction projects—that is, how attempts were made to create visions of the future in the materiality of the urban and, further, how this had unintended consequences for how such reconstructions were experienced. I argue that the material reconstructions of Batumi created what I refer to as a *heterochronic atmosphere*—that is, an atmosphere in which multiple and often contradictory temporalities came to coexist. I suggest that the affective presence of such an atmosphere can help explain why my informants repeatedly used the notions of boredom and depression to describe lives lived in the midst of social optimism. Seeking in this way to connect the material, the temporal, and the affective via the notion of atmosphere, I take my cue from a line of reasoning arguing that there is a relationship rather than an opposition between the material and the affective (Anderson 2004; Navaro-Yashin 2012; Thrift 2004). I return to this later in the chapter. First, however, we take a walk in the city.

Being Bored and in Depression

It is autumn in Batumi. It rains a lot these days. The first downpours quickly sieve into the ground and down drainage systems, but soon there is nowhere for the water to go. Originally built on a swamp, Batumi lies at sea level, and after a day or two of rain the streets begin to look like small canals. As drainage and sewage systems overflow, the water supply to the vast majority of houses in the city center becomes blocked. More and more buckets and plastic containers appear in courtyards and on pavements, collecting water for washing, doing dishes, and flushing toilets. The young men among whom I am conducting fieldwork spend as much time as they can outside, walking. It takes skill to hop puddles and intimate familiarity with the ground to miss holes in the pavement hidden under water. Some days there is simply too much water to move from one end of the city to another, and even going out on a visit becomes impossible. On such days, many are forced to sit at home, alone. In interviews and conversations the bad weather is often accentuated, as is the fact that there is little to do in a Batumi, a city of around 120,000 inhabitants. Consider the following statements:

> In the winter young people are drinking, nothing more, drinking, drinking, drinking. . . . We don't have any entertainment in the winter; we are closed in the winter. We can only drink and then go home and drink some more. Time goes slowly. So much rain, something like London. (Giorgi, twenty-one)

> I was born unhappy. It's a small town; there's no work here, no vacancies for young people. (Irakli, twenty-one)

> In autumn, winter, and spring it is always raining, you have no money, you cannot go anywhere, only a few people do anything,

people have no interest in life—for simple people it is a dark side. . . . Most young people here, during the winter, they drink, they do drugs, because there is nothing to do, they have empty lives, everything disappears. (Magu, twenty)

We call Georgia "the devil's asshole"; our dreams die in this place. (Sasha, twenty-two)

I'm bored with this life. (Goga, twenty-one, who followed this statement with silence and refused to elaborate)

A book about young people in Batumi can only be boring; you should find another subject. (Roman, twenty, referring to my fieldwork)

Boredom was often used to describe how there was nothing to do, particularly in the long and wet winter. Although the young men's statements could be read as ironic or sarcastic comments on their own situation, the experience of boredom and the lack of opportunities were a serious matter for the young men because they could lead to an even worse experience: depression. The young men spent most of their time hanging out in small brotherhoods (*dzmak'atcoba*), small close-knit groups of friends. Now and then, when a member of a brotherhood was not around for a time, the others would usually note that he was in depression. Being in depression was not a matter of mental illness, not something one *had*, but rather something one was *in* or *surrounded by*, a condition or sentiment occurring when enclosed in a particularly distressing situation rather than being a disease or an illness. There were ways to steer clear of being in depression and boredom: making sure, for instance, that one was not at home alone but rather hanging out in the company of friends (one's brother men), experimenting with nonprescription drugs thought to cure depression or engaging in creative modes of self-expression such as music, poetry, and tattoo art (Frederiksen 2013). But these were most often temporary measures. Because one was *surrounded* by depression, it did not easily go away, or rather, one could not easily step outside it.

A Bright Future?

The strange thing was that the young men were surrounded by much optimism. Political processes in the Republic of Georgia at the time of my fieldwork in 2008–2009 were built on the idea of the creation of a new historical period and a path leading toward a brighter future. In the 1990s the Ajara region, of which Batumi is the center, had been ruled as a semi-independent autonomous republic. Shortly after the revolution in Georgia in 2003, the leader of Ajara, Aslan Abashidze, was ousted and the region again came under the full control of the Georgian government. This return was highlighted by the government of the newly elected president, Mikheil Saakashvili, as one of the key symbols of the success of the revolution. Batumi had been a tourist hot spot during the Soviet period (residing on the Black Sea, it is one of the few subtropical stretches of coastline in the entire Soviet Union), but during the 1990s the tourist industry had declined dramatically because of the political situation (Pelkmans 2006). Through a state-funded multimillion-dollar reconstruction project, Saakashvili aimed to revitalize Batumi as a tourism center. In public speeches given during his visits to the city, Saakashvili enthusiastically promised that within a few years Batumi would be hosting millions of tourists and local employment would be abundant (Frederiksen 2011; Mchedlishvili 2009). At the time of my fieldwork, reconstruction and building sites were thus a prominent feature of the urban landscape. Almost everywhere one could see, hotel skeletons were slowly growing higher, streets were being dug up to be repaved, large posters were declaring forthcoming projects, and signs, buildings, and monuments associated with the 1990s were being removed. Sounds of hammers, drills, trucks, saws, and electric screwdrivers were heard constantly.

Batumi was not the first Georgian city to be renovated. In fact this had been taking place in a series of other Georgian cities, a process colloquially known as *sighnaghization*, after the small hill town of Sighnaghi in eastern Georgia, the first Georgian city to undergo reconstruction. Saakashvili had declared the renovation of Sighnaghi to be a symbol of his government and the social changes it stood for (Serrano 2010). In a speech, he referred to the reconstruction of Sighnaghi:

> There were so many sceptics in Georgia. There will be many people who will say that all this is PR, they will tell you not to believe your eyes, that this is just a flight of your imagination, that all these [reconstructions] simply do not exist, that it will go up in smoke tomorrow. There are many people telling you not to believe your eyes. But I would like to tell everybody, those of us who are willing to see and believe, let us pass and come to Sighnaghi. . . . Sighnaghi is not only our, our generation's gift to the whole of Georgia. This is our gift to the eternal Georgia. This is a gift to Georgia's future. This is a

gift to our grandchildren. This is a gift to the 30th century Georgia from the 21st century Georgia. This is the legacy we have received from our ancestors, which, now tenfold more beautiful, tenfold more distinguished, we will pass on to our future generations, to the future of Georgia. . . . Sighnaghi today will be a happy future tomorrow and from today and forever, for our country and for our people. (Georgian Media Center 2010).

This statement closely resembles a speech given by the president a few years later on the reconstruction of Batumi in which he revealed plans to build a new opera house in the city:

We will complete this project together and, as I promised, we will turn Batumi into the most beautiful city on the Black Sea coast. . . . We should give all these things to our future generations. When a future generation asks what we have given them, they will say that we built the number one tourism centre on the Black Sea coast, the most beautiful opera house in Europe, a new Barcelona in Georgia and, what is more important, a better life. (Quoted in Mchedlishvili 2009)

Absent Futures

Gia was twenty when I first met him. He was unemployed and was about to marry his pregnant fiancée. The wedding had been delayed for lack of money, and although Gia and his fiancée had a strong desire to move into their own apartment, especially when the baby came, they were still living with their parents. As the following excerpt from my field notes shows, Gia came from a family that had previously been relatively well-off:

Gia and I go to his family's house located on the outskirts of the city. The two-storey house is grand in size, almost completely square with a wide balcony with intricate woodcarvings following the contours of the entire first floor. Inside, the hallway is open all the way to the ceiling and is dominated by a massive stairway. "It's made from wood from Africa," Gia notes. "My grandfather [now deceased] was a rich man in Batumi. This is his house. He had two wives and sixteen children. Today we live twenty people in this house." His grandmother, a small lady with a toothless smile, comes in with coffee. Her clothes are worn. Not much is left of what seems to have been a grand past. Most of the furniture has been sold. We go out on the balcony. Gia's uncle owns a lot across the street from the house that is used as a parking lot for trucks. A long row of Turkish trucks steadily passes by us with goods to be transported to Central Asia, but none of them stop. On the other side of the house is a derelict mandarin juice–processing factory that stopped its activities in the early nineties. "My grandfather was in prison for five years because he drove mandarins to Moscow without permission. It was a hard time," Gia explains. Next to the factory a small shed has been erected. "A few years ago a man came and said that this part of the garden was his property. My family went to the city hall to throw him out, but he still lives there." Various pieces of trash fill up parts of the garden, but here and there small plots are used for growing vegetables to be sold at the market. "See the house over there? A twenty-year-old boy was shot there some days ago. Something about money and drugs."

Because it was on the outskirts, no reconstruction of Gia's family's house had been considered. Such reconstructions were reserved for public buildings and residential buildings located in the very center of the city (places tourists were likely to go). Gia would blankly refuse to talk about the reconstructions and buildings projects in Batumi, which he seemed to have nothing but contempt toward, but he often noted that he thought Saakashvili was a cock (*khle-a*).

In 2009 Gia and his fiancée were finally married—a grand event with hundreds of guests—but shortly after his wedding Gia suddenly started being absent when his friends and I met. When I asked, his close friend Emil explained that "Gia depresia-shi"—Gia's in depression.

During the same period, the same happened to another of the young men, Gosha. He aspired to become a musician but despite vigorous attempts had little luck. He lived with his brother and his son. He was separated from the mother of his son, and with no income he had difficulties in making ends meet. Possibly prescribed inappropriate medication following a doctor visit, he had become dependent on nonprescription drugs. He believed they were necessary for playing music, as otherwise he would become extremely restless and not be able to play the guitar (for an elaborated version of Gosha's story, see Frederiksen 2013). His situation slowly worsened, and as in Gia's case, he eventually stopped leaving the house. As he would often make clear, being outside became a burden because he might see people he did not wish to meet and, more importantly, did not want to be around the construction in the city center. Already-somber moods did not seem to go well with being surrounded by optimistic building activities.

An absent future apparently led to people being bored and in depression. But why was the future experienced as absent when it was so massively present in the state-sponsored reconstruction activities? Why was the image of the future that Saakashvili attempted to make materially present through this reconstruction not appreciated? Why did these surroundings contribute to an atmosphere of depression rather than an atmosphere of, for instance, hope? To probe these questions, I leave Georgia for a while and go on a small theoretical excursion.

Heterotopia, Heterochronia, and the Pursuit of Particular Times

In his short essay "Of Other Spaces," Michel Foucault ([1967] 2008) argues that we live in an epoch of juxtaposition and dispersion, one in which two types of spaces can be distinguished: utopias and heterotopias. Whereas the former are sites with no real place but that present society in a perfected form, heterotopias are actual places in which several incompatible sites are juxtaposed. Foucault uses the image of the mirror to illustrate the difference. In one sense the mirror is a utopia because it is a placeless place: what we see in the mirror is not reality but a virtual space—we are not actually there. However, the mirror is also a heterotopia in that the mirror does exist in reality: "It makes this place that I occupy at the moment when I look at myself in the glass at once absolutely real, connected with all the space that surrounds it, and absolutely unreal, since in order to be perceived it has to pass through this virtual point which is over there" (15). In short, heterotopias are spaces that exhibit a dual meaning. Furthermore, and more importantly for the argument I advance here, heterotopias can be connected to time in the sense of *heterochronies*, or instances in which different "slices of time," as Foucault calls them (15), are juxtaposed in a single site. The museum is a heterochrony par excellence, as this is a space in which several historical periods or times are enclosed; different times are brought together to create a form of unity in a space that is itself supposed to be timeless. However, because they are heterochronic, attempts to deliberately create either timelessness or particular times do not always succeed. Two examples, Soviet architecture and a pomegranate given to Stalin, illustrate this point.

The Soviet Union was not only constructed as a territorialized, spatially bounded, and historically self-conscious unit (see Appadurai 1991); it also rested on an idea of linear time in the sense of the perceived socialist path leading to a communist future. Hence, both territory and time were significant to the ideological formation of the Soviet Union. Time was central to the very idea of the Soviet Union as a historical entity and the way daily life became structured for its citizens. Katherine Verdery has referred to this principle as the "etatization of time"—that is, the construction of time as a political and ideological process of state formation (Verdery 1996: 39).

Nowhere, perhaps, has time been objectified (and etatized) as literally as in Soviet architecture. The grandiose project of creating an image of an eternal, ahistorical unity became manifest in both the creation of infrastructure and the erection of statues and monuments. For instance, the Narkofim Communal House in Moscow was built to overcome the social and economic contradictions of industrial capitalism and instead embody "the terms of the good life for the greatest number of people" (Buchli 1999: 2). In relation to monuments, as Mikhail Yampolsky argues (1995: 96), the installation of a gigantic figure of Lenin on Moscow Square not only represented a commemoration of the then newly deceased leader; it just as much attempted to create a sense of eternity, the immediate achievement of an ahistorical condition (namely, communism) in the sense that Lenin, and all he stood for, would always be there. Soviet building projects were "oriented precisely towards the creation of some utopian preserve of the future where time would not flow" (97). Indeed, as Bruce Grant notes, few other images of the end of the Soviet era have attracted as much attention as those of Soviet monuments and statues tumbling to the ground, signifying that a historical period that was once perceived as lasting forever had come to an end (2001: 332).

But although in this sense the Soviet Union was built on (literally and figuratively) a notion of an eternal time, this did not happen without internal contradictions. For one thing, as Caroline Humphrey demonstrates in her article on Soviet infrastructure, although Soviet building projects were constructed in the belief that they would have a transformative effect by molding "a new way of socialist life," socialist values were not seamlessly generated as intended (Humphrey 2005: 40). As she shows in relation the Soviet hostel and courtyard, the quality of these buildings was not a simple reiteration of what had been envisaged in Soviet ideology: "For all their politics of control, planners or Party organizers could not shut down the imagination 'from above'" (55). Although the built environment did contribute to the conceptual world of the Soviet people, the anticipated social and psychological metamorphosis that had been expected to take place failed to do so (40). In other words, the meanings or intentions of the built environment were often translated into something completely different as actual social life entered the picture (see Buchli 1999). But cracks in the etatization of time in the Soviet Union were not just manifest in infrastructure. This is where we turn to the pomegranate given to Stalin.

In 1949, as part of the celebrations of Stalin's seventieth birthday, gifts given to the leader were displayed in the Pushkin Museum of Fine Arts in Moscow among other places. The exhibition was to portray both the glory of Stalin and the success of the Soviet Union and its timelessness. In an article examining this exhibition, Nikolai Ssorin-Chaikov (2006) shows how the idea of state timelessness was contradicted by both the rush with which the exhibition was put together and the inability to preserve some of the gifts. As an example, six pomegranates and some fresh apples sent as a gift from an Azerbaijan schoolgirl arrived dried and rotten, making it impossible for the staff of the museum to preserve and exhibit them, although they were obliged to. The same was the case with various rugs and furs that had collected moths before arriving (370). There is no greater threat to an idea of timelessness than that of decay, and Ssorin-Chaikov's descriptions of the gift exhibits shows that this threat was immanent. As he notes, a tension between the momentary and the eternal was created that revealed "an additional linearity which was that of entropy and not teleology" (370).

In analyzing this situation, Ssorin-Chaikov makes use of Foucault's notion of heterochrony. As already mentioned, Foucault argued that one of the features of modernity is several spaces and sites that are in themselves incompatible becoming juxtaposed in a single place. Such sites can each be "linked to 'slices' of different time, thus constituting heterochrony" (2006: 357), a coexistence or simultaneity of different times. Hence, linear historicist time, as that put forth by the Soviet regime in both ideology and infrastructure, for instance, can come to border, contrast, or overlap with other temporalities. Applied to the display of gifts to Stalin, heterochrony helps explain how multiple and often contradictory temporalities were at stake within the Soviet Union, in not just the everyday lives of ordinary citizens but also the very construction of state timelessness in Soviet modernity.

As Nadia Seremetakis notes with reference to the work of Walter Benjamin, "Modernity portrays and constructs itself as an originating continuum selectively appropriating the past, and creating inattention, in order to mandate the present and the future through the idea of progress—the meta-narrative of continuous and directional historical time" (1994: 20). However, Ssorin-Chaikov's study of gifts to Stalin shows that such metanarratives of time do not necessarily go uncontested.

In presenting this example, I highlight how certain materialities, whether spaces, infrastructure, buildings, or mundane items such as pomegranates, can reveal instances of heterochronia even in the midst of official attempts to create notions of linear time. What is of importance here in relation to the empirical data from Georgia, to which I now return, is the apparent contradiction inherent in such attempts.

Decay and Deceitful Materialities

The Georgian philosopher and literary theorist Zaza Shatirishvili has referred to the national narrative put forward by Mikheil Saakashvili following the revolution as a form of cosmogony, or a vision of a new universe emerging out of the perceived chaos of the 1990s. As Shatirishvili shows, this narrative has figured in Saakashvili's presidency in political speeches, symbolic acts, and building projects (Shatirishvili 2009: 60). It is clear from President Saakashvili's rhetoric, quoted previously, that the changes made in Batumi were not merely a matter of making life better today: it was just as much a question of creating something long lasting, "from today and forever," for country and people. However, at the time of my fieldwork, the eternal Georgia being promoted by Saakashvili through the reconstruction of cities such as Batumi and Sighnaghi was beginning to show cracks. One and a half years after the reconstruction of Sighnaghi, human rights organizations reported that several residential houses in the city had to be pulled down, reconstructed balconies needed constant repair work, and residents complained that they feared for their children because of the electrical wires lying scattered in the streets. Residents who had been forced to have their tin roofs replaced with tiles suffered severe leaks when it rained, and despite appeals and petitions to construction companies and the regional governor's administration, nothing was repaired (Mtlivlishvili 2010).

Although reconstruction continued in Batumi, cracks were also appearing there. For instance, parts of the plaster decoration on the Sheraton Hotel being constructed near the shore fell to the ground, allegedly because of hasty construction. The same hotel had a grand opening in 2009, despite the president having already opened it, before it was finished. Cracks and contradictions existed in not only faulty construction work but also images that did not always reflect reality: stone-pebble coastlines contradicted brochures depicting white sand beaches, reeking sewers emptying into the sea and the smell of petroleum from the harbor contradicted the images of clear water perfect for swimming. Portrayals of "the most beautiful sunset by the Black Sea" in a brochure aimed at Turkish tourists ignored that the sunset just a few miles farther west, in Turkey itself, was the same one. Images on large posters placed in front of construction sites declaring what would be there and when were contradicted by constant delays (some buildings were never constructed). While private houses slowly deteriorated, public buildings in the city center were increasingly being decorated (albeit many only on the outside). Some private and public houses that had been decorated or renovated showed signs of anything but permanence.

As already mentioned, the highly optimistic sentiments regarding these projects and their relation to the future of the nation articulated by the government were in stark contrast to those of the young men among whom I conducted my fieldwork. Being mainly between ages eighteen and twenty-five, they had all been born around the time of the dissolution of the Soviet Union and had grown up during the time of Aslan Abashidze. Most of them were unemployed, and several had been or still were engaged in small-scale crime. Unemployment rates in the Ajara region at this time were among the highest in the country, despite the massive workforce employed by the reconstruction and building projects. One reason for this was that many of the construction sites were run by Turkish contractors, and therefore Turks were a large proportion of the workforce. Further, although there were some tourists in Batumi, their numbers were limited (partly because of the recent war), so jobs in the tourism industry were hard to find and in any case only temporary, as the summer holiday season lasted only a few months.

Affect, Atmosphere, and Materiality

How is all this related to affect and atmosphere? Affect, Sara Ahmed argues, is a surplus created between individual perceptions and the social and material worlds (2004: 119). In that sense, it is neither within nor without. The notion of affect draws our attention to the links between the social and the somatic, not in the social constructivist sense of subjects being somehow constituted by the structures of the social world but in a much more intimate way, in which the two are coconstitutive of each other (Protevi 2009; see also Clough 2007 and this volume's Introduction and Chapter 3). Groups and individuals can come together or be aligned by certain emotions, creating communities of loss (Oushakine 2009), hate (Ahmed 2004), or sorrow (Frederiksen 2013), what Ahmed terms affective economies (2004: 119). But such affective economies, I argue, can also create experiences of depression, as was the case with Gia and Gosha. The affective, in this context, is closely related to the atmosphere created by urban reconstructions. Atmospheres, writes Niels Albertsen (1999), occupy a position between the real and the virtual. They are located between our surroundings and us. Furthermore, an atmosphere is multisensorial: we apprehend it with, and it affects, all our senses. Sensing an atmosphere is not limited to an observation of material facts; it is also a matter of being attentive to how we are located in our surroundings (Albertsen 1999; see also Böhme 1993). Just like depression among the young men in Batumi, an atmosphere is something we are *in*, it is something that surrounds us.

Imagine the air in the Moscow museum, the smell of rotting pomegranates contradicting the intended timelessness. Imagine then in Batumi the first indications of autumn, cool breezes and lightning storms on the horizon, revealing that, however prosperous the summer season has been, the long dull winter is coming soon. Imagine alongside this the optimistic speeches given by the president, the posters about forthcoming buildings, the multiple construction sites. Two phenomena are at work in these images. On the one hand we have the materiality of urban space in Batumi. As in the Stalin museum, in Batumi an attempt was made to create a particular vision of time. Concrete materials were put together to signify particular ideas of time. On the other hand we have the sensations that these materials create, their visual appearance, their smell, their sounds. We see people in these surroundings and experiencing, perceiving, and being affected by them, such as a group of young men who find themselves in depression.

As mentioned previously, boredom and being in depression could best be conceived of as a mood or an affected state and a result of a seeming inertia in the unfolding of one's individual life, in sharp contrast to the processes of state-sponsored development evident in the materiality of urban space aimed at indexing a potential future. Seeing material surroundings as directly translatable into personal distress is risky and often overly simplistic analytically, yet we might miss something if we see the two as separate spheres with no intermediaries (see Frederiksen 2013). But what, then, is the link here between time, materiality, and the affective? In this final section, I suggest that this is a question of what I call heterochronic atmosphere.

Exploring experiences of discontinuity and noncontemporaneity as inherent parts of processes of development and modernity is not new. These were central themes for authors such as Walter Benjamin (1999) and Siegfried Kracauer (1969). However, as Nadia Seremetakis rightly notes, these were theoretical rather than empirical studies that did not describe such processes in terms of how particular cultures or groups deal with temporal ruptures and senses of discontinuity as a part of everyday life (1994: 21). Descriptions of the experience of boredom as an outcome of modernity have rendered it "a symptom of the 'imprint of meaninglessness' that characterizes the disenchantment of the material world." Boredom, then, becomes "a secondary epiphenomenon that stands on the side of the explained as a feeling, a matter of no consequence, to be explained as the 'social construction' of a set of named conditions" (Anderson 2004: 741). There has been a tendency, Ben Anderson continues, to make a distinction between the material and the affective in studies of sociospatial life, a distinction that has been challenged by the so-called nonrepresentational theory developed by Nigel Thrift among others (Anderson 2004: 740). As Thrift notes in relation to cities, they "may seem as roiling maelstroms of affect," and yet affect has been relatively absent in the study of the city (Thrift 2004: 57). One reason to study affect in urban space, Thrift holds, is that the creation and mobilization of affect has become an integral part of everyday urban landscapes; it is deployed not merely for aesthetic reasons but also for political ends (58). This is evident in the state reconstructions of cities such as Batumi and Sighnaghi in Georgia in the sense that they are undertaken not merely to make the cities look good but, more importantly, to symbolize the success and legitimacy of the government and create trust in both the future of the country and the government itself, leading to an atmosphere of hope and progress.

In her study of affective spaces in northern Cyprus, Yael Navaro-Yashin recounts a walk she took with an informant on a plot of land once owned by Greeks but now allocated to Turkish-Cypriot refugees. Being in a sense looted land, it was a plain of bushes and thorns. Had the ownership of the fields been uncontested, Navaro-Yashin writes, they would have been plowed and planted, producing "an affect of freshness and liveliness. Instead, in the prickly fields through which we moved, the atmosphere discharged a feeling of the uncanny, a strange feeling derived, in this instance, out of a sense of impropriety, haunting, or an act of violation" (2012: 11). As in Georgia and the Moscow museum, there is something at stake here that is both material and affective, as well as both political and personal. And it is exactly such dualities that the notion of atmosphere can help us capture. An atmosphere, writes Anderson, envelops and presses on life. In developing the notion of "affective atmospheres," he urges us to capture the tensions and ambiguities that can arise between presence and absence, the definite and indefinite, subject and subject/object (2009: 77). We see a clear reference here to the work of Gernot Böhme, who has described atmospheres exactly as intermediaries between subject and object. "We are not sure," he writes, "whether we should attribute them to the objects or environments from which they proceed or to the subjects who experience them" (1993: 114).

Conclusion

Referring to Marx's description of the revolutionary atmosphere, Anderson holds that an affective atmosphere is akin to a meteorological one in the sense that it is something that surrounds us and exerts a force on us, something that we breathe in through the air. Anderson notes that "atmospheres may interrupt, perturb and haunt fixed persons, places or things. . . . [I]t is through an atmosphere that a represented object will be apprehended and will take on a certain meaning" (2009: 78, 79). Atmospheres in this sense have a constitutive openness to be taken up in experience. Therefore they are not completely controllable: they cannot be made by erecting monuments or reconstructing an urban space, because inevitably they will also have to be perceived. Returning to Caroline Humphrey's study of Soviet infrastructure, despite massive attempts at control, Soviet planners could not "shut down the imagination" of ordinary citizens from above (2005: 55). In the same sense, I argue, the reconstruction projects of Saakashvili were not able to create an atmosphere of hope or belief in the future. This, I believe, was because they were heterochronic—they inadvertently came to suggest, on the one hand, that the vision of time proposed was anything but seamless and certain in the sense that cracks (sometimes quite literally) appeared and, on the other, that even if the vision of the future of the country could indeed be reflected in the material reconstructions, this vision was not one that everyone in society was part of. The atmosphere created by the reconstruction, then, did not merely suggest one time but also other times, lost times, and contradictory times. Walking in Batumi, the young men could not step outside this, as it was intimately bound to the materiality of their surroundings, and in this sense the materiality of the city became an affective presence in their lives. To be sure, their social situations had a significant role to play in the way they perceived their circumstances and their city, yet it was part and parcel of the picture, not unrelated to it.

Gosha and Gia sit at home, in depression. As I have suggested, exploring the notion of a heterochronic atmosphere allows us to approach and understand their situation. It gives us an opportunity to see how attempts to objectify visions of time can go awry as plans (in this case reconstructions) enter social life.

REFERENCES

Ahmed, Sara. 2004. "Affective Economies." *Social Text* 22 (2): 117–139.
Albertsen, Niels. 1999. "Urbane Atmosphære" [Urban atmospheres]. *Sociologi i dag* 4:5–29.

Anderson, Ben. 2004. "Time-Stilled Space Slowed: How Boredom Matters." *Geoforum* 35:739–754.
———. 2009. "Affective Atmospheres." *Emotion, Space and Society* 2 (2): 77–81.
Appadurai, Arjun. 1991. "Global Ethnoscapes: Notes and Queries for a Transnational Anthropology." In *Recapturing Anthropology: Working in the Present*, edited by R. G. Fox, 191–211. Santa Fe, NM: School of American Research Press.
Benjamin, Walter. 1999. "Theses on the Philosophy of History." In *Illuminations*, edited by Walter Benjamin, 253–264. London: Pimlico.
Böhme, Gernot. 1993. "Atmosphere as the Fundamental Concept of a New Aesthetics." *Thesis Eleven* 36:113–126.
Buchli, Victor. 1999. *An Archaeology of Socialism*. Oxford: Berg.
Clough, Patricia Ticineto. 2007. *The Affective Turn: Theorizing the Social*. Durham, NC: Duke University Press.
Foucault, Michel. (1967) 2008. "Of Other Places." In *Heterotopia and the City: Public Space in a Postcivil Society*, edited by Michiel Dehaene and Lieven De Cauter, 13–31. New York: Routledge.
Frederiksen, Martin Demant. 2011. "Good Hearts or Big Bellies: *Dzmak'atcoba* and Images of Masculinity in the Republic of Georgia." In *Young Men in Uncertain Times*, edited by Vered Amit and Noel Dyck, 165–187. London: Berghahn.
———. 2013. *Young Men, Time, and Boredom in the Republic of Georgia*. Philadelphia: Temple University Press.
Georgian Media Center. 2010. "Things Fall Apart: Sighnaghi 36 Months On." Previously available at http://www.georgianmediacentre.com (accessed May 23, 2011).
Grant, Bruce. 2001. "New Moscow Monuments, or, States of Innocence." *American Ethnologist* 28 (2): 332–362.
Humphrey, Caroline. 2005. "Ideology in Infrastructure: Architecture and Soviet Imagination." *Journal of the Royal Anthropological Institute* 11:39–58.
Kracauer, Siegfried. 1969. *History: The Last Thing before the Last*. New York: Oxford University Press.
Mchedlishvili, Natalie. 2009. "Saakashvili Opens Construction of New Batumi Opera House." *Georgia Today*, May 12.
Mtlivlishvili, Gela. 2010. "Movement Is Dangerous in European Sighnaghi." *Web Portal on Human Rights in Georgia*, March 25. Available at http://humanrights.ge/index.php?a=text&pid=8150&lang=eng.
Navaro-Yashin, Yael. 2012. *The Make-Believe Space: Affective Geography in a Postwar Polity*. Durham, NC: Duke University Press.
Oushakine, Serguei. 2009. *The Patriotism of Despair: Nation, War and Loss in Russia*. Ithaca, NY: Cornell University Press.
Pelkmans, Mathijs. 2006. *Defending the Border: Religion, Identity and Modernity in the Republic of Georgia*. Ithaca, NY: Cornell University Press.
Protevi, John. 2009. *Political Affect: Connecting the Social and the Somatic*. Minneapolis: University of Minnesota Press.
Seremetakis, Nadia. 1994. *The Senses Still: Perception and Memory as Material Culture in Modernity*. Chicago: University of Chicago Press.
Serrano, Silvia. 2010. "De-secularizing National Space in Georgia." *Identity Studies* 2:1–16.

Shatirishvili, Zaza. 2009. "National Narratives, Realms of Memory and Tbilisi Culture." In *City Culture and City Planning in Tbilisi: Where Europe and Asia Meet*, edited by Kristof Vann Assche, Joseph Salukvadze, and Nick Shavishvili, 391–399. Lewiston, NY: Mellen Press.

Ssorin-Chaikov, Nikolai. 2006. "On Heterochrony: Birthday Gifts to Stalin, 1949." *Journal of the Royal Anthropological Institute* 12:355–375.

Thrift, Nigel. 2004. "Intensities of Feeling: Towards a Spatial Politics of Affect." *Geografiska Annaler* 86B (1): 57–78.

Verdery, Katherine. 1996. *What Was Socialism, and What Comes Next?* Princeton, NJ: Princeton University Press.

Yampolsky, Mikhail. 1995. "In the Shadow of Monuments: Notes on Iconoclasm and Time." In *Soviet Hieroglyphics*, edited by Nancy Condee, 93–112. Bloomington: Indiana University Press.

5

Standing Apart

*On Time, Affect, and Discernment
in Nordeste, Brazil*

ANNE LINE DALSGÅRD

I know a neighborhood where at times it is all too easy to become depressed. Where there are moments of misery. Of lack of promise and movement in life. Moments like that day in 2003 when Beto looked me straight in the eye and said, "Where is the opportunity?" I had no answer to give him. He was around twenty at the time. Today he is ten years older, and when I visit the neighborhood I always look for him in front of the bar where he usually sits, drunk and skinny. On days when he is not there, I get worried. When he is there, we exchange a few words about the weather and the opportunities that never improve. In no way would I ever blame him for the situation he is in, but I think he blames himself for not having become *alguem na vida* (someone in life), as people say. He has been struggling against heavy odds, and apparently he has lost. Life in northeast Brazil has always been tough; the Nordeste region is one of Brazil's poorest, and until quite recently, young people from low-income families have had few chances to get an education or a job. To steer through the impasse faced by youth in Nordeste takes more strength and enthusiasm than any individual has. That, at any rate, is the claim I seek to substantiate in this chapter.

I focus on a few young people who, at least so far, have found and maintain a hopeful outlook among themselves: Artur, who currently works as a public servant in the environmental sector; Evinha, who is today an economically independent mother and wife; and Daví, who has joined the army and found a career, despite very nearly giving in to depression and drugs. Artur, Evinha, and Daví have somehow avoided the gloominess that has gripped Beto and many others in their age and peer group. They have managed to associate themselves with something promising and accepted that theirs was not an easy path but nonetheless a path that would be passable. As Artur once said, "*A gente* [you] have to be pragmatic; we cannot choose the best but have to accept taking a longer road." Not being able to move away from the (social and geographical) place they inhabit, they have had to work in another dimension: time. They have tried to link up to a future that is not the logical consequence of where they are in the present but one that is willfully projected and sustained by mutual affection.

An Argument on Affect and Temporality

Personal, group, or national identities involve projections of the future in terms of both the projects that current predicaments and joys instigate and the light that expected futures cast on the present. Ann Mische proposes that we see projectivity as, at least potentially, "composed of creative as well as willful foresight" (2009: 697), and I share her interest in hope as a selective attention to future possibilities, which in turn opens possibilities in the present. However, whereas Mische focuses on the cognitive structures of projection, I look more into the everyday navigation at the "emotional substratum" (694) of such projections. By asking with Michael Flaherty (1999: 153) how individuals purposely act on the social milieu in which they are embedded, to create a particular form of temporal experience, I focus on the intertwining of place, affect, and temporality. My take on the theme of this book, time objectified, is thus a discussion of temporality as a result of not only cognition but also affect and affection—or perhaps rather as a result of cognition as always already affective (Varela and Depraz 2005).

Social life is inherently affective and hence in motion; we are "moved to move" in our daily relational engagements (Harris and Sørensen 2010: 149; Leder 1990; Sheets-Johnstone 1999). These movements, internal and external, are closely linked to our sense of time. In the article "At the Source of Time" (2005), the philosophers Francisco Varela and Natalie Depraz argue that, because of human biology, value assessments structure the living present and its immediate aftereffect (which they call "micro-temporality") by dividing the world into artifacts, plants, persons, animals, and so on that ought to be approached or avoided (66–69). This moving toward or away from manifests in a like-dislike polarity and in a concomitant rapid and often unnoticed transformation from one affective toning of the body to another (70). We experience this transformation, or shift, in the body as taking place in time; that is, we experience time by way of the affection we undergo when our body moves along with the impressions it receives and assesses.

Temporality is constituted by affect also on a larger, more conscious level, in the folding of the prereflexive affection (such as a shift in muscle tone or a change in breathing or heart rate) into the awareness that a specific situation has arisen. In the moment that a sense of "I am involved"— that is, an emotion (Rosaldo 1984)—emerges, a specific timescape emerges too. Depression and anticipation; joy and sadness; shame and indignation; patience, humility, and hope: these are emotional phenomena with different degrees of immediacy, but each proposes a temporal landscape in which the past, present, and future appear with varying intensity. In a moment of shared joy the future may be attractive; in sadness the past may predominate (but in sorrow perhaps also the image of a future without a loved one). In shame and indignation, there is an eagerness to change the present (self in shame; others in indignation) into a wished-for future. In patience and humility there is an acceptance of continuity, and in hope a wish for a change that cannot, however, be effectuated in the moment.

Emotions and their associated timescapes are discernible and possible to work with. This is precisely what Ben Anderson empirically explores in "Becoming and Being Hopeful" (2006), in which he argues that the materiality of the music a young man, Steve, listens to animates his life:

> Induced by the transmission of hope between Steve and the music, and then between him and his environment, is a corporeal disposition of hopefulness felt in a renewed animation of the proprioceptive and visceral senses (rather than the determinate content of a particular hope). This is a repeated set of background feelings that enacts a good way of being which forms a hopeful site of experience. (743)

In Steve's world, "a hopeful site of experience" is found in listening to a melancholy piece of music by Radiohead, crying with it, and realizing that others have felt as he has: "I always find it . . . a solace . . . to know someone else is feeling the same . . . which is great. I listened to this album yesterday morning when I'd been feeling down—it helps because I know I'm no way as bad as Thom Yorke, but he kind of feels the same. . . . [I]t let me get on with it a bit" (742). The relief that Steve experiences is immediate and bodily (crying often involves a deep relaxation of the body) and based on the disruption of the total identification with his own emotions, "the circulation of despair" (743), through an opening to the suffering of others. But, as Anderson proposes, hope can be spoken of as "an affective relation to an open not-yet elsewhere or elsewhen" (746). What I emphasize in the following is in line with this: not only can we find hope in sharing solitude and despair with others as Steve does; we may also practice hope in a more reflective distancing from depressing surroundings while linking up to a more promising future.

In this chapter I argue that it is sometimes possible to objectify (in the sense of making it the object of one's experience) the transmission of affects (Brennan 2004) to which one is subject in the present and to take an active stand before it to keep the future open and promising. This objectification can be seen as a kind of "time work"—that is, "the intrapersonal and interpersonal effort directed toward provoking or preventing various temporal experiences . . . [an] agentic micromanagement of one's own involvement with self and situation" (Flaherty 2011: 11; see also the Introduction). It concerns the future but takes place in the present—on the level of affect and emotion—and as we shall see, it breaks with our commonsense understanding (on which much theoretical deliberation rests) that "our existence as humans is temporally structured in such a way that our past experience is always retained in a present moment that is feeding forward to anticipate future horizons of experience" (Desjarlais and Throop 2011: 88). Contrary to the idea of temporality as a progressive linear movement, my point is that a fairly detached (from past experience) future might as well act on the present moment. Or as Morten Nielsen so effectively puts it, the present moment becomes "a function of an imagined future moment which is extended backwards in time to ground the current act" (2011: 398).

However, the following is not a straightforward tribute to the power of human imagination. The question that parents, teachers, and nongovernmental organizations in Brazil struggle with, how to give young people a hope without making them feel hopelessly responsible for their own lives (and potential failures), is also an analytical predicament: how to describe some individuals' apparently successful attempts to choose their own futures without simultaneously indicating that it is possible for everyone. My stand is twofold: First, I insist on an openness of the present, doubt, if you like, regarding any analytical conclusion about the future. We simply do not know where life will take any of us, and statements about how things *are* will always be provisional (see also Dalsgård and Frederiksen 2013). Second, I contend that subjectivity is a product of intersubjective interaction. In other words, I work from the premise that only through the mediation of others (concrete or imagined, generalized others [Mead (1934) 1965]) do we experience ourselves. The only choice an individual may have is thus to direct attention toward affirming impressions of his or her present and future self, inasmuch as they exist (see also Flaherty 1999: 155). The willfully projected future mentioned above is connected to Teresa Brennan's term "discernment": a conscious examination of and decision to embrace or reject a certain affect (Brennan 2004: 11, 126). The rebuffing of negative affects requires recourse to an alternative, more promising future, which seems to be sustainable only if recognized by others who have significance in our life.

However, on neither the societal nor personal level is recognition of one's worth abundant in the neighborhood where I have done my fieldwork.

The Place

The neighborhood I am preoccupied with lies on the outskirts of Recife, a city of around 1.5 million inhabitants in the state of Pernambuco in Nordeste, one of Brazil's poorest regions. I have visited this neighborhood regularly since 1997 in connection with a variety of research projects and objectives. Recently, I have been particularly focusing on young people and their relation to the future. Artur and Daví are acquaintances from this period, and I have known Evinha since 1997, when she was around eighteen years old and I interviewed her mother for another study (Dalsgård 2004).

People living in the neighborhood often say that they live in the *periferia*, which in local terms means not only the geographical periphery but also the social periphery, the fringes of society. They are, as some residents call themselves, *a classe fraca* (the weak class). Many arrived during the great migrations of the 1960s and 1970s and established homes here on the outskirts of the big city. The lack of decent-paying work in the city left many families without proper income and is still the main cause for the prevalent poverty. Some men work in business (formal or informal), others as cab or truck drivers, mechanics, servants, watchmen, construction workers, or unskilled or semiskilled laborers. Some men and women are public servants employed by the local public administration or the local schools, but here, too, the pay is fairly low. Some men are odd-job workers, known as *biscateiros*, and many women work as maids or cleaners in low-paid jobs outside the *bairro* (district), principally in Recife. A proportion of the men are unemployed for shorter or longer periods.

Especially for the male residents of the neighborhood, the persistent lack of opportunity is humiliating. It is not unusual to see a man get drunk early in the morning on a normal weekday. A man is supposed to be the head of his family and be able to provide for it; when this is not possible, it seems easy to seek oblivion in the bottle. For younger men, drugs and crime are ways to escape the quagmire of monotony and boredom. This is reflected in the national statistics for homicide: around the turn of the millennium, Pernambuco had the highest level of violence in Brazil, with fifty-four homicides per hundred thousand inhabitants—twice the national level. While this rate has fallen remarkably since 2007, Pernambuco still holds fourth place among the most violent states in the country. Simultaneously, on a national level the homicide rate among youths (ages fifteen to twenty-five) is double the rate of all other age groups taken together. Three-quarters of juvenile deaths stem from violence, traffic accidents, or suicide, which the statistics refer to as "external causes" (Waiselfisz 2011).

A kind of resignation seems to precede these deaths: when life does not offer any progress, or when it seems too dearly paid, then thinking about tomorrow seems irrelevant. As a male sixteen-year-old said to my collaborators Monica Franch and Katherine Gough, "I have no dreams. I do not know my day tomorrow, how should I care about my future? I let things flow" (Dalsgård and Gough 2004: 106). When youth is defined as a transitional period in life in which one moves from one stage to another (Dalsgård, Franch, and Scott 2008), the impossibility of moving makes life meaningless. As Franch writes, "Paradoxically, in times of risk and uncertainty social exclusion may convert the uncertainty into its opposite: an excess of certainty. This is seen in the cases of 'fatalism of the present', where the problem is not not knowing what will happen tomorrow but knowing that tomorrow will be exactly the same as today" (2008: 254–255). In a simple way, the sense of repetition ad nauseam is captured in an expressed aversion toward *feijão e arroz* (brown beans with rice), which is a staple in Nordeste and many other poverty-stricken parts of South America but which young people sometimes cite as the epitome of boredom. When you can eat hamburgers, why eat beans every day?

The lacking promise of social mobility in the neighborhood is linked to another, and more concrete, lack of (or at least stalled) mobility, which to a large degree is generated by the social imaginary of the dangerous, poor, black young male living on the outskirts of the city (see also Caldeira 2000: 77–79; Goldstein 2003: 205). Newspaper and television reports frequently show the bodies of homicide victims, most often young black men, and problematic youth are invoked in state and civil society interventions, in cultural and educational programs, and in police activities and legal measures. When the young men leave their neighborhoods and enter the public spaces of the city, they are stigmatized, avoided, or directly excluded because of the color of their skin and their body language and gestures, clothes, and language, which reveal their low-income status. Recognized as coming from the more impoverished areas of the city, they immediately arouse suspicion.

Police routinely stop them in the street, people who are better off may cross the road to avoid coming near them, and drivers who see them are likely to close car windows when waiting for a red light.

One young man, Kleiton, told me that he used to go to college on his bicycle. Every time he saw a police checkpoint, he slowed down, knowing that they would stop him. "I was already used to it," he said, "but I often arrived late because of that." I asked him if he ever got angry, perhaps indignant, and he answered: "Me? No! That would be to fight against it. . . . [I don't want to] fight against a system that is reinforced all the time. The television shows it, every time strengthening it, and I am not going to fight against that." Artur said, "There is this invisible social barrier, like you arrive at Shopping [Center] Tacaruna, and the security guards follow you everywhere, because you are black, because you are poor. Or you go to the beach, and you think that everyone there is like you, wanting a suntan, but that's only until someone has stolen something from this *granfino* [rich and elegant person]. Then there they are, saying, 'It was that black guy who took my things, while I was out swimming!'"

In the neighborhood, days are often whiled away in a relaxed and joyful atmosphere. The sense of familiarity and the feeling of sharing a common fate are comforting. But for those who leave the area, either to study or just for recreation, it is obvious that they do not have the same possibilities as those who are better off in society (see also Dalsgård 2004: 142–149). The unequal societal distribution of hope is a glaring fact, the effect of which may well be a complex mix of guilt and resentment, as Ghassan Hage notes (quoted in Zournazi 2002: 150). However, even as I am writing this, Pernambuco is experiencing rapid development, as the Workers' Party–led government has recently invested heavily in the region. More young people are going to college and finding jobs, and families who previously could hardly get one proper meal a day now have money to make small investments. In addition, the neighborhood is located close to a 2014 World Cup stadium, and the municipal plans for the infrastructure around the stadium are impressive and give inhabitants a sense of inclusion. In general, there is more optimism in the area than I have ever seen.

Optimism, however, is not an element that has so far dominated the lives of Evinha, Artur, and Daví.

Insecurity as a Lived Experience

Evinha grew up in the favela, the poorest part of the neighborhood, in a house that had neither windows nor a proper toilet. For a long time, even after she had a child with Beto, she continued to live with her parents, unable to provide for herself and her son. This is where I met her, when I visited their home to interview her mother. At that time, back in the late 1990s, the favela had much drug-related crime. Young men shot by other young men and dying in pools of their own blood had never been an unusual sight in the neighborhood, but in those days the place had "caught fire," as people said. A short survey I did on violence among Evinha's friends showed, shockingly, that many had seen, or had been in close proximity to, more than ten violent deaths. Today Evinha is well aware of the effects of witnessing such events, and she is afraid that the violence will affect her son or that drug-related crime will attract him. As she said:

> I see it like this: We moved out of that area [the favela] because he saw everything there. He knew the smell of marijuana, saw the guys armed and everything, saw the guys counting the money. And I said to myself, "I do not want my son to be in this environment, because when I am on my job, they will call him." Because they call, they want more and more, and call. . . . Another thing is that he only sees these *boyzinhos* [literally, small boys] with this style of life, only wanting clothes of [certain] brands. I keep telling him, "Do not want that! Do not!" But it will be *a luta espiritual* [spiritual struggle] for him, because he will know that I told him and at the same time he may wish to do as his friends do. And then he will have to choose his own life, on his own criteria, and I cannot do anything, just talk and talk. I cannot change his opinion; everyone is born with a *livre arbítrio* [free will].

Evinha's worries about her son are not unfounded. His father, Evinha's former husband, is Beto. The man who sits at the street corner nearby, only thirty years old. Evinha's brother is addicted to marijuana and putting his parents' lives and his own at risk. Evinha's younger sister walks with "the guys armed," carrying their weapons and risking being associated with them when their day comes and they are killed. Where Evinha and her son live, it is not easy to stand apart. The sight of dead bodies, the smell of marijuana, the comments from people around them all boil down to a sense of invasive insecurity, a feeling that they have to learn to cope with. Evinha tried to literally lift her son over and above all this by physically moving him out of the favela and into the potential of a better future.

The sense of insecurity is related to the violence and the lack of future opportunities, but it is also nourished by the mistrust felt toward surrounding people. Life in the neighborhood is a life full of dependency on others. As I have written elsewhere (Dalsgård 2004), being recognized as a decent person and a good neighbor is a matter of survival in its very material, most literal sense. Women help each other with food, money, or other necessities, which makes the vicissitudes of life bearable. Men help each other in finding jobs, getting access to building materials, and assisting with construction work. As Unni Wikan writes about life in "a world of urgency and necessity," you are what you are by virtue of your connections to these things and this world: "The same house, the same clothes, the same darned people.... This does not mean that things are fixed, immutable. But they persist, and you have to hang on to them, not just trade in the old car for a new one" (Wikan 1995: 275). These mutual dependencies make people susceptible to the norms and evaluations of others, which may produce a "swamp of affects" (Brennan 2004: 155) in which judgment, comparison, and disloyalty feed on fear, anger, and resentment.

As Evinha once said, "People drag you down. When you tell others, with this energy, this joy, that something good has happened to you, some will say 'Fine!'—only good things. But many will put up resistance: 'But it is far from here?' 'Do you think you can make it?' 'It is five years, that's a really long time. Do you really think you can succeed at it?' Everyone gives their opinion, and it interferes with your psychology and in the end you arrive there [the job, place of education, etc.] all nervous." And Sonia, a woman in her forties, once put it in the following way: "I have many friends, but [I walk with] one foot forward, another behind, because any small thing and ... [a friend] puts you down, really steps on you." The emotional pulling down that Evinha and Sonia talk about and that "interferes with your psychology" is part of the affective toning of bodies mentioned above. Through talk, telling you that things will be difficult and that you may not be able to handle them, but perhaps even more through implicit mistrust and envy, do others enervate you and leave you depressed or anxious.

And people not only envy you but also neglect your needs by turning their back on your problems. The idea of *falcidade* (falseness) has popped up often in my talks with people. For instance, *falsa amigas* (false friends) is a concept that young women use (see also Franch 2010). Women I talked to during previous research projects usually distinguished between *amigas* (intimate friends) and *colegas* (acquaintances). *Amigas* were friends you could really trust and tell everything to. *Colegas* can chat with, share certain problems with, and help each other but never really trust each other. Often, an *amiga* turns out to be just a *colega*, a person who is not trustworthy. Daví posed the dilemma of trust: "*Colegas* are people whom you can have a lot of conversations with but who will never help you. They will think, 'Oh, Daví has problems; he will have to take care of them himself!' They will never ask if they can help; not even how things are going." The unpredictability and uncertainty about which type of person you are with makes time stand out as a decisive factor in life. Here, "time will show" is not just a casual remark but also a fact lived every day. You do not know with certainty whether you can trust people around you. It shows in decisive moments, for instance, if you lend a lot of money or confide your emotional pain in a critical situation to someone. If the money is not returned or your pain is suddenly a subject of gossip, you know which type you have been talking to. And vice versa. Friends, who keep quiet about your pain or trust you when you need a loan yourself, show themselves as real friends who wish to energize you and help you move on. Hooking up with the right kind of people is therefore a matter of concern, especially for parents who see the vulnerability of their offspring.

Daví was nineteen when I met him in 2009. At that time he was living in a house on the riverbank, which had suffered a heavy flood a couple of years before. The location was not supposed to have any human habitation, so the municipal authorities had not warned the inhabitants when the dam upstream was opened. The water had soaked everything, spoiled most of his family's belongings, and forced them to live with relatives for a while. However, they had now returned, and life had become safe again. Some years ago it had been worse, Daví explained. Gangs fought over the territory, and there was constant shooting in the neighborhood. People had to stay indoors, and children were not allowed to go to school on days when the place was too *movimentado* (bustling). Since then the police had been very active in driving out the criminals, and children could once again play in the streets. But in an episode just before carnival that year, the police passed a father who was playing with his sons outside the house. The police took him for a bandit and began beating him up in front of his own children. The man's wife heard the commotion and ran to get their identity papers, and after seeing these the police stopped. "You know," Daví said, "we are poor, and they can't see who is who."

The insecurity in the neighborhood thus relates to people living in areas for which the authorities feel no responsibility and among people they cannot trust. At times, the insecurity creeps into a person as a feeling of lack of self-worth, as when Evinha told me that she wanted to have a child to know whether she could really love and be loved in return. *Você não presta!* (you are worth nothing) is a common outburst in the neighborhood. Parents may say this to their children when they feel disappointed in them. Irina, a young woman who got pregnant when she was seventeen, was thrown out of her parents' house with exactly these words when her mother learned her daughter was expecting a child. And Fábio, a young man who became involved in drugs and theft in his late teens, had to listen to repeated comments from his relatives about his lack of a future: "You are worth nothing. A thief. You will not live to be twenty!" they would say. As Fábio recently exclaimed, "Nobody believed in me; nobody believed that I could change!"

Daví was lucky—somebody did believe in him. Before he turned seventeen he had become involved in something bad and had to repeat eighth and ninth grades. But because he said nothing of this at home, his parents were unaware. They found out when his mother was asked to come to a meeting at the school on whether they wanted Daví in school there. Daví met her when she was on her way home; she hardly looked at him, passed him as if he were a stranger, merely saying, "We'll talk about it at home." "*Puxa* [Gosh], she knew it all," he said when he told me. Daví's mother went to see a local schoolteacher named Wellington one day soon after, and Wellington contacted Daví. Wellington mentored a group of young men who were trying to help themselves by helping others. "But why should I help others? I found it a bit strange to be with them," Daví explained. "But it was a very close group, a great friendship," and gradually Daví began to understand. He left the marijuana, *por forca de vontade propria* (of his own free will), as he gradually came to understand that life could be different. He resumed his studies, "filling my head with knowledge instead of *maconha* [marijuana]," as he put it, and he even began to buy novels. Today he is the owner of a rare thing in the neighborhood: a bookshelf. Daví found it very hard to leave the company he used to keep. His old buddies used to come to his house, and even today they still watch him in the street when he passes. "They don't know what I do [these days]," Daví says, "and I don't tell them." Had it not been for Wellington's group, Daví might not have changed. Daví says he owes Wellington a lot.

Wellington explained to me that everybody has a dream in life but many people do not know how to reach it. Those who offer a young person an opportunity often forget to say that "this will be the opportunity of your lifetime." In other words, the opportunity may not be enough; somebody has to express a trust in your ability to take it. Wellington did that, and Daví responded. "He has changed a lot," Wellington recalls. "For instance, the other day he said to me, 'At that time I was lost, but not today. I have lost a lot of time; I will not lose more.'" And then Daví told Wellington that he had done something new at home, something that had never happened before, and that it had moved them all. He had proposed that they have lunch together, even though the family, as many others, rarely share a meal together. As Wellington said, it was not the financial situation that had changed. The family still lives near the riverbank in a poor house, but the relationships have changed along with Daví's new attitude. He used to never see his father; now, when his father comes home from work, Daví is there and sits down and talks to him.

Daví's "I have lost time" refers to time work and the sense of agency experienced when time is no longer an external force but something over which one has control. However, the steps Daví took were not by his merit alone but had been helped by important others around him.

A Community of Shared Endeavor

Evinha was not helped as Daví was. Instead, she found inspiration in Artur. One day, I went with Evinha to visit Artur. She had proposed to me that I interview him, but when we had been there a while I realized that she herself had an interest in meeting him. Artur is different from most of the other people in Evinha's world.

Artur lives with his mother in the favela where Evinha previously lived. He was around thirty at the time I met him, and he had lived there almost all his life. Today most of the houses in the favela are respectable: built with bricks, they have indoor toilets and a wall surrounding the property. But the streets are marked by the history of the place: narrow lanes, which are muddy when it rains and inaccessible to vehicles, including the garbage truck. There is no postal service either. People have to have postal addresses elsewhere, in care of some friend or relative. The residents themselves have gradually installed drains and sewers over time—not at all efficiently—and electricity is still supplied by illegal cables. The area is known to house drug dealers, and some years ago a gang controlled part of the neighborhood. It is an area where young men are at high risk of being attracted to criminal activities.

We sat there on the terrace, behind the tall, whitewashed wall blocking off the street and yet so close to the life unfolding around us: people just beyond the wall, the smells from neighboring kitchens, and the radio in the dark, cool room behind us. Artur was wearing the national Argentinean football shirt. And he wore it proudly, knowing it was provocative to most of the people around him. He told me that it helped him to remember his own independence. Hearing Artur's story I understood that independence is a prominent theme in his life. In the following excerpt, he tells how Duda (a diminutive of Eduardo), his friend and neighbor, helped him find the path that brought him to where he is today:

This road is called Rua Xepa. If you look in the dictionary, *xepa* means "that which is left over." Somebody at the municipality gave it that name. I think they wanted to humiliate us: *"aquele lugar lascado* [this skid row], let us put Xepa." [He laughs and explains that *xepa* refers to the leftovers of a vegetable market, which are thrown away.] But you cannot imagine how this place is a *pólo cultural* [cultural center]. It is something we ourselves have worked for. Duda and I were the same age, we went to the same school, Frei Caneca [the best public school in the area]. We were both rather *contestador* [questioning the status quo]. We had a vision a bit beyond reality; we saw the cruel naked reality of society. Then Duda and I began to walk the same path. We visited these places where you can study. I remember we went by foot to the library in Camaragibe [four kilometers away]. There was a [type of] biscuit called "Tresolo," twelve [in a packet] for me and Duda, six for each of us. At times we did not even have Tresolos. . . . [Every day] we arrived there at eight in the morning and went home at one o'clock. At that time we went to school from three to seven in the afternoon, so we went home and returned to school at three. Always with this vision. We then spoke with someone who said that it wasn't at the public library you should study but at CEFET [a technical school]. We asked around. On our own initiative. Asked A; asked B. Duda was accepted [at CEFET] first; then I was inspired by his victory. And our victories, Duda's and mine, have inspired all around here who have been accepted. Look at how many people in this place have been accepted at CEFET [Artur mentions several names].

Duda's and Artur's good fortune, and their inspiration, seems to have been their companionship and their ability to not succumb to the negative attitudes and propositions from others nearby. They had to maintain a certain distance from life around them to not accept the taken-for-granted future of the place and be affected by the negativity of others. Artur spoke of seeking his own way, finding his own path; in fact, this was a path in time, moving forward, toward something of his own. He talked about choosing, but once again, what he has chosen is a future more than a present. As he explained:

> This is a very small community; the houses are so compact, one on top of the other, but if the guy who is almost in his grave in this place sees the guy who is studying, he doesn't give any value to it.

He is finished, with his feet in the grave, unemployed, in the street talking about other people's lives, playing dominoes, *tirando onda* [showing off]. But if you pass by with a book, he will humiliate you; if you pass by with the Bible, he will humiliate you; with a new pair of shoes—"Oh, new shoes, eh?" He will soon be commenting on your finances. He himself is in such an advanced state [of decay], and even so he does not realize the state he is in. It is easier for him to observe the life of others. It is a pity, but one must continue. To study is a struggle. Those who want to [will] begin, but the road isn't easy; you have to be prepared for a defeat. Because a human being has to be prepared for the defeats. It is not only victories; the one who does not know how to lose does not know how to win. . . . I see a lot of adolescents here not helping their parents. The fathers leave at five o'clock in the morning, struggle hard to bring home ten small bread rolls for their children, and they [in return] do not even sweep the floor, do not clean a plate. They are deluded, not because they don't want to study but because they don't realize the seriousness of the thing. For them everything is fine; they don't realize they are discriminated against because of their hair, their color, their social class, the place they live, and the people they live with. . . . People say that you are a product of the environment you live in. But it isn't like that. If a person has character, he knows what he chooses. *Puxa*, I have always sought my own way. . . . You have to be faithful to your inner reality and continue forward. You need to know what you are searching for. Otherwise you get frustrated with yourself, your parents, even the dog. But this place has character, you see, knows what is good and what is bad.

Artur's thinking was not of his own invention, however. While he spoke, he sometimes referred to the Bible, and even though he is not a Protestant, his ideas about individual responsibility and persistence are not far from the neo-Protestant rhetoric heard so often in recent years in Brazil. Also, teachers and nongovernmental organization staff emphasize the importance of individual agency, and when I asked a public school teacher whether this emphasis deceived the young people, given that so many factors work against their progress in life, the teacher responded, "Yes, you are right, but if I [tell them the truth], they will soon give up and get nowhere." Even parents referred to the traditional saying "Agua mole, pedra dura, bate tanto até que fura" (soft water, hard stone, beats so much that the stone breaks) to support the young people's efforts that, at times, seemed hopeless. Vera, a mother with three sons in their twenties, sighed and said, "I do not say 'you cannot; you will never get there' because suddenly one or another will actually get there. It's like the sperm cell: people have sex, and out of a million, one reaches the ovum." The work on time, here expressed in the form of persistence and patience, is thus integrated in both the discourse of the church and in the common precepts for life.

Artur's attitude, however, was exceptional. He did not simply talk about being confident; his whole body emanated confidence. Since then I have often wanted to ask him how he could be so poised, but I have not seen him. In my view, he had managed to set himself apart from the hopelessness and disappointment of the place, which can affect one so easily there. This was not an individual effort, even though this was how he himself perceived it. It was an effort shared with friends around him, probably both through words and bodily mirroring.

A Place for Hope

In her book *The Transmission of Affect*, Teresa Brennan (2004) takes it as her starting point that affects can be transmitted from person to person, altering the biochemistry and neurology of the subject. Like Varela and Depraz (2005), Brennan states that judgment, the evaluative (positive or negative) orientation toward an object, is the moment a person is affected (2004: 5), and this affection, Brennan adds, has an energetic dimension in the sense that it can enhance or deplete the energy of the person (6). The subjective appropriation of positive effects of affection, the identification that "this is me feeling this way," may be pleasure or joy, a more distinct category than the initial enhancement of energy. The negative effects may be identified as depression, anger, or anxiety. As Ben Anderson writes, the various processes of qualification multiply a movement of affect and allow for the experience of "space-times that are enabling and constraining of distinct subjectivities and identities" (2006: 737). Evinha was affected by Artur's attitude on the day we met him. After the interview, she reflected on his words:

> I liked the way he talked, because he talked with such assurance about the things he has obtained. And I think, if he can obtain that, why shouldn't I be able to do the same? I like his way of talking, his open mind, even though he lives in there [the favela]. He does not behave like a *favelado*. For him it is a matter of not stopping but always looking out for new things. Not like others: "Finish *segundo grau* [twelfth grade—that is, mandatory schooling] and then fine.

That's it!" No, he is always looking for new people, new places; every person you meet is an open door.

Artur's physical appearance, his confidence, had impressed Evinha, as had his not being affected by living in the favela. Always moving forward: that was his strategy. In her conclusion she turned toward herself, generalizing from Artur to a more including "you." When I returned to the neighborhood a year later, she gave me a paper with these words:

I wrote these words when I was really sad, in one of those moments when everything is wrong and difficult:

Happiness and suffering supplement each other.
No one is so happy that she has never suffered.
No one is so sad that she has never been happy.
Happiness and suffering walk side by side.
Sometimes happiness walks in front, and suffering stays behind.
But then come the mistakes in life, and they help suffering overtake happiness.
And so it continues for the rest of one's life.
I cannot tell who wins or loses
Because I haven't reached that point,
and when I am there, I shall still not know,
since then I will be asleep forever, exhausted from hurrying, laughing, and suffering.

(These words make sense only more or less, but they helped me a lot when I wrote them down on the 17th of February 2010—a year ago.)

I was surprised when she gave me this text. Just the day before I had wanted to ask her how she managed to hold herself up and continue when the days were bleak, as I knew they sometimes were. But I never did ask her, and therefore her giving me the paper was not in response to a request. She must have wished to show me that at times she was sad and that she had the means to overcome sadness. Or maybe she just thought I would appreciate her words.

I remembered how, one year earlier, when we went to visit Artur, she was still unemployed. In the year that had passed since then, she had got herself a job. She and a friend had applied for a job at a mobile phone company. Her friend was asked to come for an interview; Evinha was not. But she showed up anyway on the day the interviews were being conducted, and she told them that she had been asked in as well and that the list of interviewees must be incorrect—and she got the job. Today she clings to her opportunity, summing up with a hard, triumphant laugh: "Many will try; few will succeed!" This is the slogan of the company where she works. And Evinha's personal version of that slogan ends with the strong affirmation: "I will succeed!" I am sure that Artur's confidence alone is not what made Evinha change her attitude and perspective. On the other hand, I also think she wanted to see him because she wished to be close to him at a moment in her life when she had to find a way out of an unbearable situation.

Places not only are; they happen (Casey 1996: 27), and thus, emerging in time, they are already always saturated with affect. Trust, mistrust, care, and worries; the changes in tempo; a lack of smiles or outbursts of hearty laughter all affect the biochemistry and neurology of the inhabitants of a given place if we follow Brennan. But as Brennan also writes, it is possible to detect this mutual affection:

> When one judges, one is possessed by the affects. When one discerns, one is able to detach from them, to know where one stands. . . . Discernment, in the affective world, functions best when it is able to alert to the moment of fear and anxiety or grief or other sense of loss that permits the negative affect to gain a hold. . . . On the face of it, any faculty of discernment must involve a process whereby affects pass from the state of sensory registration to a state of cognitive or intelligent reflection; this does not mean that the process of reflection is without affect, just that the affect is other than the affect that is being reflected upon (2004: 119–120).

I think that when Evinha wrote her poem about happiness and sadness, discernment was what she was exhibiting: she reflected on her depression, moving her attention from an all-encompassing experience of being pulled down by a heavy weight (one day she sighed and said, "This place is a hole!") to a melancholy state of mind in which sadness was something passing, never really total and never really gone. When Artur wore his Argentinean football shirt it was part of an act of discernment, as he knew the effect it had and liked to resist the angry outbursts it provoked. And when Evinha observed that Artur was confident, not affected by being a *favelado*, that made her reflect on her own affection by the favela. The *luta espiritual* that Evinha foresaw in her son's life was not just a moral quest but also an encounter with the smell of marijuana, the violence, and the willingness to accommodate the assessments of others. It was a direct confrontation with sensations that would affect her, were he not alert to their negative effects.

Conclusion

Everyone has a free will, according to Evinha. Artur put it differently: "You have to be faithful to your inner reality." But looking more closely at their situation, none of the young people described in this chapter stood alone. Artur and Duda had parents who believed in them, got them into the best public school in the area and allowed them to spend their time out of school at the local library. Artur and Duda also had each other. Daví had a mother who made contact with Wellington and a father who welcomed his son's new attitude. And Daví had Wellington and his group, who helped him sustain his new life perspective. Evinha had not had much support from her family, but she linked up with Artur (and me) and began to trust that she too could succeed. Much in line with Flaherty's (use of G. H. Mead's) notion of a selective attention, they generated "a loop of mutual determination" among themselves (Flaherty 1999: 155), which, as I see it, was transmitted as much through mutual affection as through the spoken word.

The time work done by these young people is a continual intersubjectively maintained discernment of and standing apart from anxiety, depression, and other emotional drawbacks in their immediate surroundings. By not taking notice of the discrimination by the police, when going to college on his bicycle, Kleiton stands apart; when calmly passing people in the street commenting on his striving to get an education, Artur stands apart; when not accepting the habitual relationship to his father but willfully changing it, inspired by his new relationship with Wellington, Daví stands apart. And by moving her son away from the criminal environment and insisting on her own worth, Evinha certainly stands apart too. To be met with "Você não presta!" is a heavy burden, and to hold on to the openness of the moment, the uncertainty of its ending—in that one has not yet reached the end point, as Evinha puts it—depends on the capacity to surpass the immediate present that overwhelms with negativity and diminishes one's energy. Standing apart is an imaginative move that, by way of its change on the level of affect, manifests physiologically as a change in the composure of the body. It is a movement in which the place, and the future it offers, is no longer something that one is fully absorbed by. An alternative future, unspecified but promising, radiates into the present as confidence, literally vibrating one's body here and now.

ACKNOWLEDGMENTS: *I thank Jacqueline Kennelly at Carleton University for constructive comments on an earlier version of this chapter.*

REFERENCES

Anderson, Ben. 2006. "Becoming and Being Hopeful: Towards a Theory of Affect." *Environment and Planning D: Society and Space* 24 (5): 733–752.
Brennan, Teresa. 2004. *The Transmission of Affect*. Ithaca: New York University Press.
Caldeira, Teresa P. R. 2000. *City of Walls: Crime, Segregation, and Citizenship in São Paulo*. Berkeley: University of California Press.
Casey, Edward S. 1996. "How to Get from Space to Place in a Fairly Short Stretch of Time." In *Senses of Place*, edited by Steven Feld and Keith H. Basso, 13–52. Santa Fe, NM: School of American Research Press.
Dalsgård, Anne Line. 2004. *Matters of Life and Longing: Female Sterilisation in Northeast Brazil*. Copenhagen: Museum Tusculanum Press.
Dalsgård, Anne Line, and Katherine V. Gough. 2004. "Et spørgsmål om forskel: Ungdom, vold og overlevelse i Recife." *Den Ny Verden: Tidsskrift for Internationale Studier* 37 (3): 99–108.
Dalsgård, A. L., M. Franch, and R. P. Scott. 2008. "Dominant Ideas, Uncertain Lives: The Meaning of Youth in Recife." In *Youth and the City in the Global South*, edited by Karen Tranberg Hansen with Anne Line Dalsgård, Katherine V. Gough, Ulla Ambrosius Madsen, Karen Valentin, and Norbert Wildermuth, 49–73. Bloomington: Indiana University Press.
Dalsgård, Anne Line, and Martin Demant Frederiksen. 2013. "Out of Conclusion: On Recurrence and Open-Endedness in Life and Analysis." *Social Analysis* 57 (1): 50–63.
Desjarlais, Robert, and C. Jason Throop. 2011. "Phenomenological Approaches in Anthropology." *Annual Review of Anthropology* 40:87–102.
Flaherty, Michael G. 1999. *A Watched Pot: How We Experience Time*. New York: New York University Press.
———. 2011. *Textures of Time: Agency and Temporal Experience*. Philadelphia: Temple University Press.
Franch, Mónica Lourdes. 2008. "Tempos, contratempos e passatempos: Um estudo sobre práticas e sentidos do tempo entre jovens de grupos populares do Grande Recife." Ph.D. diss., Universidade Federal do Rio de Janeiro.
———. 2010. "Amigas, colegas e 'falsas amigas': Amizade e sexualidade entre mulheres jovens de grupos populares." *Sexualidad, Salud y Sociedad—Revista Latinoamericana* 4:28–52.
Goldstein, Donna M. 2003. *Laughter out of Place: Race, Class, Violence and Sexuality in a Rio Shantytown*. Berkeley: University of California Press.
Harris, Oliver J. T., and Tim Flohr Sørensen. 2010. "Rethinking Emotion and Material Culture." *Archaeological Dialogues* 17 (2): 145–163.
Leder, Drew. 1990. *The Absent Body*. Chicago: University of Chicago Press.
Mead, George Herbert. (1934) 1965. *Mind, Self and Society*. Chicago: University of Chicago Press.

Mische, Ann. 2009. "Projects and Possibilities: Researching Futures in Action." *Sociological Forum* 24 (3): 694–704.
Nielsen, Morten. 2011. "Futures Within: Reversible Time and House-Building in Maputo, Mozambique." *Anthropological Theory* 11 (4): 397–423.
Rosaldo, Michelle. 1984. "Toward an Anthropology of Self and Feeling." In *Culture Theory: Essays on Mind, Self and Emotion*, edited by R. A. Shweder and R. A. Levine, 137–157. Cambridge: Cambridge University Press.
Sheets-Johnstone, Maxine. 1999. *The Primacy of Movement*. Philadelphia: John Benjamins.
Varela, Francisco J., and Natalie Depraz. 2005. "At the Source of Time: Valence and the Constitutional Dynamics of Affect." *Journal of Consciousness Studies* 12 (8–10): 61–81.
Waiselfisz, Julio Jacobo. 2011. *Mapa da Violencia 2012: Os novos padrões da violencia homicida no Brasil*. São Paulo: Instituto Sangari.
Wikan, Unni. 1995. "The Self in a World of Urgency and Necessity." *Ethos* 23 (3): 259–285.
Zournazi, Mary. 2002. *Hope: New Philosophies for Change*. London: Lawrence and Wishart.

6

Certificates for the Future

Geographical Mobility and Educational Trajectories among Nepalese Youth

KAREN VALENTIN

Perhaps more than any other institution, modern schooling offers hope—for social mobility, for a place in the symbolic universe of modernity, and for a predictable, stable future. This is especially true in contemporary Nepal, where prospects for many young people are uncertain. Yet investments in formal education tend to pay off—economically as well as symbolically—only in some distant future. Such delayed rewards have encouraged an increasing number of young people to make other choices in their lives, including that of transnational migration, especially in economically and politically unstable regions of the world, where educational and professional promises for young people tend to be bleak not just for all those without education but also for a growing mass of educated unemployed youth (Jeffrey 2010). Education is a strong driving force in the interrelated processes of geographical and social mobility (see, e.g., Fong 2011; Pan 2011; Rao 2010; Valentin 2012): young people migrate with the aim of pursuing formal education, and academic skills and formal qualifications in the form of diplomas acquired before and during the migration process are instrumental in young migrants' aspirations for further mobility.

In contemporary Nepal, ideas of education and the outside world are embedded in a powerful narrative of modernization, which, with its insistence on a linear, forward-looking form of thinking, implies an idealized future (see Zerubavel 2003). Ordinary Nepalese people have experienced this modernization narrative through the ideology and institutional practices of planned development, which have permeated both political and public discourse since the mid-1950s, when the country became the recipient of foreign aid (Ahearn 2004; Pigg 1996). One of the most significant mediators of this narrative has been the introduction of formal education, through which Nepalese children and young people have come to envisage "the modern" as science-based knowledge, in contrast to local knowledge, and as something that is synonymous with the "foreign" (Valentin 2005; Liechty 1997). Schooling thus is one gateway to an imagined modern world, in the sense of both going abroad to the modern and of bringing the modern to Nepal. Educational migration as a global mass phenomenon available to an increasing number of young people from the world's poorest regions not only synthesizes these ideas of the modern; it also provides a lens through which to comprehend the symbolic realm of modernity. In terms used by Mark Liechty in his study of urban middle-class youth in Nepal (1995: 168–169), "state modernism," understood in terms of a state ideology of progress, development, and modernization, is conflated with a "consumer modernity" embedded in the global capitalist political economy, which manifests itself in, among other things, an increasingly commercialized international education market, where hopes for the future are for sale.

As a technology of the imagination, migration makes people envisage better lives in other places and other times (Vigh 2009: 94). In the contemporary world, such imaginaries become reinforced by the enduring public and political faith in formal education as the means to progress, both nationally and individually (Valentin 2005), and make migration for education appear particularly promising. Seen in this perspective, it is not surprising that a large number of young Nepalese people, especially from the urban upper-middle and upper classes, are attracted by opportunities to acquire an education abroad. "Abroad" (*bidesh*) has become a trope for imagining particular places and the qualities ascribed to them through the temporal idioms of progress and backwardness (see Pigg 1996: 163). This is reflected in a hierarchy of migrant destinations, in which some countries are perceived as being "ahead" of others and are therefore more attractive as potential places to obtain an education and its ultimate product, a diploma or degree from a foreign university.

While spatiality remains a central analytical category for exploring geographical mobility, the aim of this chapter is to emphasize temporality in the study of Nepalese student migration to Denmark. To look at this through the specific lens of educational migration compared to other forms of migration is relevant because of the strong inbuilt future orientations of both migration and education, individually as well as collectively. This is especially pronounced for youth, which, more than any other age category, is ascribed transformative potential and is therefore a central point of symbolic investment for families, communities, and even nation-states. The hope of change, coupled to fear of failure and uncertainty, is fundamentally linked to the category of youth (Cole and Durham 2008). Many young people are therefore willing to take chances that might improve their own and their family's situations and seek out new opportunities through migration and other routes.

Adopting a transnational perspective on the study of migration, with its emphasis on networks, social relations, and the multiple connections that migrants develop (see, e.g., Levitt and Glick-Schiller 2004; Brettell 2008), this chapter sheds light on the relationship between geographical and educational trajectories through a focus on different interrelated temporalities, which either facilitate or constrain young people's mobility and thus circumscribe ideas of the possible and the impossible. It draws on ethnographic data collected in a research project on educational migration from Nepal to Denmark.[1] Since 2009 I have followed the Nepali student community in Copenhagen with increasing intensity through classroom observations, participation in various political and cultural events, and less formal social interactions in homes, trains going back and forth to college, cafés, and so on. In addition, I conducted twenty-five recorded in-depth interviews (twenty-two single and three group interviews) with students.[2] In all, I have communicated and interacted with approximately a hundred Nepalese, males and females, most of them living in Copenhagen. Around half of these, mostly males, are students; one-fourth are dependents (mostly female spouses); and the remainder are a mixture of green card holders (a residence permit also used in other countries that grants a person the right to seek work in Denmark for three years), small-scale entrepreneurs, and those who have come for other reasons. I also interviewed educational coordinators and administrative staff from four of the colleges concerned and had numerous informal conversations with teachers. Finally, I spent one month in Kathmandu in the summer of 2012, where I met returnee students and relatives of students still living in Denmark, as well as representatives of

---

1. The project is part of the collaborative project Education, Mobility and Citizenship: An Anthropological Study of Educational Migration to Denmark (2010–2014), financed by the Danish Council for Independent Research.
2. Interviews quoted here were conducted in English with occasional use of Nepali and Danish terms. All translations of terms are mine.

political and civic organizations engaged in the mobilization of Nepalese abroad. This amounted to an additional sixteen formal interviews.

The current project is further informed by my long-standing academic interest in Nepal, since the mid-1990s, including extended periods of ethnographic fieldwork among urban squatters in Nepal (Valentin 2005) and among Nepalese in India (Valentin 2012). While these projects have been conducted in different settings and have been guided by different research interests, there are several cross-cutting issues of relevance to the study of time and migration, such as common family-migration histories, the continuous references that people make to other, hierarchically ordered places as both past experiences and imagined future destinations, and not least the importance of possessing—or in some cases of not possessing—different kinds of documents and identity papers with which to engage in geographical and social mobility. Attaining particular meanings and expressions depending on social class and regional context, these issues seem no less relevant to the study of educational migration to Denmark.

Conceptualizing Time in Nepalese Migrations

Central to the argument of this chapter is the notion of temporality—that is, empirical and analytical conceptualizations of time—in processes of geographical and social mobility. As an empirical category through which people order their lives and an analytical concept through which we, as researchers, understand social processes, time is relevant for the study of migration in several respects (Cwerner 2001). I approach migration from the perspective of three different forms of time—historical, bureaucratic, and biographical—which are intertwined in subjective experiences of migration and in different ways become manifested in various kinds of documents. First, mobility inevitably involves a reshaping of past-present-future relations, which are integral to temporalizations in general (Munn 1992: 115). Second, migration is about timing in fairly concrete terms and rests on the capacity of people to know when and where to move at particular points in time. Third, a life-course perspective can shed light on migration as a timed event, a turning point, in the life of an individual (Brettell 2002). I chose these three forms of time as analytical categories because they encompass both the structural and experiential dimensions of specific migrant trajectories. Furthermore, they help us comprehend how practices of migration are shaped by a combination of short- and long-term considerations—that is, the long-term expectations of an education abroad and the actual possibilities of migrating, including the immediate concerns of being admitted to an educational program abroad and getting a visa. In the following section, I unfold these three temporal notions of time through a discussion of Nepalese student migration to Denmark.

Historical Time and Current Patterns of Nepal–Denmark Migration

The notion of historical time may be understood as "a linear chronological movement of changes in a society over decades or centuries" (Hareven 1977: 59), referring to actual historical events, which, through subjective and collective interpretations, are likely to impinge on structural conditions in a given society and thus contribute to shaping social practices, ideologies, and institutional arrangements. Situating current migration patterns in relation to factors in historical time, at both the sending and receiving ends, can help us explain how changing structural circumstances may provide avenues for culturally meaningful turning points in the lives of young people (see Brettell 2002). Here I use "historical time" to refer to a set of specific political, economic, and institutional circumstances in Nepal and Denmark that fueled and made possible migration for a cohort of young Nepalese who have come to Denmark since the early 2000s, either directly from Nepal or via other countries.

The number of Nepalese migrating for educational or labor reasons has increased dramatically over the past two decades (NIDS and NCCR North-South 2011). This was facilitated partly by a relaxation of Nepal's emigration rules following the reintroduction of democracy in 1990, which opened up migrant destinations beyond India (Gurung and Adhikari 2004) and partly by the emergence of a distinctly urban and highly consumer-oriented middle class able to purchase education (Liechty 2003). This has resulted in a substantial marketization of education, not just nationally but also internationally, rendered visible in the vast numbers of educational consultancies operating in large cities of Nepal, all competing to attract prospective students for study abroad, especially in North America, Australia, and Europe.

Furthermore, an armed conflict between Maoists and government forces, the People's War, swept across the country from 1996 to 2006 and contributed to general political and economic instability. During the years of conflict, the educational system came under ideological attack and was severely affected, especially in the rural areas of the country: Maoists abducted students and targeted them for indoctrination programs, private schools were forced to pay protection money to Maoists, schools had to shut down for prolonged periods because of strikes, and in Maoist-controlled areas the government curriculum was replaced by a "people's education" curriculum

(Cadell 2006; Eck 2010). Although very few of my informants reported having been directly involved in or affected by the armed conflict in terms of military actions, threats, or reprisals, they expressed a more general concern about the lack of educational and occupational opportunities available to them as middle-class youth in postconflict Nepal.

The above-mentioned factors have led to a drastic expansion in the number of young people, males and females, leaving Nepal. "Going out" (*bahira jane*) has therefore become part of everyday discourse and refers to countries other than India, the country accounting for the largest number of Nepalese migrants by far, mostly undocumented. Implicit in this is, as mentioned above, a hierarchy of destinations in which India is lowest, then come the Middle East and Far East, then Europe, Canada and Australia, and finally the United States at the top, a hierarchy that correlates with modernistic ideas of developed countries.

While Nepalese do not have a significant history of migration to Denmark before the first decade of the 2000s, and the current figure according to official statistics only amounts to about 1,951,[3] a number of factors have contributed to making Denmark part of the imaginary of Nepalese youth at this point in history. In Europe, decreasing populations and a lack of workers in certain sectors, combined with the internationalization and commercialization of education, have made it both possible and attractive for young Nepalese to come to Europe to study. The Danish government, to make Denmark competitive in the global economy by securing a highly qualified work force, has attempted to attract talented international students (UVM 2008). This branding of Denmark as an education destination in the 2000s resulted in an increasing number of students from developing countries, including Nepal, being enrolled in self-financed educational programs, especially the two-year academy profession programs at business colleges or three-and-a-half-year professional bachelor's programs at so-called university colleges, whereas only a very limited number enter regular universities. Enrollment in higher education is one of few the legal gateways to Denmark for non–European Union citizens, hence Nepalese granted education visas in 2008 and 2009 are the third-largest group of students from outside the EU. At the same time, and especially before the global economic crisis, there was a demand for unskilled labor in certain sectors in Denmark, including the service sector, in which foreign students could find employment that

---

3. See Danmarks Statistik (Statistics Denmark) at http://www.statistikbanken.dk/FOLK1, November 2013. The number includes all students, green card holders, and other categories of Nepalese citizens living in Denmark.

could be combined with their need for part-time jobs, although often at a lower wage than their Danish counterparts.

Thus, a number of factors—especially the postconflict situation in Nepal and the global marketization of education, which Denmark has strategically joined in recent years—have fostered new migration routes and practices. Education has become one such route, which has opened up new destinations like Denmark. Combined with the pervasive modernization discourse that continues to shape the imaginations of young Nepalese people, these factors feature "the times we live in" (see the Introduction) and provide an example of how particular historical moments offer different opportunities for shaping individual life courses.

Bureaucratic Time: Between the Categories of Student and Immigrant

As a second form of time I suggest bureaucratic time, or the temporalities built into administrative processes connected with the particular category of international students, with their identities as both foreigners and students. The notion of bureaucratic time is intimately linked with power and control and extends what Sunaina Maira, in the context of South Asian migration to the United States, terms "immigrant time," a temporal encounter between the state and the migrant bound up with a preoccupation with, and fear of, documents (2009: 122). A few scholars have addressed these issues through a focus on the intersection of student migration with unskilled labor migration from the global South to the global North, showing how this is embedded in structural global inequalities (Pan 2011; Mapril 2011; Neilson 2009). Through their focus on the blurred processes of legality and illegality that circumscribe this kind of migration, these studies draw attention to the urgent issues of having or not having papers, waiting for papers, being given or denied papers, and so on. Permits that entitle foreigners to temporary or permanent residence are by nature temporal as time becomes a key tool with which to regulate and control immigration (Cwerner 2001). Embedded in specific historical times and shaped in response to those times, immigrant time is often marked by prolonged periods of waiting, an effect of the state's attempts to control and fix people in time through documenting practices (Ferme 2004). Certain documents are particularly relevant for transnational migrants, most obviously passports, visas, residential permits, and social security cards, but for an increasing number of young people, academic documents such as admission papers and diplomas may serve as another form of travel document, either as a pass to new destinations or as an expected outcome of the move itself. International students, especially those coming from outside the EU, face rigid bureaucratic regulations in the intersecting fields of education and immigration policy (Valentin 2012), and it is therefore relevant to explore potentially conflicting temporalities of obtaining different kinds of documents—for example, admission papers to a college versus a visa—and how this may contribute to opening up or closing certain pathways.

As Maira's "immigrant time" captures only temporalities associated with students' status as foreigners, it may be appropriate to expand it to include also the temporal aspects of bureaucratic processes related to being a student under the broader bureaucratic time. In contrast to the temporal experiences of, for example, refugees and asylum seekers, who conceive of waiting as meaningless and without any direction (Vitus 2010), student and immigrant time implies a more purposeful waiting, which, similar to what Craig Jeffrey (2010) has described in the context of educated unemployed northern India youth, also offers opportunities to acquire new skills. In the case of Nepalese students in Denmark it is not a waiting that is translated into experiences of boredom. Most of the students I have met express a different concern about time—namely, not having enough of it to be able to study, work, and maybe take Danish lessons, all of which may help them secure a future life in Denmark. This is reflected in, among other things, tight daily study and work schedules and recurrent references to examination dates and deadlines for assignments. Waiting time for these young Nepalese thus acquires different meanings because it is related to a social category that is imbued with hope and future prospects, that of "student," a category with which they can claim a legitimate affiliation by their enrollment in formal institutions of education and that provides the legal basis of their stay. However, an inherent tension between everyday and long-term experiences of bureaucratic time and the different forms of waiting it implies becomes especially salient in the context of foreign students coming from outside the EU. As self-paying students they have to not only meet academic requirements, passing examinations and actively attending classes, itself a precondition for renewing visas, but also work for extended hours during their studies to pay student fees and living expenses. Thus, students' investments made in obtaining an education in Denmark, in time and money, are inextricably bound up with their status as temporary immigrants and not just as students. The expected outcome of this is an academic degree, which makes these investments appear meaningful from a longer-term perspective but also makes for uncertainties about the future: where to go and what to do afterward with a diploma?

Biographical Time: On the Route to Adulthood

Migration as related to the life course of an individual calls for an analytical focus on generation and, more specifically, on how intergenerational relations within families and local communities are shaped and reshaped in response to changing institutional structures and broad-scale economic, political, and social processes (Cole and Durham 2007). Labor migration, especially within Nepal and from Nepal to India, has been a common practice for young Nepalese males for generations as a survival strategy and because of the sociocultural meaning attached to it as a rite of passage for young men in the family (Sharma 2008). Migration is a transitional process (Cwerner 2001: 27), which in the context of youth migration often coincides with the passage to adulthood. Many therefore leave at a point in their lives, in their teens or twenties, when they would generally be expected to take on more responsibilities and secure the future of the household, through their wages and by getting married and having children. In accord with observations made by Filippo Osella and Caroline Osella (2000) in their study of masculinity and migration from southern India to the Gulf states, moving away temporarily is an expected step in the transition to adulthood signified by a shift in status: young males leave as minors and return as adults ready to take over the responsibilities of the household (Sharma 2008: 312).

While the character of Nepalese transnational migration has changed radically over the last two decades, some of the elements described above are still recognizable in current practices of educational migration to Denmark. Young Nepalese coming to Denmark for higher education differ from so-called labor migrants described by other scholars (e.g., Graner 2009–2010; Kollmair, Manandhar, Subedi, and Thieme 2006; Sharma 2008; Thieme and Müller-Böker 2004), especially with respect to social-class background. Judging by the conversations I have had with them and by their relatively high social and economic positions in Nepal, most come from upper-middle-class families: many report close male relatives (fathers, uncles, grandfathers) being politicians (both locally and as members of parliament, mayors, or union leaders), lawyers, businessmen, government officials, and teachers; they refer often to family-owned landholdings outside Nepal; and not least, in many cases the family has had the economic or social capital needed to pay travel and study fees, either by using savings, by selling land, or through loans. On the basis of their surnames, many of the students come from high-caste families (for example, Bahun, Chetri, and high-caste Newars), which reflects historically produced, caste-based privileges to formal education in Nepal. However, caste does not appear to be an empirically central feature in my study, and therefore I do not deal with it in detail.

Although the entire period of organized student migration from Nepal to Denmark is less than ten years, certain demographic waves can be traced, partly through my observations and partly through conversations with a representative of the Danish embassy in Nepal about visa-issuing practices. The first group of Nepalese students were mainly young males. Some had married before coming to Denmark, whereas others returned to Nepal on short-term visits to marry Nepalese women and later brought them to Denmark. By 2013, according to official statistics, about 40 percent of the Nepalese population in Denmark was female, mostly dependents, as they term it themselves to refer to their status as spouses accompanying their husbands. And finally, as the couples have started to have children, the number of grandmothers, especially, applying for short-term visas has increased. Despite the longer periods of education and the hope for a secure job tending to delay marriage, especially among the urban middle class in Nepal (Liechty 2003: 211), informants still report marriage and childbearing as significant moves toward adulthood in the Hindu-based society of Nepal, though student identity and the relatively free life abroad, far from the daily social obligations in the often-extended families in Nepal, keep them in the desirable position of being young people for a while longer. In addition to the existential aspects of being with a partner and the social obligations of establishing a family, marrying is also a way of securing a full income because spouses are allowed to work full time. Moreover, there is a long-term benefit from this because it allows the couple to alternate between being students and full-time breadwinners. The residence permit is conditioned by enrollment in an educational program, so once the husband has finished his two-year course he can start working while the wife takes up her studies, this being a legal way of extending one's stay whereby both parties receive access to education. Migration for education thus provides young people with an opportunity to prepare for adult life through the potential accumulation of economic and symbolic capital, but similar to Vanessa Fong's observations among transnational Chinese students (2011: 171), it also allows them to postpone the obligations of social adulthood through prolonged stays away from home. At the same time, they have to meet the expectations of supporting their families in Nepal, either by sending financial remittances back home, which is difficult because of the high cost of living and studying in Denmark, or in a longer perspective through the more extended outcome of having an education, which they hope can pave the way to upward social mobility for the entire family.

While the migration process is stretched out in time in the life course of an individual and thus difficult to date in terms of an absolute beginning and end, particular events such as obtaining a visa, receiving an admission letter, or getting on a plane are often remembered as significant, defining moments. Such moments carry hopes for a different and often better future and, from a life-course perspective, are potential turning points that recast past experiences in the light of future opportunities.

Interweaving Times in the Trajectories of Youth

The three forms of time I have discussed point to some of the temporal structures that frame young migrants' maneuvering, not just in the present but also with respect to future life. The following three cases, each with a different emphasis, of young Nepalese males illustrate how such different notions of time are integrated into and contribute to shaping subjective experiences of migration and how experiences of leaving create a new sense of the past, against which the present is evaluated and the future is modeled. Whereas the past is often articulated in terms of nostalgia and romanticization, the future is envisaged in terms of progress (Zerubavel 2003). While migrant narratives often refer to a place of origin, to the idea of a spatially defined starting point for the migration, there is usually also an imagined endpoint as the cases below show. This is both spatially defined in terms of fairly well-defined hierarchies of migrant destinations and temporally mediated through certain future achievements—a job, a degree, a residential permit, a refuge, or just a better life. These work as identifiable objects for future hopes (Crapanzano 2003) and thus as strong driving forces for further mobility, both geographical and social. All three cases are in some sense typical of high-caste Nepalese male students in Denmark and thus illustrate how different notions of time are interwoven in the trajectories of educational migrants.

Laxman: Moving Ahead or Wasting Time

Having noticed me at several events in the Nepalese community in Denmark, Laxman introduced himself to me through a friend request on Facebook in late 2009. I first met him in person the following year at a concert on the occasion of Dasain, the largest annual Hindu festival celebrated by Nepalese. He was there with his Nepalese girlfriend, whom he married the following year, and some Danish friends. A few months later I had an interview with him in which he revealed how he left Nepal and came to Denmark via extended stays first in India and then in the Middle East.

Laxman grew up in a village near one of the large cities in the southern plains of Nepal in an obviously well-to-do family. His father, who had died recently, had retired from the army, and in addition to his pension, the family had large landholdings. In 1995, just before the onset of the People's War, Laxman left for India to study business management and stayed there for six years. Around 2002, at age twenty-two or twenty-three, he went to the Middle East to work in a restaurant, after a tough competition in which he and five others were selected from among three hundred applicants. Once in the Middle East he received training and was promoted, first to crew leader, then to team leader, and then to supervisor and manager, a position in which he remained for two years. He was striving to become an area manager, which would mean a good salary and a company-provided apartment and car. However, a junior colleague whom he himself had trained was given the position, apparently because the colleague had a bachelor's degree in hospitality management, which Laxman did not. This, according to Laxman, became an incentive to move on. He returned to Nepal, where he met a friend who was studying in Denmark. With the help of a wealthy cousin, whom Laxman refers to as a brother, he set off: "So my brother said, 'Okay, you go there first, find out what the country [is like], because once you go there you will get the Schengen visa, [which allows travel throughout Western Europe, and] you can travel to two or three countries. You find out whichever country is good to settle in for you or if you will like to explore about some business education, and I will support you.'" The first stop on his route was a *Folkehøjskole* (folk high school), a part of the Grundtvigean tradition of adult education that arose in the mid-nineteenth century in Denmark with the aim of educating the peasantry. Focusing on democracy, active citizenship, and lifelong learning, several of these folk high schools nowadays have preparatory programs lasting three to four months for young foreigners who wish to study in Denmark.

After a stay at the *Folkehøjskole*, Laxman moved on to a business college and later enrolled in a so-called top-up bachelor's degree course in hospitality management. When I met him he had just started his internship in the course, for which he was paying DKK 32,500 per semester (about 4,400 euros). He mentioned no plans to return to Nepal, saying that all his friends were abroad in high positions as engineers and medical doctors and that what he termed "the level of thinking" in Nepal with respect to people's lack of dedication to developing their country was too low for his taste. If, he asserted, his fellow villagers gave him ten years, he could develop a "model place with a model school and high living standards," but they did not care.

As the following quotation illustrates, he linked this level of thinking to wasted time and indirectly addressed his fellow villagers in Nepal:

> I want to change the education system also, [to be the same as] here in DK [Denmark]. I want to gain some influence from here [Denmark]. I say, take some good things that I have, the knowledge I paid for being here. When I tell them that for one lecture, one hour, I am paying 550 DKK, . . . when they convert it, they say, "Uuuh" [indicating that it is a huge amount of money]. I say, "Get something from me! What I am getting I know you guys cannot afford . . . , but at least I am there. I am getting an education there, I am getting the lectures, but we can transfer the knowledge. It is transferable; get some good knowledge, try to change, make the change." They just waste time; I count[ed] . . . in the morning when I walk[ed] all the way in the villages, two thousand hours were wasted. Everybody [was] grouping, talking, grouping, talking, grouping, talking. I didn't tell them anything; I was simply walking, observing the people, and in the evening I made the report. I said, "Well, one morning our village is wasting two thousand hours."

What is particularly noteworthy here are Laxman's reflections about wasted time and the implicit message that those who stay behind waste their time by just sitting together talking, in contrast to those who go abroad to buy knowledge, which, he asserted, could be transferred from him to his home community. Feeding into the dominant understanding of development and its inherently modernistic ideas of linearity, progression, and rationality, the perceived link between time and progress is further supported by his statement that in ten years' time he could develop a model village provided the villagers let him do so. Moreover, Laxman illustrates how academic and geographical trajectories converge: the lack of and the demand for degrees and diplomas becomes a driving force for continued geographical mobility and acquisition of skills proceeds with destination, from Nepal to India, the Middle East, Denmark, and potentially the United States or Canada, where he hopes to pursue a master's degree. This clearly reflects the aforementioned hierarchy of destinations and thus the spatial and temporal interconnectedness of migratory flows, where movements in space are conceived of as movements in time. The modernization narrative is indeed a reflection of a historical time in Nepal, which, for young Nepalese students in Denmark, as the following case of Dilip shows, translates into a discourse of strongly felt obligation to transfer some of the skills and knowledge gained from abroad to their homes, whether they themselves plan to go back or not.

Dilip: The Returns of Invested Time and Money

A teacher from a Danish business college suggested I contact Dilip because, according to the teacher, he was an extraordinarily dedicated and talented student. When I first met Dilip in the spring of 2011, he was just about to graduate with a certificate in leadership and was thus searching for further opportunities. He had just given tuition classes to some junior students, an obligation he had to fulfill in return for the scholarship he had received from the college. In the two interviews I had with him he told me about his background and how he came to Denmark. Having finished his undergraduate studies in engineering in Kathmandu, in 2007 he had the chance to go to Greece, where he completed one semester in hotel management studies. During the summer vacation he went to Denmark to look for a place for an internship as part of his studies in Greece, but having met other Nepalese in Denmark he changed his mind and decided to apply to a business college in Denmark instead. In particular he emphasized that, unlike most of the other Nepalese students in Denmark, he came from a poor farmer's family from Jumla, an underdeveloped region with few educational opportunities in western Nepal, which furthermore had been badly affected by the armed conflict. He also stressed that his father, who had never gone to school as a child, had nonetheless managed to acquire some education through a private teacher, a *gurukul*, and that later he was somehow awarded a degree in India, which allowed him to teach and clearly also gave him some status. Dilip spoke about the situation in his home community:

> They have no education . . . and they have hunger. You know, they all work . . . seventeen to eighteen hours [a day], and [still] they do not have enough [money to buy necessities]. And education now—there is now a trend to educate. They want to learn, they want to go to school. But they don't have that kind of environment, no college. And if they go to school, there is not enough to eat at night. So all the children who are above ten or eleven years used to work.

Dilip himself emphasized his dedication to studying and said that he regularly attended class and was very disciplined, but he also said that he wanted to complete his studies quickly so that he could give back to his home community in Nepal some of the things he had learned. A little later he returned to the question of the expectations others held of him in terms of a return on the investments made in his education and how this was linked to his engagement in community development in Nepal through a youth club that he had founded while still in Nepal and that he currently supported with about DKK 600–700 (approximately 100 euros) every two or three months. He said that he was sponsoring two children through this club and continued:

> [Yeah,] that is my first responsibility. And the second responsibility is to give my money to my mum and sometimes to my sister if they really need some money. But they also don't have that kind of expectation. They struggle for themselves, but they . . . have high expectations [of me]. You know. That is the thing. They always push me, you know. They never want money. I know they have problems, but they only ask me, "How is your education?"

This quotation illustrates a recurrent theme in the two interviews I had with him, that of others' high expectations of him in terms of his potential contributions to the home community. But he also acknowledged that it could be difficult for him to return because his habits had changed during his years abroad, such as using a machine to wash his clothes. I was in contact with him on Facebook at the end of 2011, where he told me that, since our last meeting, he had been admitted to a master's program at a business school.

Dilip's case illustrates how his drive to obtain an education abroad is linked to previous experiences in Nepal and to the expectations of his family and home community in an area of Nepal that has been badly affected by the armed conflict. Dilip described himself as the son of a poor family, corresponding with the impression I received when I later had the opportunity to meet some of his close relatives in their rented room in Kathmandu. While Dilip's socioeconomic background is not at all typical of the students I have met in Denmark, in his self-representation this was exactly what motivated him to pursue an academic career, not just to secure a future for himself in terms of a position but also to contribute to educating those left behind, in other words, to confer some of his cultural capital on the community. Because economic as well as symbolic investments made in education are expected to be paid back in the near or distant future, "return" (understood as a wide range of economic, political, and civic contributions to the homeland) has a strong temporal dimension binding past experiences with future orientations.

One may have the impression that the world is open to these young migrants and that it is up to themselves to decide their futures—where to be and what to do. This is not the case, for although many of these Nepalese students come from well-to-do families, they are still subject to tight immigration laws and financial constraints that result from the prevalence of low-paid jobs and high education fees. As a reminder of the need to understand also the restricted character of social and global mobility (see Vigh 2009: 93), the case of Kedar illustrates the working of bureaucratic time, showing how future orientations are intimately linked with and constrained by it.

Kedar: The Costly Waiting

Kedar was one of the first students I connected with in the summer of 2009. He had come to Denmark in 2003, when formal education for people from outside the EU was still free, and was among the first Nepalese students in Denmark to enroll in a business college, first in an academy profession program (which is shorter than a bachelor's program) and later in a bachelor's program in economics and information technology. Having completed these, he was admitted to one of the universities to obtain another bachelor's degree, this time in business and communication studies, and in late summer of 2011 he graduated from a master's program in the same field of study. Unlike many others (especially in the early years) he did not come to Denmark through the auspices of an agency but had searched for a destination on his own on the Internet. To my question, "Why Denmark, a tiny European country?" he answered that he was always being asked this question. The reason, he asserted, was that he always received prompt replies from the Danish institutions. In response to my question about how long the immigration process took, he replied:

> It all depends on the immigration service in Denmark. Before, [when I came in 2003,] it only took me three months. It took me three months; I got the pass. But I came to know of someone . . . [who has] been waiting for one year or more in Nepal. The money was held in Denmark, and they have been waiting for the reply [from the Danish immigration service]. It is also a problem. A lot of Nepalis, they send money first to the school, and then they have to wait for one year, and they [representatives from the immigration service] say, "We don't want you." . . . They didn't give them the visa.

Kedar's family is originally from Pokhara. His family home is now in Chitwan, in the southern plains of Nepal, but his widowed mother lives with his brothers in Kathmandu, where they also have a house. Kedar had an arranged marriage four years earlier with a Nepalese woman who had never been to Kathmandu before her marriage at age twenty-two. Soon after the marriage they went to Denmark, where they had a son. While Kedar did kitchen work in cafés during his studies, his wife had a full-time job as a maid in a hotel, from which she was given paid maternity leave. Some months later, at the end of 2011, I met them both in their home. As a graduate he was now looking for a job in his field of study and had sent off numerous applications but so far had had no positive replies. He did not have any income, and his wife was on sick leave recovering from a broken arm, receiving just enough allowance to cover the expense of the two-room flat. Their account was overdrawn, and they could make it only thanks to a bank loan. Kedar seemed to be ambivalent regarding his future. His visa would expire soon, in January 2012, and he had just spent DKK 10,000 (about 1,400 euros) to apply for a green card, which is awarded on a points system, points being given according to educational level, language skills, work experience, adaptability, and age. According to his own calculations he had about 15 points above the necessary 100 points, which made him assume he would get the card. However, if he could not find a job that matched his qualifications in Denmark, he assured me, he wanted to return to Nepal and not move on to Spain or Portugal as many others had. Although he had a very different class background than Dilip, with a widowed mother who was able to pay the expenses of his first year in Denmark (transportation plus living costs) without having to sell any family land, Kedar expressed a similar concern for using the skills he had acquired through his education in Denmark to contribute to building up Nepal, if necessary on a voluntary basis. Three months later, in February 2012, I met him incidentally, and he told me that he had been given a green card, happily, but that he still did not have a job.

That Kedar had invested DKK 10,000 applying for a green card despite having received only negative replies to numerous job applications is an example of waiting characteristic of bureaucratic time, or waiting that is bound up with not only legal requirements but also financial concerns. Not only do the documents themselves cost money (and become more and more expensive) but the time spent waiting is also calculated in monetary terms, either as time in which the debt increases (as was the case with Kedar) or when money is being withheld and potentially lost, as in the case of all those waiting in Nepal to obtain visas and admission.

The young students' concerns for the future are obviously related to their current situations as migrants on temporary visas in a Europe with tightened immigration rules for certain nationalities. This in turn affects their everyday lives and is reflected in their continuous preoccupation with official papers—visas, work permits, invitation letters, academic certificates, and so on—which they hope, in either the shorter or longer term, can secure their stay, if not in Denmark, then somewhere else in Europe, or help them build a future in Nepal. For an international student coming from outside the EU, completing an educational program and being awarded a degree inevitably raises the question of "What then, and where," because the temporary residence permit is conditioned on their enrollment in an academic program. That means that six months after graduation they automatically lose their visa unless they find some other way to stay on—for example, by obtaining a green card, enrolling in another educational program, or having a spouse who does so.

What these three stories have in common is, first, the way different notions of time are interwoven and become salient in the lives of ordinary people. Second, they all represent a male version of the migrant trajectory, one that has its own temporalities. All three left Nepal as unmarried men at a point in their lives when they would generally be expected to marry and gradually take on adult responsibilities. They were part of a wave of single males leaving Nepal at a point in its history when educational and employment opportunities for young middle-class people were decreasing because of the armed conflict and its aftermath. After a couple of years, many young men married and brought their wives to Denmark as dependents who were therefore eligible to work full time. While many of the young women were students or recent graduates from Nepal, some later continued their studies in Denmark, whereas others had to give up their educational ambitions to devote themselves to a full-time job as a kitchen assistant or a hotel maid. Analytically, this compels us to explore the relationship between geographical and educational trajectories, how such trajectories are embedded within and framed by different temporal horizons, and how this contributes to shaping young men's and women's ideas about and prospects for the future.

Conclusion

An overall question in this volume is how time affects the daily lives of young people and how they themselves make sense of time (see the Introduction). Exploring the issue of youth and temporality through a focus on the historically recent phenomenon of educational migration from Nepal to Denmark, this chapter sheds light on the role of education as both an aspiration and a strategy in processes of geographical and social mobility. A temporal perspective on mobility compels us to pay attention to the multiplicity, intersections, and ruptures of different times inherent in experiences of migration (Cwerner 2001). I have here approached the issue of migration through three different notions of time—historical, bureaucratic, and biographical—to illuminate how young people's lives are framed by overlapping and often contradictory temporalities. Where and how do young people, in this case young Nepalese students in Denmark, encounter time in its various forms, and how does this shape individual trajectories and subjective experiences of migration? As the empirical examples have shown, time becomes salient in both the form of strong future orientations—hopes, expectations, and obligations—through which the investments made in an education abroad can be repaid and made meaningful, and the materialized form of different documents such as visas, passports, and diplomas, which, as markers of time, bind together these three different notions of time.

However, while acknowledging that migrants are simultaneously engaged in overlapping economic, social, political, and educational spheres and that one should therefore be cautious in making sharp distinctions between different forms of migration, I also argue that a focus on education as the primary motivation for migration offers a new lens through which to explore the relationship between youth and temporality. In addition to the global intensification of educational migration being itself a product of historical times and student status, not by definition but in practice, being mostly associated with the period of youth, educational migration also accentuates the tensions between the long-term and short-term outcomes of migration, expected as well as actual. There is a strong belief, or at least a hope, that the economic and human investments made to acquire an education abroad will pay off in the future, but at the same time the immediate demands of living expenses and the expectations of one's family back home, combined with repeated bureaucratic restrictions, may lead to ruptures in expected educational and geographical trajectories.

ACKNOWLEDGMENTS: *I thank Jeevan Sharma at Edinburg University and Tristan Bruslé at Le Centre National de la Recherche Scientifique for constructive comments on earlier versions of this chapter.*

REFERENCES

Ahearn, Laura. 2004. "Literacy, Power, and Agency: Love Letters and Development in Nepal." *Language and Education* 18 (4): 305–316.
Brettell, Caroline. 2002. "Gendered Lives: Transitions and Turning Points in Personal, Family, and Historical Time." *Current Anthropology* 43:45–61.
———. 2008. "Theorizing Migration in Anthropology: The Social Construction of Networks, Identities, Communities, and Globalscapes." In *Migration Theory: Talking across Disciplines*, 2nd ed., edited by Caroline B. Brettell and James F. Hollifield, 97–135. New York: Routledge.

Cadell, Martha. 2006. "Private Schools as Battlefields: Contested Visions of Learning and Livelihood in Nepal." *Compare: A Journal of Comparative Education* 36 (4): 463–479.

Cole, Jennifer, and Deborah Durham. 2007. "Introduction: Age, Regeneration, and the Intimate Politics of Globalization." In *Generations and Globalization: Youth, Age, and Family in the New World Economy*, edited by J. Cole and D. Durham, 1–28. Bloomington: Indiana University Press.

———. 2008. "Introduction: Globalization and the Temporality of Children and Youth." In *Figuring the Future: Globalization and the Temporalities of Children and Youth*, edited by J. Cole and D. Durham, 3–23. Santa Fe, NM: School for Advanced Research Press.

Crapanzano, Vincent. 2003. "Reflections on Hope as a Category of Social and Psychological Analysis." *Cultural Anthropology* 18 (1): 3–32.

Cwerner, Saulo. 2001. "The Times of Migration." *Journal of Ethnic and Migration Studies* 27 (1): 7–36.

Eck, Kristine. 2010. "Recruiting Rebels: Indoctrination and Political Education in Nepal." In *The Maoist Insurgency in Nepal: Dynamics and Growth in the 21st Century*, edited by Mahendra Lawoti and Anup Pahari, 33–51. London: Routledge.

Ferme, Mariane. 2004. "Deterritorialized Citizenship and the Resonances of the Sierra Leonean State." In *Anthropology in the Margins of the State*, edited by Veena Das and Deborah Poole, 81–115. Oxford: James Currey.

Fong, Vanessa. 2011. *Paradise Redefined: Chinese Students, Transnational Migration, and the Quest for Citizenship in the Developed World*. Stanford, CA: Stanford University Press.

Graner, Elvira. 2009–2010. "Leaving Hills and Plains: Migration and Remittances in Nepal." Special issue, *European Bulletin of Himalayan Research* 35–36:24–42.

Gurung, Ganesh, and Jaganath Adhikhari. 2004. "Nepal: The Prospects and Problems of Foreign Labour Migration." In *Migrant Workers and Human Rights: Out Migration from South Asia*, edited by P.-S. Ahn, 100–130. New Delhi: International Labour Organization.

Hareven, Tamara. 1977. "Family Time and Historical Time." *Daedalus* 106 (2): 57–70.

Jeffrey, Craig. 2010. "Timepass: Youth, Class, and the Politics of Waiting in India." Stanford, CA: Stanford University Press.

Kollmair, Michael, Siddhi Manandhar, Bhim Subedi, and Susan Thieme. 2006. "New Figures for Old Stories: Migration and Remittances in Nepal." *Migration Letters* 3 (2): 151–160.

Levitt, Peggy, and Nina Glick-Schiller. 2004. "Conceptualizing Simultaneity: A Transnational Social Field Perspective on Society." *International Migration Review* 38 (3): 1002–1039.

Liechty, Mark. 1995. "Media, Markets and Modernization: Youth Identities and the Experience of Modernity in Kathmandu, Nepal." In *Youth Cultures: A Cross-Cultural Perspective*, edited by V. Amit-Talai and H. Wulff, 166–201. London: Routledge.

———. 1997. "Selective Exclusion: Foreigners, Foreign Goods, and Foreignness in Modern Nepali History." *Studies in Nepali History and Society* 2 (1): 5–68.

———. 2003. *Suitably Modern: Making Middle-Class Culture in a New Consumer Society*. Princeton, NJ: Princeton University Press.

Maira, Sunaina Marr. 2009. *Missing: Youth, Citizenship, and Empire after 9/11*. Durham, NC: Duke University Press.

Mapril, José Manuel Fraga. 2011. "The Patron and the Madman: Migration, Success and the (In)Visibility of Failure among Bangladeshis in Portugal." *Social Anthropology* 19 (3): 288–296.

Munn, Nancy. 1992. "The Cultural Anthropology of Time: A Critical Essay." *Annual Review of Anthropology* 21:93–123.

Neilson, Brett. 2009. "The World Seen from a Taxi: Students-Migrants-Workers in the Global Multiplication of Labour." *Subjectivity*, no. 29:425–444.

NIDS (Nepal Institute for Development Studies) and NCCR (Nepal Centre in Competence in Research) North-South. 2011. *Nepal Migration Year Book 2010*. Kathmandu: NIDS/NCCR North-South.

Osella, Filippo, and Caroline Osella. 2000. "Migration, Money and Masculinity in Kerala." *Journal of the Royal Anthropological Institute* 6 (1): 117–133.

Pan, Darcy. 2011. "Student Visas, Undocumented Labor, and the Boundaries of Legality: Chinese Migration and English as a Foreign Language Education in the Republic of Ireland." *Social Anthropology* 19 (3): 268–287.

Pigg, Stacy Leigh 1996. "The Credible and the Credulous: The Questions of 'Villagers' Beliefs' in Nepal." *Cultural Anthropology* 11 (2): 160–201.

Rao, Nitya. 2010. "Editorial Introduction: Migration, Education and Socio-economic Mobility." *Compare* 40 (2): 137–145.

Sharma, Jeevan Raj. 2008. "Practices of Male Labor Migration from the Hills of Nepal to India in Development Discourses: Which Pathology?" *Gender, Technology and Development* 12 (3): 303–323.

Thieme, Susan, and Ulrike Müller-Böker. 2004. "Financial Self-Help Associations among Far West Nepalese Labor Migrants in Delhi, India." *Asian and Pacific Migration Journal* 13 (3): 339–361.

UVM (Undervisningsministeriet). 2008. "Tilsynsberetning om udenlandske studerende på Roskilde Handelsskole, Køge Handelsskole, Selandia—Center for Erhvervsrettet Uddannelse og Professionshøjskolen Metropol/SUHR's." Available at http://www.uvm.dk/Aktuelt/-/UVM-DK/Content/News/Udd/Videre/2008/Dec/-/media/UVM/Filer/Udd/Videre/PDF08/tilsyn_17december08.ashx.

Valentin, Karen. 2005. *Schooled for the Future? Educational Policy and Everyday Life among Urban Squatters in Nepal*. Greenwich, CT: Information Age.

———. 2012. "The Role of Education in Mobile Livelihoods: Social and Geographical Routes of Young Nepalese Migrants in India." *Anthropology and Education Quarterly* 43 (4): 429–442.

Vigh, Henrik. 2009. "Wayward Migration: On Imagined Futures and Technological Voids." *Ethnos* 74 (1): 91–109.

Vitus, Katrine. 2010. "Waiting Time: The De-subjectification of Children in Danish Asylum Centres." *Childhood: A Global Journal of Child Research* 17 (1): 26–42.

Zerubavel, Eviatar. 2003. *Time Maps: Collective Memory and the Social Shape of the Past*. Chicago: University of Chicago Press.

7

The Normativity of Boredom

Communication Media Use among Romanian Teenagers

RĂZVAN NICOLESCU

No, I don't call when I'm bored. I send text messages when I am bored!
—ANDREEA, FOURTEEN YEARS OLD

Modern boredom has been described as emerging with Romanticism as an impulsive individual reaction to the rapid and continuously changing flows of life. Romantic literature mostly described boredom as a passive but essential feeling of the human soul as it strove to grasp its dreams (Sagnes 1969). Almost simultaneously, philosophy added transcendental punitive suggestions: boredom was the "root of all evil," a dark "demonic pantheism" (Kierkegaard [1843] 1946: 228, 231). At the beginning of the twentieth century, Georg Simmel famously described the blasé mood as an immediate consequence of an emotional life intensified by the continual shift of external and internal stimuli in the modern world ([1908] 1971). Today the discussion has moved from the academic realm to an almost commonsense claim about modern life. Boredom is associated with so many things that the main political and ideological accusation is that these shallow relations leave us with no real commitments that would lead us out of our state of lethargy.

In this chapter, I depart from this perspective of boredom as a usually unproblematic witness to the emotional existence of modern humans to interrogate specific social relationships that are shaped by the emergence of boredom. Looking at everyday boredom in relation to communication technology used by a group of Romanian teenagers, I suggest a fundamentally active understanding of boredom that is instrumental in establishing and negotiating social relations.

An Ethnography of Boredom

There are very few ethnographic works on boredom. If boredom appears in an ethnography, it is often discussed in relation to the researcher; while informants must *do* or *engage with* something, the ethnographer may allow himself or herself to be bored quite often. I believe this attitude often conceals a particular concern with what is a priori considered worthwhile or rewarding for the discipline. Important exceptions exist, however. Throughout his work Emile Durkheim regarded emotions as part of the collective consciousness and related them, for example, with religious sentiment ([1893] 1984) or with social exclusion ([1912] 1995). In his famous study on suicide, Durkheim conducted an extensive examination of feelings and showed that they were reflections of the structure of society ([1897] 1970). In this perspective anomie, one of the main affects identified as potentially leading to suicide, is generated by a lack of regulation of the individual by modern society.

In the sparse ethnographic works on boredom (e.g., Kopytoff 1994; Musharbash 2007) or idleness (Corrigan 1993; Nafus 2002), boredom emerges mostly in relation to fundamental social and historical change, such as colonialism or postsocialism. Such transformations often led to cultural maladaptations to the quality of time and opportunities brought by the new social imperatives. Michael Herzfeld's work on the Cretan mask of boredom (2003) noticeably stands apart from this view. In his ethnography, boredom has a clear role in the community and is practiced and transmitted as a skill. I argue for a similar active and assumed understanding of boredom as acquiring social significance essentially because of the extent it is resisted and contested.

This chapter is based on fieldwork I conducted in 2008 on the experience of everyday boredom in relation to the use of communication technology. I worked in a central, affluent neighborhood in Bucharest, Romania. I focused on teenagers between fifteen and eighteen years old who lived with their families in the dense blocks of flats in that neighborhood. Most of them were in high school and tended to spend much of their after-school free time in their media-rich bedrooms (Livingstone and Bovill 1999). Compared to the rest of the Romanian population, the families I worked with were more affluent and had greater access to consumer goods, including new technology and media. However, my findings from the research do not interpret boredom as necessarily related to technology; rather, technology is used only to frame (Goffman 1986) a particular instance of boredom.

In this chapter I focus on what teenagers described as after-school boredom, as experienced individually and especially at home during their long hours of solitude. Almost unanimously teenagers I worked with agreed that this was real boredom, the most feared type and the one they resisted most strongly. This boredom was not the inconsistent and contingent kind of boredom experienced, for example, during long and empty vacations, while engaging in less useful activities such as going shopping or watching TV with their parents, or at school. At the same time, this kind of boredom was largely regarded as an opportunity for reflexivity, when one looks within a rather limited realm for solutions. During this period, teenagers complained that "there [was] not much to do," that time was "still," and that they "[didn't] have the faintest idea what to do."

I do not assert a social distribution of boredom but rather explore it with respect to three main social factors fundamental for understanding the background of this research: work, education, and technology use. Regarding work, I follow Monica Heintz's writings on work ethics in post-socialist Romania (2002, 2004). Looking especially at highly competitive business sectors and the emerging middle class in urban centers, she finds that Romanians quickly embraced the hierarchically imposed capitalist value of work, despite it being against most of their more egalitarian and lenient work relations. In my research, the adults' understanding of boredom was related to their practical understanding of work (as a respected capitalist value) and not of actual work relations. It was also rooted within the dichotomized perspective of work and leisure. Specifically, adults regarded boredom largely as a negation of work values.

Education was highly valued by the families I worked with. With few exceptions, the teenagers were preparing for undergraduate studies in Bucharest. These educational ambitions were driven and supported by their families by personal example, an insistence on quality in their current education, and enormous investment in private tutoring and other extracurricular activities. Many of these options were available primarily because of the material means and the cultural capital of the parents. Drawing on Pierre Bourdieu's "predispositions" (1977: 72), I suggest that parents' strict attitude toward work and education shaped their children's behavior during free time. For example, a particular display of wealth by parents seemed to encourage in their children a more intensive use of technology, and the children of parents who valued time and efficiency tended to have fewer but closer relationships with their peers during free time.

Relatively easy access to technology and its use was particularly important. Most of the teenagers I worked with received, directly or indirectly, their technological devices from their parents, who supported in moral and economic ways the use of this technology. From the first mobile phone to broadband Internet connection, teenagers had gradually intensified their use of such media over the years. At the time of my research, all of them had a mobile phone, and most owned a personal computer and were part of at least one social media network. All the teenagers usually had access to other media shared by the family, such as a personal computer, television, stereo, or landline phone. My fieldwork suggests that the diverse and intense media consumption was related to Romanian middle-class wealth and profusion of goods. The teenagers' use of free time in relation to communication technologies was diverse and unpredictable; for example, they could talk on their mobile phones between a half hour and one hour a day and spend between one and eight hours a day in front of their computers. The longer they were bored, the longer they used social media.

Boredom, or How Does Anxiety Build the Social Group?

> [Boredom] is like some small, little worms that come to your feet, like that [*gestures with her fingers*], and simply don't let you stay in bed. . . . You don't have peace! So you don't have peace, and you must do something in that moment to consume your energy somehow, or at least to get on Mes [Yahoo! Messenger], for example, or talk on the phone, to let your thoughts go in some other direction, not to stay and think, "God, I'm staying in my room, like, between four walls [*laughs*], and I cannot stand anymore; I cannot stand it!" And I am looking for flies!
> —Beata, sixteen years old

I consider two main perspectives on boredom: boredom as a feeling and boredom as discourse. First, I show how the underlying conflict between boredom and excitement as subjective emotions drives a fundamental perception of the self in relation to the world. Second, I show how boredom as discourse stands for a more active method for accumulating and sharing knowledge. I then argue that what brings the two perspectives together is the practice of experiencing and dissipating boredom. Indeed, it is through practice that teenagers turn this unsolicited and detested mood into a recognizable and shared expansion of the self toward a particular available social group. Thus, for them, boredom unexpectedly accounts for the creation of social meaning.

Feeling Bored

> [To be bored is] to have nothing to do, to finish all the things you have [to finish] that day and to want to do something and come up with no idea! . . . You haven't the faintest idea what to do! And there is nobody there to tell you [what to do]. —**Miruna, sixteen years old**

In boredom's stillness and usually confusing nature, teenagers feel an inner urge to overcome it. They do this in myriad ways, ranging from calling peers to going out "to look for something to do" (according to fifteen-year-old Traian) and to passive initiatives such as going to sleep to wake up "refreshed . . . with more taste for life" (in the words of sixteen-year-old Dana). When teenagers cannot find something new to do, they look for activities that are considered interesting. Most of the time, determination and motivation are external for these teens; the self simply feels a vague wish to dissipate boredom and usually does not follow a specific objective.

In contrast, their parents and professors thought teenagers' relatively long periods of unwanted solitude should be filled either with productive activities that corresponded to their ideals, such as homework, sports, and cultural occupations, or by technology, such as the computer, the Internet, music, or television (without necessarily giving thought to what the teenagers did with it). However, the teenagers felt that these values imposed by others contradicted their own values. As the quotation that opens this chapter suggests, teenagers knew exactly what boredom was. They also shared an understanding of it and strategies for overcoming it, mainly because they *recognized* and *used* boredom in their virtual groups according to specific norms. As I suggest in this chapter, boredom and its particularly exigent needs were instrumental in teenagers' choice of a system of normativity that would respond to their needs. For example, Andreea preferred to send text messages when bored because this asynchronous communication assured a longer and unpredictable interval of excitement. Waiting eagerly for responses and writing back were her best strategies for combating boredom. Other teenagers chose to announce that they were bored on social networks and to a long contact list when they wanted bigger opportunities to find excitement. In this way, by specific uses of communication media, teenagers translated their uncertainties, fears, empty feelings, misunderstandings, and refusals to do what their tutelary institutions expected from them into a familiar, recognizable, and therefore socially comfortable sphere. The process in which trapped individuals meet their social peers is the process by which boredom becomes social.

Following psychology's notions of emotions and affects, Willard Gaylin argues that feelings represent our subjective awareness of our own emotional state (1979: 1). Consequently, feelings are what we experience, through which we *know* our current emotional state. Gaylin identifies three classes of "vital signs": the first class is the feelings that aid individual survival and group living: anger, anxiety, guilt, shame, and pride. The second class warns us of potential or imminent bodily or life-course malfunctions, indicating that we are not achieving our goals, are not serving our ends, or are depleting our resources. Examples are being upset, being tired, being bored, being envious, and feeling used. The third class of feelings are those that acknowledge that existence of the individual or the group must have some meaning beyond the mere fact of surviving, for instance, being touched, being moved, and feeling good (8).

Thus, boredom is vital because it awakens our consciousness. My ethnographic material suggests that boredom cannot be dispelled unless it occurs in a familiar context and familiar means to eliminate it are available. This leads me to ask how familiar a context needs to be and when a social context becomes familiar. A useful answer is in Donald Winnicott's theory of "potential space" (1971). Winnicott defines potential space as the "intermediate area of *experiencing*, to which inner reality and external life both contribute" (1971: 3; emphasis in original). Potential space is the result of a dialectical process between fantasy and reality: while potential space is the place where we live, it belongs to neither the realm of reality nor the realm of fantasy (Ogden 1988: 257). I suggest that bored teenagers situate themselves in such an ambiguous space, where reality is granted by either the novelty (or, in contrast, the mastery) of the technological object or the comfort of a particular social sphere. My ethnographic research suggests that usually novelty and comfort collaborate in dissipating the profoundly undesired state that the individual experiences; the teenager looks frantically in his or her available peer groups for any strategy likely to dismiss boredom rather than for a specific alternative. Thus, the feeling of boredom is objectified through discourses and practices.

Discourses on Boredom

Teenagers use two main strategies to overcome after-school boredom. The one most used is orienting themselves toward the exterior through communication or social media. They employ various tactics, but the immediate aim is always to contact somebody, preferably not another bored person, to drag the self out of boredom. I asked fourteen-year-old Rareş what he does when he is bored. He replied:

Yes, you try to escape! You're, like, trapped in a prison, the prison of boredom, and you are trying to escape! And lots of the time you can, so it is possible, but some other times you cannot. I mean, no, you literally don't have the strength to succeed. You cannot be entertained; you cannot entertain yourself because you are tired. You don't feel like doing anything. . . . So you call a friend!

Rareş is a dynamic teenager. He has played soccer since he was six years old and dreams of playing professionally, and thus far his family has supported him in this attempt. He also has excellent school grades, which greatly pleases his family. For Rareş, boredom typically emerges after an activity loses its momentum. He is one of the few teenagers I worked with who could also become bored doing homework. This particular type of boredom is generated not by idleness or a discontented search for meaning but rather by a temporary mismatch between his dynamic attitude or high expectations and an activity's monotony. Rareş is one of the many teenagers who rely on close friends to overcome boredom. Because his mobile phone plan does not provide many talk minutes, he prefers to contact them over the Internet. However, mobile phones are renowned as the most reliable media to use when bored. Their ubiquity and the likelihood and predictability that close friends will answer calls make mobile phones the most effective and appreciated tool to fight boredom.

Another popular tactic is for the bored self to publicly announce that he or she is bored. This announcement is explicit and made most often on social media, such as Yahoo! Messenger, hi5, or Skype. Other methods include making random prank calls or sending text messages about the bored condition to all the contacts in one's mobile phone. The bored person broadcasts his or her mood by either a specific status message in his or her system profile or a special message sent to an extended list of contacts, which is allowed by most social media. Depending on user settings, the status message can be seen by some or all on the user's contact list of possibly a few hundred. Such messages could be simple and unfocused ("I am boooored . . .") or a direct invitation to a specific activity ("I am bored. Who wants to play Counter Strike?"). By publicly acknowledging they are bored, teenagers begin a collective game with simple rules: In the first phase they offer their peers the option to adopt the attitude they expect. In the second, both senders and receivers have an opportunity to engage in conversation. Peers receiving the message choose whether to respond and at what intensity. The responses decide whether the relationship is to be continued. After people respond, the initiator of the message, as the bored person, chooses at his or her leisure the persons and the modality to continue the conversation with. Consequently, this method of dissimulated inquiry leads ultimately to a selection base for the conversation that is broader than calling certain people. The apparently passive activity of keeping an Internet social media site open for hours, hoping that eventually something interesting will happen, is a dynamic method of exploration. In this strategy, the prime concern for the bored person is who and how many embark on the rescue boat as well as how intense and innovative the response to the declaration of boredom is.

I suggest that the best way to understand the discourses on boredom is to see boredom as a metaphor for teenager culture. I use Christopher Tilley's argument that metaphor provides a "basis for an interpretative understanding of the world" (1995: 4), in the sense that metaphors generate knowledge and practice. Therefore, even if each teenager experienced boredom in a different way, their attitudes and practices when bored suggest that they all shared the same meaning of boredom.

My fieldwork also suggests that, at the level of experience, teenagers view everyday boredom in relation to the potentiality for excitement offered by their various communities. For example, Rareş's attempt to materialize boredom constitutes an attempt to turn his emotion into a distinguishable material form. "Prison" speaks of Rareş as he speaks of boredom. For Rareş as for many other teenagers, his description of boredom as prison objectifies the solitude of the individual, the centrality of the individual's condition, and the immense difficulty to overcome that solitude. His account of boredom might be inspired by the many computer games he is fond of, but the delimitation of his personal space is driven by boredom and becomes almost tangible; it is reinforced by the description of recurring escape attempts: the untrapped and experienced friend should be there to help him out. They should both fight boredom until physical and psychical exhaustion occur.

Drawing on Michel Foucault's account of the modern obsession for confession (e.g., 1978), Nikolas Rose argues that, in confessing, one is subjectified by another: "In the act of speaking, through the obligation to produce words that are true to an inner reality, through the self-examination that precedes and accompanies speech, one becomes a subject for oneself" (1990: 240). Through this subjectification we affirm our identity and our attachment to a peer group. A relationship *is* active despite boredom or any other existential anxiety, while media represents a mere means to relieve boredom. At the same time, boredom is fundamental to the way teenagers understand relationships. A "proper" relationship can dismiss boredom.

Social Media and the Normativity of Boredom

We have seen that most strategies for overcoming boredom involve a sort of communal ethos to drag the bored self and its closest bored peers out of boredom. Teenagers actively engage with the peer group they think will most rapidly dispel boredom while following rigorous sets of rules, interdictions, and exclusions for such an engagement.

But technologies can *create* boredom as quickly as they *dissipate* it—for example, when there is a gap between the expectation people invest in a technology and the level of excitement it actually delivers. Social media accessed at the wrong time or long conversations on a landline phone are considered boring. Many teenagers told me that they feel bored especially while connected to social media in the mornings or late evenings, when most of their peers are not available or are engaged in other activities. Nevertheless, they persist in spending many hours on uninteresting Internet social networks, hoping somebody to share their boredom with will appear. Therefore, communication technology is not a magical trick employed to cheat boredom. Instead, it offers a more subtle opposition between boredom and the possibility of excitement. Each of the two states creates the conditions for the other to emerge and become socially visible: when one state reaches too high a level, the other comes into play. This perpetual balance assures the stability of the teenagers' social relationships. Although boredom and excitement could each exist without the other, teenagers perceive a continuous tension between the two because technology makes it possible for both to exist. Boredom and excitement become expressive social manifestations, as in accepting or refusing help from within their social sphere.

Messages from teenagers advertising their boredom can be annoying to those who receive them, but teenagers have precise techniques for avoiding this, such as the use of response times that correspond to the level of intimacy between peers. The techniques maintain a balance between overenthusiasm and aloofness, between constancy and instability, and ultimately between boredom and excitement. The result is that by wider communication teenagers explore multiple ways to equilibrate their emotions and to relate to different peer groups in an appropriate way.

Teenagers were usually more anxious when they were home for long periods in the absence of their parents. During these times they directed their anxieties toward their peers. They would seek to engage in any sort of relationship but mostly looked to their social groups and technology. Less frequently, they tried to dissipate boredom by themselves during periods of predetermined duration that were recognized as transitory to some sort of potential excitement. Following Lars Svendsen (2005), this corresponds to "situational" boredom. During such periods of less intense boredom, which is considered bearable, teenagers might listen to music, watch television, or play computer games. In these cases, engagement with a technological object or media is individual, even if its consumption is part of a particular social process. Teenagers I interviewed were clear that such activities could be interesting but certainly do not offer the same level of excitement as similar activities conducted within their peer groups do.

My research suggests that various media are important not because of what they enable people to do (relate, play, entertain) but because of how people articulate their individual or collective selves through them. Social media is a safe shortcut to socializing and thus out of boredom. How then do teenagers choose from the available possibilities? We have seen that the type and frequency of contact is usually not important as long as expectations respect each group's limits. More important is the possibility of such contact and consequently its very existence. What is essential in tactics to fight boredom is a distinct concern with responding to explicit or implicit demand. Therefore, different means to communicate while bored stand for a constant practice of a full set of mutually recognizable rules.

We see that boredom becomes not just an enemy for the self but a threat that could jeopardize an individual's entire system of social relationships. Teenagers believe that if boredom is not treated at the right moment, and according to rules specific to each social group they are part of, deeper anxiety could result, which would be an unacceptable departure from the norms accepted within that group. For example, when somebody announces to a social group that he or she is bored, that person expects another member from the group to spend time and effort dispelling that boredom. If this does not happen within a certain time that depends on the type of social network, the bored person feels estranged from that group. This social recognition and the safety provided by the peer group constitute a normative system that individuals consider fundamental for being dragged out of boredom.

I suggest that simple things such as when and how fast to respond to a bored person, how much time to spend in different social groups, and the type of information exchanged during specific periods constitute ethical norms for the teenagers' peer groups. Teenagers create social arrangements while being bored or excited because they insist on normative schemes driven by group expectation.

Therefore, to be bored is not really a problem of connectedness; rather, what is at stake is how the individual (trapped or untrapped) recognizes and *deals with* more subtle categories of specific connectedness situations. The teenagers I worked with would engage with social media because it offered the best possibility for extending the self at almost any time. Boredom is just one of myriad conditions they experience. Media bridge these experiences and activate the latent possibilities of enchantment that exist in the self and in the individual's peer group. From this perspective, communication technologies and media are instrumental to these teenagers' relationships, specifically for constantly reshaping the collective set of values these relationships are built on. The ultimate goal is not the enchantment itself but the periodic reassurance that its possibility is there, unaltered, and ready to be activated within the teenagers' current social norms.

For example, when parents return home after work, the existential anxiety that vexes teenagers during the day usually disappears. It is not transformed or mediated; they simply are not bored: they are either happy to engage with their parents or annoyed by the parents interrupting or threatening their private activities. Parents and their children give fundamentally different definitions of boredom, resulting in misunderstanding between them. For example, when fifteen-year-old Silvia complains to her mother that she is bored, her mother is exasperated: "What? Read! Do something!" Silvia accuses her mother of a profound and unwarranted lack of understanding: "It would be the last thing to do when you're bored—to read! [*Laughs*] It would be a punishment!" Reading represents to the mother an idealized norm envisaged for, and to a certain extent imposed on, her child. Daily, parents compare their ideals of what their children should do with what their children actually do. In this evaluation, most parents overlook the boredom in their children's daily activities or at least downplay its significance: boredom is generally referred to as incidental, occurring when something is delayed or postponed. Parents argue that it is not a normal situation and should be dispelled by normal means.

The teenagers' actions while bored articulate their own idea of normal: a certain collective ethical realm, constantly adjusted to meet a set of shared values. Media perpetuates this set of values by successfully relating the entrapped self to its social world. Therefore, boredom is not an individual feeling anymore. It has been argued (e.g., Goffman 1975, Bourdieu 1977) that many of our behaviors are dictated by expectations determined by the context in which they occur. In my understanding of normativity I draw on Bourdieu, who insists that the objects and practices people habitually engage with implicitly command their socialization. In these terms, I understand the normativity of each peer group as being produced by a set of common practices and their revisions and pursuits. As Bourdieu puts it, the subtle indeterminacy of *habitus* comprises a full range of predictable expectations (1977: 9, 78).

At the same time, it has been argued (e.g., Foucault 1979; Rose 1990) that, through specific mechanisms of modernity, various types of regulations of the self have been spelled out. These arguments may be true for the production of communication technologies or social media or the regulative norms that control their usage. But when we look at how media is actually used by teenagers, we see that instead of being subject to a dominant normativity, they erect a peer system of ethical norms to follow. These norms are accepted or rejected also because teenagers are excited or bored and usually outside the guidance of their families or teachers. I argue that teenagers produce a reliable system of relationships by constantly verifying the ability of these norms to dismiss boredom and maintain an acceptable level of entertainment or attention. Reliability is assured by the efficiency of these relationships for responding to an anxious peer.

Conclusion

In psychology it is assumed that boredom informs us whenever something wrong happens or is about to happen and indicates the nature of the impending danger (Gaylin 1979: 7–8). From an anthropological standpoint, I suggest that boredom is important primarily because of an individual's capacity to interpret this information using social norms. Interacting with someone when bored and within a certain social group represents the validation and potential renegotiation of that group's norms. Therefore, this chapter is about the normativity not of boredom in itself but of expected social answers to boredom.

We have seen that media creates special environments in which teenagers contested the ambiguous space-time interval of boredom. Teenagers judged such media's reliability by its efficacy for responding to their boredom. Their anxious efforts articulated this interval into a decipherable and thus recognizable form of sociality. Therefore, this distributed intimacy became the instrument that could efficiently fight boredom. Instead of establishing an always-on domain, as celebrated by most media theories, the teenagers I studied preferred one that was consistently on. I suggest that social media plays a key role in not only mediating the self or the collective awareness of specific social subjectivities but also creating and insisting on ever-new and gratifying social relationships.

I further argue that teenagers negotiate the terms of their social relationships according to a stable and contended set of ethical self-made norms by appropriating communication technology within the collective accumulated expertise. Teenagers are able to reproduce their social arrangements especially because while bored or excited they insist on those normative schemes driven by group expectations.

REFERENCES

Bourdieu, Pierre. 1977. *Outline of a Theory of Practice*. Cambridge: Cambridge University Press.
Corrigan, Paul. 1993. "Doing Nothing." In *Resistance through Rituals: Youth Subcultures in Post-war Britain*, edited by Stuart Hall and Thomas Jefferson, 103–105. London: Routledge.
Durkheim, Emile. (1893) 1984. *The Division of Labor in Society*. 2nd ed. Basingstoke, UK: Macmillan.
———. (1897) 1970. *Suicide: A Study in Sociology*. Edited by George Simpson. London: Routledge and Kegan Paul.
———. (1912) 1995. *The Elementary Forms of Religious Life*. New York: Free Press.
Foucault, Michel. 1978. *The History of Sexuality*. Vol. 1, *An Introduction*. New York: Pantheon Books.
———. 1979. *Discipline and Punish: The Birth of the Prison*. New York: Vintage.
Gaylin, Willard. 1979. *Feelings: Our Vital Signs*. New York: Harper and Row.
Goffman, Erving. 1986. *Frame Analysis: An Essay on the Organization of Experience*. Boston: Northeastern University Press.
Heintz, Monica. 2002. "Changes in Work Ethic in Postsocialist Romania." Ph.D. diss., University of Cambridge.
———. 2004. "Time and the Work Ethic in Postsocialist Romania." In *The Qualities of Time: Temporal Dimensions of Social Form and Human Experience*, edited by Wendy James and David Mills, 171–183. Oxford: Berg.
Herzfeld, Michael. 2003. *The Body Impolitic: Artisans and Artifice in the Global Hierarchy of Value*. Chicago: University of Chicago Press.
Kierkegaard, Søren. (1843) 1946. *Either/Or*. Princeton, NJ: Princeton University Press.
Kopytoff, Igor. 1994. "Leisure, Boredom, and Luxury Consumerism: The Lineage Mode of Consumption in a Central African Society." In *Consumption and Identity*, edited by Jonathan Friedman, 163–187. Reading, UK: Harwood Academic.
Livingstone, Sonia, and Moira Bovill. 1999. *Young People, New Media: Report of the Research Project Children, Young People and the Changing Media Environment*. London: Department of Media and Communications, London School of Economics and Political Science. Available at http://eprints.lse.ac.uk/21177/.
Miller, Daniel, ed. 2005. *Materiality*. Durham, NC: Duke University Press.
Musharbash, Yasmine. 2007. "Boredom, Time, and Modernity: An Example from Aboriginal Australia." *American Anthropologist* 109 (2): 307–317.
Nafus, Dawn. 2002. "Time, Sociability and Postsocialism." Ph.D. diss., Sidney Sussex College, UK.
Ogden, Thomas. 1988. "Playing, Dreaming, and Interpreting Experience: Comments on Potential Space." In *The Facilitating Environment: Clinical Applications of*

Winnicott's Theory, edited by Gerard Fromm and Bruce Smith, 255–278. Madison, CT: International University Press.
Rose, Nikolas. 1990. *Governing the Soul: The Shaping of the Private Self.* London: Routledge.
Sagnes, Guy. 1969. *L'Ennui dans la Littérature Française de Flaubert à Laforgue, 1848–1884.* Paris: A. Colin.
Simmel, Georg. (1908) 1971. *On Individuality and Social Forms.* Chicago: University of Chicago Press.
Svendsen, Lars. 2005. *A Philosophy of Boredom.* London: Reaktion Books.
Tilley, Christopher. 1995. "Discourse and Power: The Genre of the Cambridge Inaugural Lecture." In *Domination and Resistance*, edited by Daniel Miller, Michael Rowlands, and Christopher Tilley, 40–62. London: Routledge.
Winnicott, Donald. 1971. *Playing and Reality.* London: Tavistock.

8

Making a Name

Young Musicians in Uganda Working on the Future

LOTTE MEINERT AND NANNA SCHNEIDERMANN

Lucky walks into a small hotel, where we are staying in Gulu, Uganda, wearing aviator sunglasses, a red cap, and Nikes. Lotte does not recognize him right away, looking so cool, stylish, and older than his seventeen years. With a wide smile he enjoys her surprise and pulls out two brand-new CDs with his latest music and video productions. His photo is printed in color on the CDs, and the text gives his name, the album name, and the price:

LU[C]KY DAVID WILSON
Album name: Kuc odugo/Peace returned in Northern Uganda
150,000/= UGX [Ugandan shillings; $60]
Original audio CD

"Very expensive! Who will buy this?" Lotte asks Lucky. "I know," he says. "I will negotiate. But just wait and see; they will buy it! My name is known now in northern Uganda. My songs are on air. Haven't you heard me?"

This incident epitomizes what we explore in this chapter: young musicians' attempts to create desired personal futures by making a name for themselves through musical products, which they promote and hope other people will recognize and buy. Throughout the chapter we shed light on the specific time work (Flaherty 2011) involved in these musicians' creation of artist names. We are interested in what the young men are trying to do when they take artist names, and we explore this practice of self-naming as temporal and relational work. We argue that naming is generally a process in which time and social relationships are condensed, as multiple times and relationships may be actualized in a person's name. Self-naming, such as taking an artist name, represents a decisive break from social ties of a given name, and we see the taking of an artist name as being an attempt to form new social relationships and devise a potential future for oneself. When fashioning themselves as music artists our young interlocutors project their dreams of who they *could be*, defined not by kinship, tribe, or religion, as their given names are, but by popular culture and fans' consumption of their cultural products as artists. In this world of popular music, the young men produce objects—music and images burned into CDs and DVDs—to create the person they wish to be. Musicians succeed in becoming this person, at least momentarily, when fans buy their products, pay to see their performances, and call them by their artist names.

We discuss these practices, drawing on ideas from the anthropology of naming (Bodenhorn and vom Bruck 2006) and the philosopher Ian Hacking's concept of "dynamic nominalism" (1998: 165; 2006). We are inspired by the sociologist Michael Flaherty's idea of time work (2011) and by notions of the subjunctive (Whyte 2002; Frederiksen 2013). We stress the material and economic side of this relational time work when these artists create material objects such as a CD as extensions of their potential future selves. We further argue that what pulls young musicians toward the potential person they hope to become, and momentarily actualizes it, is their *relation to others*—namely, their fans and audience. In the time work and "reversed progress" (Nielsen 2011) toward becoming the potential of the name they have taken, the artists need others—an audience—to call their names and consume their products. Most of these young men do not succeed. Perhaps they do not have the exceptional talent and ability to conjure the future that it takes to stand out from the crowd of young people trying to make a name in the informal music economy. Furthermore, the audience—other young people, who have to buy the music products for the artist to succeed—has limited purchasing power. Many are poor.

In this chapter we first situate our analysis in the historical context of northern Uganda and then discuss the temporal aspects of naming practices, using the two cases of Lucky and his friend Lay-C as our basis, before developing our argument further. The chapter is based on our collaboration through shared informants. Nanna Schneidermann has been doing long-term fieldwork in Uganda since 2006, focusing on young people in the informal music industry. For this specific study Nanna conducted fieldwork for four months in Gulu in 2009 and 2010. Lotte Meinert has been doing long-term fieldwork in Uganda since 1993. For this study Lotte conducted four months of fieldwork from 2008 to 2013 among young people who attempted to make innovative paths to the future. We followed a small group of young Acholi men hanging out at a video library, a shop renting out DVDs and selling music as burned CDs or mp3 files from a stationary computer in the center of Gulu. Lucky, Lay-C, their friends, parts of their social networks, their employers, and later some of their family members became our common informants in Gulu. We repeatedly visited these young men at their workplaces, music studios, hangouts, and homes; had conversations with them and interviewed them; followed their production of music and videos; and went to some of their performances.

Background

In northern Uganda, young people's possibilities for a livelihood have changed significantly over the last twenty-five years. First, the armed conflict between the Lord's Resistance Army and government forces forced the civilian population to live in camps, which they were later forced to leave with the suspension of the conflict. Second, universal primary and secondary education programs have made access to further education possible and salaried jobs something young people intensely hope for (Meinert 2009). Last, and perhaps most important, the population has doubled in recent decades, and about 80 percent is estimated to be under thirty-one years old (UBOS 2006: 9). The pressure on educational institutions and the need for jobs and land have increased tremendously.

Young people's disadvantages are particularly pressing in relation to land issues in northern Uganda. Because of population growth and demographic changes, less land is available for young people since the war. In the postconflict land resettlement, some young people have been squeezed out by older generations and people with big names and money, like prominent politicians or businessmen, who grab the land. Young men who have lost their fathers are particularly vulnerable because land is inherited through patrilineal kinship (Whyte, Mpisi, Mukyala, and Meinert 2013). Despite recurring obstacles of war and postconflict crisis and prolonged youthhood as described in other African contexts (Christiansen, Utas, and Vigh 2006; Utas 2003; Langevang 2008; Ralph 2008; Sommers 2001, 2010), the young men we met in Gulu do not give up the dream of becoming *someone* important and wealthy enough to contribute to society, own his own house, pay bride wealth (*luk*), and provide for his family. They struggle to find ways to perform socially and attain socially invoked and desired obligations and goals.

Gulu bustles with young people's creative strategies for making a living in the informal urban economy: they are street vendors selling eggs, chapatis, and secondhand clothes and shoes; they run video libraries and music shops and provide hairdressing services; they work in self-made nongovernmental organizations (NGOs) and on building sites; and they drive the swarms of *boda bodas* (motorcycle taxis) buzzing around town. These are seen as transitory occupations for young people rather than a basis for providing for a family (see Goodfellow and Titeca 2012; Hansen 2004: 72). Young people may have more options for urban livelihoods now than they did before the conflict, but in reality most options turn out to be dead ends. As the number of graduates from secondary schools, colleges, and universities explodes, the labor market is flooded with young people seeking paid urban white-collar and blue-collar jobs. The unrealistic implied promises of employment following education, coupled with demographic changes, creates discrepancies between expectations and possibilities for those young graduates who do not have the connections, family name, or money to gain entry to the labor market. In Uganda "working class" has come to refer to people who have a job with the attributes of a formal job (though it might not actually be one), like a contract, office with desks and computers, dress code, and salary paid into a bank account. "Working class" refers to the middle and upper tiers of society, in contrast to informal workers like *boda boda* drivers and street vendors.

Dreams of a modern middle-class life compel many young people to seek economic independence from their families, with cash to spend on luxury and lifestyle items like fashion clothing, electronics, and home decoration. Their ideal future is not to live in rural villages farming the land but to make enough money through farming with hired help to start businesses and build a home in town. But with no access to land, tertiary education, or jobs, prospects are bleak. Many of the young men we met in Gulu have ambitious dreams: they want to be a bank director, soccer-team owner, lawyer, or music star. Meanwhile, a discourse of boredom and inactivity, of laziness, surrounds the youth in Gulu that is coupled with a sense of anxiety about young people being rebellious and potentially threatening. The labor surplus spills into the streets, and young men especially are very visible in public spaces, waiting for something to happen, for customers, or for work. A young man of this type is commonly labeled by older generations as a *muyaye* (a loan word from Luganda meaning "thief," "thug," or "hoodlum") and a lazy youth who refuses to go to school or refuses to work.

For some of these young men (and a few women), playing and producing music has become a way to pursue an alternative approach to the good life (Meinert 2001). The local music scene in Gulu has been growing since the early 2000s (Wadiru 2012: 178). An informal market for performing and selling digitally produced popular music in local languages and English has emerged through nightclubs and school dances, small music studios, local FM radio stations, and music shops where attendants "cut" CDs by burning costumers' selections of songs onto blank CDs from a computer. Young singers are the drivers of this music economy as they try to make a name in music. They hope to make money and make an impact on people's lives as well as on their own. To become artists, they try to stand out and fashion themselves as stars and celebrities by taking humorous, imaginative, or provocative artist names, such as Lay-C, Lucky, Agenda, Equatoria Triple Stars, Smoky Allan, Sherry Princess, and His Excellency TAM Noffy. In the following two sections we describe two cases of self-naming by tracing Lay-C's and Lucky's history of their other, given names and the making of their new names.

Lay-C: Abola Geoffrey Bex

Lay-C was nineteen years old when we first met him. He worked at the video library, managing the shop, selecting music tracks, cutting CDs, doing computer repairs, and sometimes editing work for customers. Later he got a job behind the counter at a business-services (known as secretarial services in Uganda) shop making campaign posters for an upcoming national election. Smiling behind the counter, he repeats his motto, "You have to be multipurpose." His given names were Abola Geoffrey.

Lay-C's mother had a bar where she sold locally made beer. She had a strict cash-only policy, so when her baby was born, customers nicknamed him "Bol Cash," meaning "drop some money," and later this was turned into Abola. Conventionally, the Acholi name Abola is associated with the mother experiencing rejection or being "thrown away," but Lay-C explained that his name was associated with "dropping cash," at least in the beginning. Lay-C's mother died two months after he was born.

After living with his maternal aunt for six years, Lay-C's father collected him one day, saying, "This is not your home; you don't belong here." His father paid his school fees and other expenses, but because of insecurity during the war, he sent his son to his sister in a safer, neighboring district. In school the teachers called Lay-C by his Christian name, Geoffrey. He completed primary school and then came back to Gulu, which by then was relatively safe. A paternal uncle helped pay his fees for secondary school. In school Lay-C got another nickname, Bex. He remembers, "I played football like someone. . . . His name is David Beckham, from England. So I played that number that that guy also played, and my style is like for that guy. Only that I was down here [in Uganda], local. So they nicknamed me to become Bex." A leg injury prevented Lay-C from pursuing his dream of becoming a soccer player.

In 2004, at age fifteen, Abola became an orphan when his father died. He graduated lower-level secondary school the following year and started doing odd jobs, such as being a porter for builders. He was also a hip-hop music fan and started rapping. He had an opportunity to earn a certificate in information technology, and eventually he found an unpaid job at the video library where Lotte first met him. Lay-C told us that if he had had the financial backing of his family, he would have studied to become a lawyer. His father had owned a piece of land, which he was supposed to inherit, but because of the conflict in northern Uganda his father did not show him the land before he died. Lay-C's uncles now occupied the land, and he did not feel that he was in a position to claim it. Moreover he was not interested in living as a farmer in the village.

In late 2006 Lay-C heard on the radio that a hip-hop organization, with ties to North America and the capital Kampala, was starting a project to promote local hip-hop in Gulu. He went to the auditions with a rap verse he had written and was accepted into the project. A prominent Ugandan rapper led the workshops that followed, and the same week he and three other young people from Gulu recorded a rap song in the Acholi language and a music video. This was a generative moment for Lay-C, who now saw a future for himself as an artist on stage, knowing that the visitors would show his music video in Kampala and North America. But the relationship with the hip-hop organization did not last.

When Lay-C was working in the video library, he and the other young guys spent a lot of time simply waiting for customers to come and rent a film. Or they waited for the power to come on, so the computer would work. Or they waited for Jack, the owner, to come with the key and open the shop. While waiting, they invented their artist names. Abola called himself Lay-C and explained that he derived it from the famous American rapper Jay-Z because he liked his music and style of rapping. Jay-Z was from Brooklyn, had been abandoned early by his father, and had been involved in selling crack when he was younger. Later he became one of the most successful hip-hop artists in the world. In a sense, with this artist name, Lay-C was attempting to link himself with a line of kin other than his biological descent—to create a musical kinship.

Lay-C also took his name in a comment on the discourse of laziness and inactivity that surrounds young people in Gulu. To call himself Lay-C seems a metaphorical inversion of and resistance to the older generation's negative categorizations of youths but also a reminder to other young people not to be lazy. Lay-C himself says of the predicament of young people in Gulu that "the youth should be sharp, not lazy. They shouldn't be lazy; they should think ahead. So that they find their way out."

After months of courtship, Lay-C's girlfriend became pregnant, and he was now faced with new responsibilities. He was expected to provide for his girlfriend and coming child. He also had to pay some of the *luk*, the initial bridewealth, to his in-laws. Becoming a father, Lay-C acquired yet another name (a teknonym) and status: Wǒn Clara, meaning "the father of Clara." Around this time Lay-C stopped working at the video library, where music was blasting from big speakers at all hours, and singers and cool youths would come to cut CDs and rent movies. Through an uncle he got the job at the secretarial-services shop, which was also a photo studio, where local business people came to print, photocopy, and have passport photos taken for ID papers.

With his new status as a father, husband-to-be, and wage earner, Lay-C no longer had time to make music. Though he recorded some songs and performed in Gulu, his name as an artist had not taken him where he once wished to be.

Yet he still used his artist name and ranked his three names and their value according to how they associate him with the different spheres of his life: the *local* (childhood and family), the *civilized* (school and the new serious job), and the *international* (the hip-hop organization, night clubs, and the video library) realms. "When I am called Bol, that means I am at home, with my people, like the aunties and the uncles. So that means they're like, I am that real person they used to know. That's Bol. But now [*laughs*], when they call me Lay-C, that means they are taking honor, or like they are saying [about me], '[He is a] musician.'"

In public space, like his workplace and in the compound where he lives, others call him by his second name, his Christian name, Geoffrey. "When you call me Geoffrey I feel more like someone, *someone* who is, like, let me say, civilized, you understand? But then you are calling me, 'Eh, Abola!' [*laughs*] on the street. [That is] so local. And nowadays, most people don't want to be local. So when you call me Abola, that means it's like you are localizing me." When he is called Lay-C in the street, he says, "[I feel]very happy! Very, very good, and I feel like someone is promoting me again. Like my music, and [they] try to remind me of what I was doing. . . . I feel really good 'cause mostly now I use that [name] for my music, and I feel like that person is encouraging me more to continue with giving out the good messages to the people through that music." He keeps reminding others and himself that he still is—or rather could be—Lay-C in the future, as if he is keeping a door open for the potential to be realized if the opportunity arises.

Lucky: Abola David Wilson

Lucky was sixteen years old when we first met him. He was one of the young men hanging out at the video library where Lay-C worked. Lucky became friends with Lay-C when he was selling copies of his first music video to video libraries in town. Lay-C gave Lucky 5,000 shillings (about 2 USD at that time) to copy Lucky's video to the video library's computer. The two have since helped each other out in times of need, and in some ways Lay-C became Lucky's mentor. Lucky became the most productive and successful of the group of young men from the video library in terms of making and performing music.

Lucky's Acholi name is also Abola. He was told that when his mother was pregnant, she had a conflict with a neighbor. The neighbor had given her seeds for the garden but subsequently kept reminding her and other neighbors about the obligation to return the gift. The mother consequently named her baby Abola to "recall the neighbor's backbiting in the past." Lucky and Lay-C share the name Abola, but the name comes with different histories and meanings.

Lucky's Christian name, David, was chosen by his mother from a variety of suggestions given by visitors during the first days after the birth. Wilson was added when Lucky fell sick as a baby. At the hospital an American health worker named him Wilson because Lucky reminded her of her own son of the same name.

Lucky was the first-born child in his family. His father died when he was young, and the family suffered from his absence. Lucky, his mother, and Lucky's three siblings lived in a refugee camp thirty kilometers from Gulu. In times of hunger and scarcity, Lucky and his family moved out of the protected camps and back to their village to farm the land. Lucky was abducted by the rebels, or rather, handed over reluctantly by his mother, when he was seven years old and spent two years with the rebel army. After his escape, he returned to his family. His story of survival in the refugee camp and with the Lord's Resistance Army inspired his artist name: "You see, I *am* Lucky!" he proclaimed.

Later in his childhood he came to Gulu to stay with relatives, and as he grew up he saw less of his mother, who had started a business in Sudan. In Gulu he and his young siblings commuted to night shelters set up by an international NGO in the center of the town to avoid rebel attacks. Lucky joined the choir at the night shelter. Being in the choir was prestigious and made him visible to the aid workers in the shelter, opening up new opportunities, such as becoming a leader and taking part in NGO activities. In the singing and dancing lessons at school, Lucky was also one of the best. The recognition he won might have sparked his hope to become an artist.

As Lucky matured, he decided to try to get into the music industry and said about his name Lucky, "I chose it myself when I was about to enter the music industry, to start singing. I was thinking—people were telling me, 'If you are going into music you need to change your name.' I was like, 'Ah? How can I change?' . . . I'm Lucky 'cause I have passed from dead, when I was not even supposed to remain in this world."

After he adopted his artist name, he refused to answer to the old Abola because he wanted people to recognize his new name. His mother sometimes said that the artist name was "a joke," but when they were having fun and life was easy, she would call him "Lucky."

Like Lay-C, Lucky assigns different values to his Acholi name and his artist name:

> [There is a] very big difference. You know, when I am out and they are calling me Lucky David, I feel like I am now a big person. Because when I am out, I feel like people are respecting me. You know? . . . When you call me Lucky, I will see that "Eh, this guy likes me." So I will also give you some soft voice to answer your call. Eh! That one is a very big difference. 'Cause when you call me Abola, . . . I might say, "Mwong?" "Mwong" is like "What's it?" It doesn't sound good. . . . When you call me Lucky, I might say [*speaking softly*], "Yes, please?"

Like Lay-C's names, Lucky's names connect him to different times and spheres of life. Lucky was the primary provider for three younger siblings who needed school fees, since his mother had moved to Sudan. He struggled to continue his own secondary schooling and sat twice for his primary school exit exams. When Lucky was not in school because he had not paid his school fees, he was working as a singer, recording and performing in Gulu, and as a casual worker at a video studio, filming weddings and the like.

Since the time we met Lucky in 2008, he had gradually become more popular in northern Uganda and even in Southern Sudan. After distributing his first song, when he befriended Lay-C, he continued to pursue music and became affiliated with a music and video recording studio where he could record for free or at a discounted rate. The producers agreed to this because they believed in Lucky's talent and hoped he would promote the studio to other prospective clients. Sitting in his mud hut in December 2010 with Nanna, he and his younger sister Grace discussed the dynamics between the musical product and the name of the artist:

> Lucky: See, [here in northern Uganda] they don't think of these big, big artists [from the capital Kampala]. You know this video of "Ileng Calo Ature" ["You Are Beautiful like a Flower"]—you know the one we have made is selling me! . . . It's selling me like nothing [else could].
> Grace (*smiling*): People like it! . . .
> Lucky: See, so I'm becoming now, at least—
> Grace (*cutting him off excitedly*): You organize a show. . . . You go to Sudan, you'll get money from people. People like that song "Ileng Calo Ature." Ah! They *like* it. We stayed there, like, for one week, and—ah!—everywhere, every radio, [was] playing [it].
> . . .
> Lucky: I have never been there before. I don't know how my song got there.
> Grace: Even they don't know the Lucky David they are calling [for]. Everywhere [they say], "I want the song for Lucky David. Lucky David!" Eh!

In other words, the artist Lucky was called into being by fans in distant places, and this created new possibilities for becoming a famous singer and becoming Lucky. In media products like songs or music videos, sold in small video libraries like the one where we met Lay-C, Lucky, and others and played on radio, the name of the artist was promoted, and the calling of the name reflected who the bearer of the name *could be*. Later in the conversation Grace advised Lucky to "make himself scarce" and not let local music promoters use his name on posters and radio ads to attract customers for a music show. A person who was common would quickly lose his good name. In other words, she suggested that, by withholding his product—his performance and name—demand for him would rise. The making of the name and the time work involved was both a relational and an economic endeavor, as was also apparent from Lucky's remark about the song selling him.

In the following we explore some of the theoretical challenges that the kind of name making that Lay-C and Lucky do pose for the anthropology of naming.

Self-Naming as Time Work

The stories of Lay-C and Lucky show how names relate people to spheres of life and situate them in time. Here we have focused on the artistic names of Lay-C and Lucky; names that they themselves have chosen and actively invested in, both socially and economically.

As pointed out by Michael Lambek, writing about spirits in Madagascar (2006), self-naming is a rare kind of naming. Self-naming as a practice is described in a number of places (Bodenhorn 2006; vom Bruck 2006) and in different historical periods (Benson 2006), but it is always something unusual, the exception to normal naming practices. An example of this extraordinary practice of self-naming, which may be globally widespread, is artist names in contemporary creative professions. What makes these names stand out? What can these names do that other names cannot?

First, we have some thoughts on conventional naming practices, or personal names given by others. The naming of a child is one of the first and fundamental acts of sociality in a human being's life. Rituals that mark the entrance of a new member into society manifest that, through naming, persons are defined and identified as such by others (Pina-Cabral 2010, 2013). The "gift of a name" is what Pierre Bourdieu calls the imposition of a name, whether a noble title or a defamatory label, and one of the central "acts of institution." On the one hand a given name is a gift of sociality that inaugurates the actor's identity, while on the other hand it informs the actor in an authoritative way what she or he is and what she or he must be (1991: 121). The gift of a name thus is ambiguous in nature and powerful in effect (Bodenhorn and vom Bruck 2006).

Because names are usually imposed on us, the act of naming oneself, as described by Gabriele vom Bruck (2006) among Yemeni women, can be a way of breaking the social strictures imposed by naming. Consequently, self-naming may be seen by others as defiance and disrespect of those who gave the original name, and new names are obstructed, just as Lucky's mother jokes with his artist's name and does not fully accept it. Thus, the question is whether one can ever truly name oneself (Benson 2006). You can name yourself, but a name is effective only if someone else calls you by this name. What stands out clearly from our study in Uganda is that for self-naming to work the nominee needs others to recognize, legitimize, and use the name.

When the young singers in Gulu name themselves, they are working on the world through naming, attempting to use a dynamic between the name and what is named. They use, in other words, the potential that the world can be manipulated by the way we talk about it or name it, as the anthropologist

Michael Jackson puts it (2005: 79). They play with the magical power of words (described early on by Bronislaw Malinowski in the coral gardens of the Trobriand Islands, 1935: 233), believing that the idea or power in the name will somehow affect the world or transfer to the person.

The singers hope for a positive effect, similar to what Hacking calls "the looping effect" (1999: 160; 2006). Hacking describes the development of categories of various deviants in society, like the gay, the obese, and the child abuser (1998, 1999, 2004, 2006). He argues that interactions between the name (category) and the named (categorized) form a dynamic nominalism in which kinds of people come into being in the same processes by which they are classified and named (2004: 279–280). The process of naming a kind of people changes the possibilities of choice and practice for the people named. In turn, these choices and practices feed back into the meaning and possible meanings of the name. This is what he calls the looping effect, an interaction between the name and the named that creates subtle shifts in practices. In other words, "Making up people changes the space of possibilities for personhood. . . . Hence if new modes of description come into being, new possibilities for action come into being in consequence" (1998: 165, 166). Where Hacking deals with the making up of groups or kinds of people from etic perspectives, we are concerned with the making up of individuals from emic perspectives, but we nonetheless believe that the same kind of dynamic is at play in the young singers' self-naming practices in Gulu. When the young singers take artist names, they need others to use these names for the names to work and for their products to sell.

Our Ugandan musicians do not de- or rename themselves; they add another name to the ones they already have. They add another possibility of who they could be, another possibility of what kind of person they might turn out to be. There is an aspect of breaking with norms and perceived structures through a detachment from the old name and identity when they stand on stage or proclaim their name as Lay-C or Lucky David. There is an aspect of self-fashioning and paternal disavowal, described by Susan Benson among former slaves (2006), in taking artistic names. But this is also a matter of reaching out to future potential selves and unsettling—or at least bracketing—blocked trajectories to the future. The artist name becomes an anchor to a desirable modern future life in the city. This reaching is done when dreaming out loud about grandiose futures as big artists with the other boys at the video library and partly done in shiftings between the projection of their names and themselves. These processes take place in both strategically planned events in efforts to get a bigger name, like Lucky's performances, and more subtle situations, passing through the realms of everyday lives, like Lay-C using his name to connect to different contexts with different future potentials. It is these shiftings between whom they are and whom they could be that form the time work of self-naming.

Condensing Time in Acholi Naming

Ideals and practices of naming in Acholiland vary greatly, yet there are some interesting shared features across eastern Africa that are worth noting for our argument here. Common traces can be found in the old Nilotic literature (Girling 1960) and in contemporary Acholi naming practices. As described by Edward Evans-Pritchard for Nuer names (1940), Acholi names often correspond to or comment on the circumstances under which the child was born: for example, Atim, "born in the bush or far away"; Ocheng, "born in the day"; and Akech, "born during famine." Or the name may be a comment from or about the mother during the pregnancy, like Abola, when the mother felt rejected. A name may also describe the social position of the baby, like Apio, meaning "the first born of twins," or Ojok, meaning a "special child with spiritual powers." All these names may also be inherited as patronyms or matronyms, thus not describing the child or birth but a kin tie. Yet they all refer to the past in some sense or other. The names condense particular times.

After childbirth, the mother usually stays in the labor hut for several days, with the helpers. The first name is usually given by the mother when she is still in her labor hut. When the mother is about to take the child out of the hut, paternal and maternal kin come and suggest a second name for the baby. They knock on the door of the hut and say the names. The mother and her helper sit inside the house watching the baby at the mother's breast. If the child sucks the breast, it is a sign that the name has been accepted. We might say that there is a staging of the child being granted some agency in choosing the name. People say that a name should not be imposed on a child; it should suit the child. Christian and Muslim names are also suggested at this ceremony or may be chosen after the ceremony. The Christian names are often chosen to remember a friend or somebody the parents admire, such as a public figure or a movie star, or to indicate a foreign connection, such as a friend abroad, a Hollywood movie star, or the current president of the United States. Later on the child is given nicknames, which may depend on joking relationships or particular characteristics (e.g., Munno, "behaves like a European"). Adults acquire a teknonym when they become parents—for example, becoming the father of their eldest child (such as Lay-C becoming Won Clara, the father of Clara).

The Acholi practice of naming a child according to the circumstances under which it was born is a very explicit strategy to make another time (and place and atmosphere) present through naming. Inherited names are also ways of bringing a person and a time from the past into the present. Names have this capacity to bridge boundaries between the past and the future, the living and the dead (Bodenhorn and vom Bruck 2006). For the self and others the Acholi name is a tribal identifier, a reference when the name is heard to where the person comes from, which can hardly be escaped. The Christian and other given names also carry this aspect of history. "Individual lives thus become entangled—through the name—in histories of others" (Bodenhorn and vom Bruck 2006: 3) In this way Acholi names are central to becoming a person within a society; connecting to the past; referring to the mother's experiences at the time around the birth; remembering people in past events, times, and places; referring to the parents' aspirations on behalf of the child at the time of birth; and referencing histories of the clan and the tribe. As Barbara Bodenhorn and Gabriele vom Bruck write, names are entangled in histories and have the capacity to place the individual in time and in a set of social relations, but they suggest that names can also work in time in different ways (2006: 26).

Making Names: Working on the Future

Our contribution to this debate about how names are entangled in time emphasizes that names are entangled in not only histories but also futures in various ways. Names may condense time, as well as extend and open time into the "could be" subjunctive mode. Names have the capacity to facilitate memory, permitted a genealogical account of social time. We have seen how the individual life trajectories of the two young men named Abola are marked by name shifts that place the individual in historical time and in a set of social relations. But names also have the capacity to evoke possible futures, depending on being called into being by others.

Lay-C is making the past and future simultaneously present through his self-naming, both as Bex and as Lay-C. He is creating a kinship with the global icons that inspired him to pursue soccer and, later, music. The names connect him to international, high-profile soccer and the American hip-hop scene, anchoring him in a particular tradition and history.

Lucky took his name to remind himself of his history of luck. He did so before recording any songs and becoming famous but with the hope of being so in the future. The name condenses his personal history but also evokes a musical genealogy. "Lucky" is a name he shares with significant predecessors; it embodies desired musical trajectories into his future as a star. Since the early 2000s Lucky Bosmic Otim has been a leading singer in northern Uganda, and he in turn was inspired by the late South African reggae icon Lucky Dube. The name is therefore directed toward a specific future as an African singer with roots in reggae and Afropop.

By condensing the impossible future stardom into tangible objects, like CDs and DVDs with songs and music videos, Lay-C and Lucky are inviting others to buy into their dreams. Taking an artist name in this sense is an attempt to evoke a projection of who they might be. The artists hope that, when fans buy their products, the projection materializes and the artists can then make a living and continue to try to live up to the name they have proclaimed.

Names, we suggest, are entangled in futures, and the processes of making a name may be regarded as a kind of time work. The sociologist Michael Flaherty (2011) introduced the concept of time work, referring to the various ways humans preclude, craft, and produce certain temporal experiences. Flaherty makes a distinction between different analytical categories of actors' work on time: duration, frequency, sequencing, timing, allocation, and taking time (2011: 12). We see the creation of artist names in Gulu as a kind of future time work that condenses a desired aspect of the future into their names and their CDs and music videos.

Let us return to the opening of this chapter, when Lucky walked into our hotel with his new CD. The CD itself was a result of Lucky's ability to get others to invest in his future as a famous artist: others at the studio where he recorded, the photographer and graphic designer who made the CD cover, and the friends who contributed to the cost of recording the songs. At the same time, the CD condenses a desired future, with the name "Lu[c]ky David Wilson" written in gold letters across a photo of Lucky, with short, neat hair, posing and smiling confidently at the buyer or fan. He is wearing a red, shiny sportswear jacket with the sleeves rolled up above his elbows and a black leather vest, a reference to the singer Michael Jackson's iconic red leather jacket with rolled-up sleeves. The photo also shows the straps of a backpack on his shoulders. These two fashion statements express Lucky's potential: the red "leather" jacket shows how he could be a global superstar, while the backpack shows that he is truly part of the local, well-educated media elite and "working class," potentially carrying a laptop or other gadgets in the modern, fashionable backpack (and not on the head or in a plastic bag). After all, he is "Lucky," like the other stars named Lucky. Next to the smartly dressed young man, the album name and the CD's price of 150,000 UGX are stated in blue and black. Under the price it says "original audio," suggesting that this is not an ordinary CD from a CD-cutting shop, where songs are written on blank retail CDs. Rather, it is an *original*.

In the informal music economy of Uganda, songs circulate in networks of CD-cutting shops, like the one that Lay-C, Lucky, and their friends frequent. CDs that people buy are normally burned at the shop with a personal selection of songs, and a CD therefore usually starts as a blank, maybe with a title written in permanent marker (the cost of these is 1,500–5,000 UGX). Only a few artists from the central region in Uganda have more or less formal contracts with local music distributors, who press CDs with front images and sell them in jewel cases with cover images (usually sold in up-town supermarkets at 10,000–20,0000 UGX). There are no international recording companies in Uganda. While these CDs are considered more original and authentic than the CDs from CD-cutting shops, they do not earn the artists royalties when they are sold. Rather, they are original because they resemble the products of the formal music industries, like those of Jay-Z and other global stars. Thus Lucky's CD, presenting itself as an "original audio CD," suggests that he *could* be an artist with a name known all over Uganda, all over the world—a name big enough to sign a recording deal with an international recording company. With what the owner of the studio Lucky records in calls a "strong product," Lucky's CDs appear attractive when they are distributed to local radio stations. The airplay on radio makes Lucky's name known, as Grace said, in places he has never been. The quality of the songs and their messages, the styles communicated through the music, establishes Lucky David as a name in music when fans request the songs on air. The result of the airplay was that Lucky started getting calls from music promoters in both Gulu and the rest of northern Uganda to come and perform at their music variety shows. Promoters learned that Lucky gives energetic performances and is a skilled entertainer. Within a year Lucky had gone from earning 10,000–30,000 Ugandan shillings (4–12 USD) to earning up to 400,000 Ugandan shillings (160 USD) per show. The profits were invested in what Lucky described as "being a better person," like fashionable dress as seen on the CD front and gadgets and home décor like mobile phones, cameras, and a home theatre with DVD player, external speakers, and subwoofer (though Lucky's hut was not connected to the electrical grid). In other words, the profits of music went back into materially establishing the name and prestige of the artist Lucky David rather than directly attending to the material and social conditions of Abola, who lives in a mud hut and has to provide and pay school fees for three siblings and his own secondary school. The two names emplace the person in different times: Abola David is a rather unsuccessful person, in terms of following traditional trajectories toward respect and social recognition. He has not yet made it, has weak kinship ties (he has no father, his mother has abandoned her children), lives in rented huts without legitimate claims to clan land, and has missed many years of schooling, failing to progress toward adulthood in a linear fashion. He is out of time, somehow. But the same person, with a different name, Lucky David Wilson, the artist, has made it. He is an artist, making money from music, hanging out in nightclubs, bars, and other performance venues and in music studios. He has fans approaching him for friendship and favors, wears smart clothes, and shows off gadgets, and his music career enables him to help his siblings with their needs. The work that goes into the name in gold, Lucky David Wilson, has a looping effect, but it is an effect that depends on the social recognition of the potential of Lucky David. The time work of the artist's name is in many ways nonlinear, as both Abola and Lucky David, like Abola Geoffrey and Lay-C Bex, exist simultaneously. The time work is subjunctive in nature and involves an openness toward what might happen. It is a mood of action that involves uncertainty and doubt, as well as hopes and the potential of the future (Whyte 2002). And the direction things may take depends to a large degree on the relationship to the audience—will they invest in the his artist name and his products? Lucky's CD itself represents a kind of material subjunctiveness, an extravagant future hope embedded in a mundane everyday thing in the present. If the CD sells and the artist name becomes famous, it will be worth more than the CD itself. If the CD and the name fail to make it, it will be worthless. The CD is an object that depicts the future star Lucky David Wilson; it makes the audience aware that this person has a potential future as a star, someone whose name might be selling everywhere.

In quite another setting, among unemployed young men in urban Georgia, Martin Demant Frederiksen and Anne Line Dalsgård describe how a business card can be a "'hook into the future', manifesting a business which is yet to be. By making business cards they mimic something that does not yet exist, as the business card contains . . . hope of something coming into being, a not-yet that, although non-existent, provided . . . an incentive to keep striving" (Dalsgård and Frederiksen 2013: 51–52). The difference between Frederiksen's analysis and the one we have presented here is that a name more intimately *is* a person, not just the business of the person. The name is a virtual extension of the person (see Munn 1986), and CDs are objectified forms of the name, as if it were burned into the shiny plastic discs, depositing the future person on their hard, waiting plastic.

What we add to the discussion of the future time work and the condensation of time in names is a focus on the importance of relations to others: the names and the futures as stars can only be called into being if an audience, fans or customers, uses the artist names and buys their products (Bodenhorn 2006). The calling into being by others is most obvious during performances when the audience cheers the artist's name and creates a generative moment when the person singing actually becomes the potential of his or her adopted name. The potential is further actualized if after the performance the fans buy the products made by the artist. The importance of the audience for the future time work to be effective is painfully evident when the audience does *not* recognize the artist. Having named oneself with an artist name does not mean one has made it. A name can only work through others. The hip-hop organization that had initially sponsored Lay-Cs recordings did not settle in Gulu, and while Lay-C helped other singers and music producers by cutting CDs and giving advice, first in the video library and later, and less frequently, in the secretarial-services shop, they "left me behind in music," he says. Still, he keeps his opportunities open. His artist name still circulates among his friends in music, though it has not gained wide recognition, a recognition that depends on mediation by CDs, performances, radio air play, and music videos. His musical career has caused serious conflicts between Lay-C and his wife, as she suspects that Lay-C on stage will attract the wrong kind of attention from unattached women in bars and nightclubs. Being a mother, Lay-C's wife cannot accompany him into the nightlife, and his new role as father and husband seems incompatible with becoming Lay-C. But even if the artist name does not make it big, as in Lucky's case, it remains a subjunctive reminder in life, a reminder of what life could or would be like if he met success. Throughout both Lucky's and Lay-C's lives, traces of multiple futures keep appearing in the present.

Conclusion: Naming the Future— Calling the Potential into Being

In the realm of popular music in Gulu, young people can take on new names that condense the potential of the future. For the young men we have met, this is a desired quality in their artist name, as their future as social adults in society is jeopardized by their history and surroundings. They are breaking away from the reminders of the past, creating new possible public personas with flamboyant possibilities. They are creating new pasts and kinships with global popular music and the music industry associated with affluence. The possible names are not limited by ties to family and clan but depend on the creativity of the name maker when making up new relations to musical kin though the names. This allows the young singers to reimagine their potentials and futures (Weiss 2009). Traditional Acholi names, we argue, condense time by reminding one of something or someone from the past.

Though artistic naming is self-naming, the project of taking an artist name is not a self-project but rather a social project. An artist name works only if others call the artist into being. For the young and relatively unknown artists in Gulu, making a name is an economic endeavor, because they are making a living for themselves and often a large family of dependents. There is a concrete side to the informal music economy in encounters with gatekeepers like studio owners, producers, radio hosts, and music promoters, as well as with audiences of potential fans that the musicians have to manage. Making a name and being famous does not simply make life easier; the young artists also experience the pressure to maintain a name and to continuously perform fame, living up to the audience's expectations of an artist's affluence and lifestyle.

Whether the name and fortune of the new stars in Gulu will materialize and stay with them for life or falter and fade as the singers grow up or just grow older is an open question. Lay-C's future, for the time being, seems to be going in a different direction, that of being a father, earning money, and aspiring to working-class office jobs. Here an artist name may be a disadvantage rather than a benefit. Lucky's artist name and CDs have succeeded in Gulu and are spreading to other parts of northern Uganda and even Sudan, where his music is heard by many listeners, potential fans. Like many other young people in Gulu, both young men are continually looking for life—that is, opportunities to make a living. Other avenues may also open up for Lucky, or circumstances might force him to leave the music scene, which is, after all, uncertain terrain. Other young musicians are constantly coming up and trying to make a name in northern Uganda because music is one of the few options that talented young people have for making it. But they cannot make it on their own.

Our overall point is that creating an artist name is a form of objectifying time that works only through *relations*. It may be that all time objectified works through relations, but the relational aspect is particularly clear in the time work of names. Time is objectified—the future of the name (the artist) is written into material objects, such as a CD, in a subjunctive manner. The artist name and the artist are *not-yet* what the CD attempts to predict. Whether the artist becomes the potential of the artist name depends to a large degree on whether others—an audience—believe in the artist's potential and buy the product of the future. The relationship between the artist name and others is what may drag the future into being present.

ACKNOWLEDGMENTS: *We thank Tuulikki Pietilä for her fruitful comments and suggestions to earlier versions of this chapter.*

REFERENCES

Benson, Susan. 2006. "Injurious Names: Naming Disavowal and Recuperation in Contexts of Slavery and Emancipation." In *The Anthropology of Names and Naming*, edited by G. vom Bruck and B. Bodenhorn, 178–194. Cambridge: Cambridge University Press.

Bodenhorn, Barbara. 2006. "Calling into Being: Naming and Speaking Names on Alaska's North Slope." In *The Anthropology of Names and Naming*, edited by G. vom Bruck and B. Bodenhorn, 139–156. Cambridge: Cambridge University Press.

Bodenhorn, Barbara, and Gabriele vom Bruck. 2006. "'Entangled in Histories': An Introduction to the Anthropology of Names and Naming." In *The Anthropology of Names and Naming*, edited by G. vom Bruck and B. Bodenhorn, 1–30. Cambridge: Cambridge University Press.

Bourdieu, Pierre. 1991. *Language and Symbolic Power*. Cambridge, MA: Harvard University Press.

Christiansen, Catrine, Mats Utas, and Henrik E. Vigh. 2006. "Youth(e)scapes." In *Navigating Youth, Generating Adulthood: Social Becoming in an African Context*, edited by C. Christiansen, M. Utas, and H. Vigh, 9–28. Uppsala, Sweden: Nordic Africa Institute.

Dalsgård, Anne Line, and Martin Demant Frederiksen. 2013. "Out of Conclusion: On Recurrence and Open-endedness in Life and Analysis." *Social Analysis* 57 (1): 50–63.

Evans-Pritchard, Edward Evan. 1940. *The Nuer: A Description of the Modes of Livelihood and Political Institutions of a Nilotic People*. Oxford: Clarendon Press.

Flaherty, Michael G. 2011. *The Textures of Time: Agency and Temporal Experience*. Philadelphia: Temple University Press.

Frederiksen, Martin Demant. 2013. *Young Men, Time, and Boredom in the Republic of Georgia*. Philadelphia: Temple University Press.

Girling, Frank K., 1960. *The Acholi of Uganda*. London: Her Majesty's Stationery Office.

Goodfellow, Tom, and Kristof Titeca. 2012. "Presidential Intervention and Changing 'Politics of Survival' in Kampala's Informal Economy." *Cities* 29 (4): 264–270.

Hacking, Ian. 1998. "Making Up People." In *The Science Studies Reader*, edited by Mario Biagioli, 161–171. London: Routledge.

———. 1999. *The Social Construction of What?* Cambridge, MA: Harvard University Press.

———. 2004. "Between Michel Foucault and Erving Goffman: Between Discourse in the Abstract and Face-to-Face Interaction." *Economy and Society* 33 (3): 277–302.

———. 2006. "Making Up People." *London Review of Books* 28 (16): 23–26. Available at http://www.lrb.co.uk/v28/n16/ian-hacking/making-up-people.

Hansen, Karen Tranberg. 2004. "Who Rules the Streets? The Politics of Vending Space in Lusaka." In *Reconsidering Informality, Perspectives from Urban Africa*, edited by K. T. Hansen and M. Vaa, 62–80. Uppsala, Sweden: Nordiska Afrika Institutet.

Jackson, Michael. 2005. *Existential Anthropology: Events, Exigencies, and Effects.* Vol. 11. New York: Berghahn Books.

Lambek, Michael. 2006. "What's in a Name? Name Bestowal and the Identity of Spirits in Mayotte and Northwest Madagascar." In *The Anthropology of Names and Naming*, edited by G. vom Bruck, and B. Bodenhorn, 116–138. Cambridge: Cambridge University Press.

Langevang, Thilde. 2008. "'We Are Managing!' Uncertain Paths to Respectable Adulthoods in Accra, Ghana." *Geoforum* 39 (6): 2039–2047.

Malinowski, Bronislaw. 1935. *Coral Gardens and Their Magic: A Study of the Methods of Tilling the Soil and of Agricultural Rites in the Trobriand Islands.* Vol. 2, *The Language of Magic and Gardening.* London: Allen and Unwin.

Meinert, Lotte. 2001. "The Quest for a Good Life: Health and Education among Children in Eastern Uganda." Ph.D. diss., University of Copenhagen, Denmark.

———. 2009. *Hopes in Friction: Schooling, Health and Everyday Life in Uganda.* Charlotte, NC: Information Age.

Munn, Nancy D. 1986. *The Fame of Gawa: A Symbolic Study of Value Transformation in a Massim (Papua New Guinea) Society.* Cambridge: Cambridge University Press.

Nielsen, Morten. 2011. "Futures Within: Reversible Time and House-Building in Maputo, Mozambique." *Anthropological Theory* 11 (4): 397–423.

Pina-Cabral, João. 2010. "The Truth of Personal Names." *Journal of the Royal Anthropological Institute* 16 (2): 297–312.

———. 2013. "The Core of Affects: Namer and Named in Bahia (Brazil)." *Journal of the Royal Anthropological Institute* 19 (1): 75–101.

Ralph, Michael. 2008. "Killing Time." *Social Text* 26 (97): 1–29.

Sommers, Marc. 2001. *Fear in Bongoland: Burundi Refugees in Urban Tanzania.* New York: Berghahn Books.

———. 2010. "Urban Youth in Africa." *Environment and Urbanization* 22 (2): 317–332.

UBOS (Uganda Bureau of Statistics). 2006. *2002 Uganda Population and Housing Census Final Report.* Kampala: UBOS.

Utas, Mats. 2003. *Sweet Battlefields: Youth and the Liberian Civil War.* Uppsala, Sweden: Uppsala University.

Vom Bruck, Gabriele. 2006. "Names as Bodily Signs." In *The Anthropology of Names and Naming*, edited by G. vom Bruck and B. Bodenhorn, 226–250. Cambridge: Cambridge University Press.

Wadiru, Stella. 2012. "Sounding the War: Acholi Popular Music in the Peace Process in Northern Uganda." In *Ethnomusicology in East Africa: Perspectives from Uganda and Beyond*, edited by Sylvia Nannyonga-Tamusuza and Thomas Solomon, 177–188. Kampala, Uganda: Fountain.

Weiss, Brad. 2009. *Street Dreams and Hip Hop Barbershops: Global Fantasy in Urban Tanzania.* Bloomington: Indiana University Press.

Whyte, Susan Reynolds. 2002. "Subjectivity and Subjunctivities: Hoping for Health in Eastern Uganda." In *Postcolonial Subjectivities in Africa*, edited by Richard Werbner, 171–190. London: Zed Books.

Whyte, Susan Reynolds, Babiiha Mpisi, Rebecca Mukyala, and Lotte Meinert. 2013. "Remaining Internally Displaced: Missing Links to Security in Northern Uganda." *Refugee Studies Journal* 26 (2): 283–301.

Afterword

MICHAEL G. FLAHERTY

In societies dominated by tradition, the future resembles the present just as the present resembles the past. The people in these societies observe the rising and setting sun, phases of the moon, and recurring seasons. Thus, their experience of time is typically cyclical (TenHouten 1999). In modern and postmodern societies, however, there is a linear perspective on time. The prevailing assumption is that the future will be not only different but better. We are taught to plan for the future and bring about its realization. For the last five hundred years, these two orientations toward time have been colliding around the world as a result of two processes: colonialism and neocolonialism.

In modern and postmodern societies, moreover, time and emotions are closely related. We anticipate the future with "hopes and fears," not as disinterested onlookers (Schutz 1964: 282). This is especially true of that liminal period called youth. Young people have more days in front of them than behind them (or at least this is the socially constructed expectation—even in societies with high rates of mortality among youth). Characteristically, then, they look forward with anticipation and anxiety. A year is one-fifteenth of a fifteen-year-old's life, but it is one-sixtieth of a sixty-year-old's life. The mathematical relationship between age and experience affects our perception of time. It makes for the impatience of youth and their tendency to perceive time passing slowly as they await transitions to adult roles.

With globalization, problematic temporal issues increasingly afflict the youth of diverse nations in parallel ways. At home and abroad, this parallelism in temporal experience is an artifact of the dialectical relationship between two great social forces: structure and agency. Structure is implicated because time is, always and everywhere, a "social institution" (Durkheim [1915] 1965: 23). As such, it is "capable of exercising on the individual an external constraint" (Durkheim [1895] 1966: 13). The structural relationship between generations is a fundamental manifestation of time as a social institution. Members of a particular generation share "a common location in the social and historical process," argues Karl Mannheim, "predisposing them for a certain characteristic mode of thought and experience, and a characteristic type of historically relevant action" ([1927] 1952: 291).

Ironically, one characteristic form of action will be agentic efforts to oppose or change the structural arrangements a particular generation stands to inherit from its predecessors. Unlike Pavlov's dog, our behavior is not simply a product of our environment. By means of selective attention, "we open the door to certain stimuli and close it to others" (Mead 1934: 25). Our capacity for selective attention enables us to take a self-determined stance toward the demands of our social context. Anthony Giddens views this capacity for self-determination (or "agency") as an irrevocable attribute of human conduct: "It is a necessary feature of action that, at any point in time, the agent 'could have acted otherwise'" (1979: 56). It follows that we do not passively accept fate as victims of our temporal circumstances. On the contrary, we modify or customize various aspects of our temporal experience and resist external sources of temporal constraint or structure. I call such effort "time work" or temporal agency (Flaherty 2011: 3).

Structure and agency are the paramount themes that emerge from the studies in this book. These phenomena are often misrepresented in the social sciences as unrelated or even antithetical concepts, but the contributions to this edited collection make it clear that they are actually two aspects of the same process: social interaction. With structure, we refer to enduring patterns of interaction. With agency, we refer to self-selected forms of interaction. The preceding chapters examine people in different societies, but all of them are self-consciously concerned with time because, in one way or another, their temporal experience is problematic. Global processes confront the youth of these societies with common structural impediments to the realization of their hopes for the future. In response, they have developed diverse agentic strategies in an effort to adapt themselves to or challenge these temporal structures.

In what follows, I discuss major variations on the themes of structure and agency. It will become apparent that separating structure and agency in this fashion is an analytical fiction, but doing so helps us see underlying commonalties beneath superficial differences.

Structure

Enduring patterns of interaction are socially constructed, but no less real for that. Of particular relevance is the fact that, typically, they are not constructed by the people who now find their temporal desires thwarted by these structures. What is more, the elements of social structure are arranged like dominoes standing close together, such that pushing over the first one sets in motion a causal chain of subsequent effects.

With the transition from modernity to postmodernism, there is a profound change in the economy from production to consumption (Bell 1976). It is tempting to say that young people in Denmark "choose" to have fewer children (as if they could do whatever they want). Yet, once productive, children are now economic liabilities, and having them impedes one's ability to purchase the good life. In truth, young couples in Denmark (indeed, throughout Western Europe) are "choosing" the sensible path. As a result, the birthrate in Denmark is below replacement, which, as Karen Valentin shows us, leads to governmental efforts to keep Denmark competitive in the global economic system by importing labor. In turn, this policy creates opportunities for agentic emigration from Nepal. It is equally tempting to say that youth in Nepal can emigrate to any country, but the sensible path results in a hierarchy of options, and given its willingness to facilitate their education, Denmark is at the top of the list. We make agentic choices, but our choices are structured by the presence or absence of certain opportunities. In short, our choices are constrained by structure.

How do young people in Nepal know that Denmark will welcome them? How do the youth studied by Lotte Meinert and Nanna Schneidermann know that their lives in Uganda could be more successful? Why do Răzvan Nicolescu's teenagers in Romania know that their afternoons could be more exciting? Neoliberal capitalism requires an unfettered technological connectedness. This connectedness is part and parcel of a social context that occasions various types of temporal dissatisfaction. Globalization proceeds via trade, tourism, and telecommunications. Along the way, sophisticated forms of entertainment become commodities, and the global marketing of these commodities creates chronic dissatisfaction with what was, what is, what will be. One of the young men in Uganda, for example, tells Meinert and Schneidermann that he and his peers are no longer satisfied by the prospect of traditional lives within their "local" culture. The ceaseless creative destruction caused by global capitalism reduces cultural diversity and, as Jennifer Johnson-Hanks points out, makes for a social environment where everything is temporary. This restless and always provisional existence produces parallel forms of temporal experience in developed as well as less-developed nations. The upshot is that young people in the United States, like those in Cameroon, lead temporary lives while waiting for entry to real careers. We are witness to the globalization of time as a self-consciously problematic experience.

Global capitalism is concerned with the multinational maximization of profit, not local development. Martin Frederiksen reports that the Georgian government hires Turkish contractors for its reconstruction projects, and many of the workers hired by these contractors are also Turkish. In turn, these policies bring about high rates of unemployment in this region of Georgia, crushing the hopes of young people who live there. Similarly, a music company with representation in North America looks for talent in Uganda, but, for the vast majority of local young men, the lure of wealth and celebrity it offers is a mirage. Athletic organizations function in much the same way. Most of the people in this edited collection grapple with the fact that they cannot find adequate work. Unlike music and sports, education is touted as a sure path toward a rewarding career, but this is simply not the case in many underdeveloped nations, and it is increasingly uncertain in postmodern societies. The kind of education that changes lives is not available for most of the youth in Georgia and Manila. From Anne Line Dalsgård's research in Brazil, we learn how racial and ethnic discrimination makes access to education more difficult for dark-skinned segments of the population. There is primary and secondary education in Uganda, but not the tertiary education that leads to real jobs. Young women in San Francisco and immigrants to Denmark from Nepal purchase advanced educations, but they cannot find subsequent entry to full-fledged careers. In the United States, these young people are called "boomerang kids" because, unable to support themselves, they return home after their education is completed. Like their peers in Cameroon, they must wait for their mature lives to begin.

Our conclusions must be tempered by the complexities of these case studies. There are, it would seem, multiple vectors from youth to time objectified. In Steffen Jensen's Manila, Frederiksen's Georgia, Dalsgård's Brazil, Meinert and Schneidermann's Uganda, we see a lack of opportunity for schooling and jobs (often exacerbated by surplus labor and racial or ethnic discrimination). These factors lead to impoverishment and thwarted desires for the better future promised by modernity. In the studies by Valentin and Johnson-Hanks, children from the upper-middle class in Nepal and the

United States find it difficult to launch their careers, which forces them to endure the uncomfortable circumstances of a provisional lifestyle. In Stine Krøijer's Denmark and Nicolescu's Romania, the problematic experience of time is structured by one's place in the life course. Because of their age, the affluent students in Nicolescu's chapter lack autonomy, not employment, and consequently find that their schedules are constrained by external demands from parents and teachers. Likewise, the activists studied by Krøijer are too young for conventional participation in Denmark's governance, but their middle-aged compatriots are too old because, once they assume mature responsibilities, they no longer have time for political activism. These vectors can be related. Temporal norms in Brazil dictate that, at a certain point in the life course, a young man should have a job with which he can support a family. And, in Uganda, a pregnant girlfriend makes for incipient responsibilities and constrained choices.

Armed conflict is another structural factor that shapes the temporal experience of youth in many nations. While this factor is not universal, the studies in this edited collection certainly suggest that it merits our attention. Two types of armed conflict figure in the objectification of time. First, there is the organized violence of warfare. Armed conflict keeps Turkish tourists away from the redevelopment sites in Georgia, which contributes to unemployment. In Uganda, armed conflict brings about the forced recruitment of young men as soldiers and the massing of displaced people in refugee camps, where they cannot earn a living from the land. In Nepal, armed conflict impedes economic development and drives emigration to other countries. To the studies in this edited collection, we must add Javier Auyero's (2012) analysis of Argentina's state-sponsored violence against its own citizens. Second, there is the disorganized violence that spills out of urban areas beset by unemployment, poverty, frustration, and substance abuse. Some of this violence is gang-related, and therefore at an intermediate level of organization, but most of it results from interpersonal conflict among people with very little to lose. This type of violence confronts the inhabitants of Recife as well as the Philadelphia ghetto studied by Elijah Anderson (1999). Whatever form it takes, violence always narrows our attention on the here and now, thereby creating the sensation that time is passing slowly (Flaherty 1999).

Like Valentin, Auyero (2012) shows us how time is used as a tool in the regulation of people. These studies concern power and a politics of time. With its bureaucratic requirements, the state makes immigrants and its own citizens wait for all manner of social services. In so doing, the state constructs political dominance through control of people's time and temporal experience. By making immigrants and the urban poor wait for whatever they need, the state creates subordination and political resignation. Dispossessed of temporal autonomy, these people can only wait. A sense of powerlessness is neither a random nor a natural phenomenon; rather, it is cultivated by those in power. Moreover, these processes are not unique to Denmark and Argentina. The state-sponsored reconstruction of urban areas in Georgia disregards the pressing needs of unemployed citizens. In vain, they wait for governmental policies that actually improve their lives, and this powerlessness breeds a corrosive alienation. The young activists studied by Krøijer succumb to futility and alienation because the Danish state stands in the way of their desired future. What can the young women of San Francisco and Cameroon do about their circumstances except adapt as best they can to the reigning temporal regime?

On road trips, parents drive the cars while children, sitting helplessly in the back seats, can only ask impatiently, "Are we almost there?" Who waits? The one with less power or autonomy (Schwartz 1973). Youth waits. Prison inmates wait, as do the young unemployed men of Manila in Jensen's study. The citizens of Georgia wait for the bright future promised by their government. Nepalese immigrants to Denmark wait for visas, residential permits, admission letters, diplomas, and the careers promised by their education. Young women in the United States wait for the right opportunity, while their peers in Cameroon await whatever comes next. Young activists in Denmark wait for radical but unspecified change. The dispossessed youth of Brazil wait for a way to make a living. Students in Romania wait for their friends to get out of school (because their vaunted electronic devices are ineffective when those friends are unavailable). Young would-be pop stars in Uganda wait for the owner to open the shop where they work, wait for customers, wait for others to appreciate their music, and wait for success.

Waiting and boredom are different but not unrelated forms of experience. We may await the realization of our hopes or a dreaded fate. Typically, however, waiting is also boring. Boredom represents frustration with the present and self-consciousness in regard to the passage of time. It combines impatience with impotence. Benedikt Rogge (2011: 289–290) argues that, with modernity, excitement becomes a commodity as well as an expectation. He distinguishes between two types of boredom. Situational boredom results when one feels "constrained" by one's circumstances. Agentic boredom occurs when one "does not know what to do" with one's free time. Both types are evident in this edited collection. In Manila, Georgia, Brazil, and Denmark (among political activists), we see situational boredom evolve into apathy, inactivity, fatalism, and depression. Like young women in the United States and Cameroon, young men in Uganda cannot afford the excitement they have been taught to desire. We see agentic boredom among students in Romania, especially when they are alone. Young Nepalese immigrants to Denmark are the sole exception. As with middle-aged people, they do not have time to be bored (Flaherty 1999: 126).

Max Scheler ([1912] 1961) has established that widely dispersed members of a social aggregate can feel the same sense of resentment as a result of their separate reactions to common circumstances of discrimination or exploitation. His insight suggests that our emotions are neither private nor idiosyncratic. Thus, with Arlie Hochschild, we must conclude that emotions have a "signal function" in that they enable one to recognize the implications of an event or situation for oneself. Put differently, our emotions represent "a way of knowing about the world" (1983: 29). They signal what our circumstances mean for us. No one volunteers for waiting and boredom. Who puts up with such conditions? Only those who cannot rectify their circumstances. Unrewarded and endless waiting signals subordination and powerlessness. Chronic boredom signals that one's experience is insufficiently exciting or challenging. Unpleasant emotions are pervasive in this edited collection, and they are crucial to our understanding of time objectified. These studies reveal uncertainty, anxiety, futility, depression, misery, humiliation, ambivalence, loneliness, frustration, and disappointment. The temporal experience of youth is shaped by these emotions.

In concert, waiting, boredom, unpleasant emotions, and other kinds of suffering constitute a precise recipe for intensified time consciousness and the experience of protracted duration (Flaherty 1999). Hours, days, weeks, and months (the finite moments of one's life) appear to pass only with excruciating slowness. Standard temporal units become bloated by the dense experience of subjective involvement with one's plight. Time itself becomes the focus of one's attention and, thereby, a problematic object of consciousness. Time objectified is a form of temporal distress. Individuals perceive a troubling difference between what they have and what they want. Imbued with modern sensibilities, they long for a better life, but their desired future is out of reach or impossible to plan for, and tomorrow will be just like today.

People at diverse points in the life course may confront the objectification of time, but youth are particularly at risk for reasons that are at once nomothetic and idiographic. The inescapable predicament of youth is that they occupy a liminal space. They are neither this (children) nor that (adults); as Victor Turner puts it, "They are betwixt and between the positions assigned and arrayed by law, custom, convention, and ceremonial" (1969: 95). Be that as it may, the studies in this edited collection make a persuasive case that, because of global and historically specific dynamics, contemporary youth are especially afflicted by the objectification of temporal experience.

Agency

It would be most disquieting if youth simply resigned themselves to their temporal fate, but, of course, they do nothing of the sort. As Frederiksen and Dalsgård point out, time objectified is not the last domino in the causal chain. On the contrary, it is the domino that sets in motion countervailing processes. Motivated to redress their disagreeable experiences, individuals and groups develop innovative strategies for temporal agency, or "time work" (Flaherty 2011). Some of these practices involve intervention, whereas others require forbearance (Giddens 1979: 56). Some of them are ingenious and efficacious, whereas others are sad and self-destructive. Some maintain the status quo, whereas others challenge it. Some succeed, whereas others fail. Disregarding these particulars, all forms of time work represent self-conscious effort to modify, customize, or resist temporal structure.

The effort of time work is not entirely overt. There are cognitive as well as behavioral facets to temporal agency. Indeed, the individual may be engaged in time work despite there being little or nothing for the rest of us to see. To begin with, one must care about, plan for, or somehow orient toward the future. A different future must be envisioned before one can bring it into being. Yet this is no easy task when most of the people around oneself are ensnared by the problems of the present. In the United States, Angela O'Rand and Robert Ellis report that "lower-class youth . . . have a more circumscribed notion of future time than youth from the middle class and their outlook on the future is less systematically ordered" (1974: 53). Anderson adds that, within the desperate and dangerous circumstances of ghetto life, "some young people bereft of hope for the future have made their peace with death and talk about planning their own funerals" (1999: 135). With a constricted or fatalistic outlook on the future, one can only imagine replicating the past and the present.

Given such conditions, to believe in the possibility of an alternative future requires a leap of faith. Dalsgård's observations suggest that religious rhetoric can provide Brazilian youth with hope or optimism where there are plenty of reasons for pessimism. Her findings dovetail with Anderson's analysis of those who strive for decency in the midst of inner-city violence: "The family unit, often with the aid of a strong religious component, instills in its members a certain degree of self-respect, civility, and propriety and even, despite prevailing impoverished living conditions, a positive view of the future"

(1999: 144). An imagined future can motivate or guide one's conduct in the present. Individuals may choose to do something (or refrain from doing something) because it makes a particular version of the future more likely. Dalsgård and Frederiksen (2013) describe a young man in Georgia who has business cards printed for a business that does not exist. It is tempting to dismiss his behavior as self-delusional, but to imagine a different future for oneself is an indispensable step on the path toward temporal agency. From Meinert and Schneidermann, we learn that traditional naming practices in Uganda condense time by linking one's identity to the present (i.e., the circumstances of one's birth) or the past (i.e., one's predecessors in the kinship system). Likewise, self-naming condenses time, but, with self-assertive and insurrectionary intent, it does so by linking one's identity to a hoped-for future. Both of these naming practices represent temporal agency, but the former reproduces the status quo while the latter challenges it.

Time work can support or oppose social structure because temporal agency emerges from, and is conditioned by, existing circumstances. There is, then, an opportunity structure that makes specific forms of time work more or less feasible. Ann Swidler argues that one's culture provides "a repertoire or 'tool kit' of habits, skills, and styles from which people construct 'strategies of action'" (1986: 273). It follows that the resources for particular types of temporal agency will be available while others are not. Time work is contingent on the interplay between person and situation. It requires, for example, a certain level of self-efficacy that, as is apparent with Krøijer's activists, may or may not be on hand. They lack access to conventional political participation but have the "habits, skills, and styles" they need for public protests and improvisational communes. Why do young men in Uganda want to be singers and pop stars instead of lawyers and architects? At least in part, we can attribute their aspirations to recognition in the choir at school and the presence of a music industry.

Global dynamics provide young people parallel opportunities to accept or even advocate that which is temporary. The young women of San Francisco engage in time work by embracing the "flexibility" of temporary jobs, but, in so doing, they make a virtue of necessity. Their vaunted flexibility is illusory, as they cannot afford extended unemployment (Henson 1996). They adapt to their circumstances and bolster their self-esteem by celebrating provisional lives as au courant. Nepalese immigrants to Denmark have only temporary residence permits, and young men in Uganda strive for success by being multipurpose rather than evincing commitment to a particular career. With their related forms of adaptation, these groups bear a striking resemblance to the agricultural peasants of European feudalism whose time work consisted of becoming habituated to the new temporal regime of industrial capitalism (Thompson 1967).

Agency does not represent the triumph of self-determination. Choosing to conform with temporal norms is only a shade less agentic than choosing to resist them. It is apparent that some types of temporal agency involve personal or collective accommodation to existing cultural trends. As we have seen, one can elect to embrace or even celebrate a provisional life. This may seem to be a rational course, but it is certainly not the only path one can take. Indeed, we must acknowledge that temporal agency is not necessarily beneficial or even in one's own self-interest from a rational standpoint. To do so, we must broaden our understanding of time work to include a wide array of unsavory, disruptive, or even self-destructive forms of conduct. At first glance, such conduct has little or nothing to do with temporal agency, but closer inspection suggests that that is exactly what it concerns.

Tea Bengtsson (2012) has examined the relationship between boredom and risk-taking behavior among juvenile delinquents in Denmark. These young men confront the problem of boredom (or nothing to do) when they are in juvenile detention centers as well as when they are at liberty on the streets. In secure care, they seek to alleviate boredom by means of resistance to institutional rules. On the streets, they avoid boredom by participating in various types of petty crime. With Bengtsson, we must view *both* lines of action as time work, and we must also acknowledge some degree of irrationality in these endeavors. Resisting institutional rules can lengthen one's sentence in secure care; engaging in petty crime can get one sentenced to secure care. Either way, one spends more time in boring circumstances. Yet this rational calculus is less compelling for these young men than is *making their time* (in secure care or on the streets) more exciting, albeit temporarily so. To refrain from this temporal agency would leave oneself at the mercy of caustic boredom. Simultaneously, this behavior is and is not in one's own self-interest. It is misleading, then, to classify it as rational or irrational, for at the heart of the matter is the fact that "a person is a thing of which too much can be asked" (Goffman 1969: 42).

Outsiders often view the ghetto or barrio as a dangerous area filled with violence and drug abuse, but perhaps the most fearsome aspect of life in these places is the ubiquitous and dispiriting boredom. Robert Levine describes what one witnesses there: "Many of these people are unemployed, have little prospect of employment, and . . . almost no future time perspective." Consequently, the inhabitants (especially young men) "congregate loosely each day and wait for something to capture their interest. Their problem is not so much finding time for their activities as it is to find activities to fill their time" (1997: 95–96). By recognizing the exigencies of time work, we can discern that much of what outsiders find fearful about these places is, in fact, a by-product of efforts by the inhabitants to manage the contours of their own temporal experience. The studies in this edited collection provide valuable evidence for this interpretation.

Dalsgård reports that it is not unusual to observe public drunkenness on a weekday morning in the poorest *bairros* of Recife. Likewise, Frederiksen tells us that the young men of Georgia have recourse to drugs and violence as ways to mitigate their despair. With drugs and alcohol, one can customize temporal experience as a timeless stupor. With violence, one can transform empty intervals of time into exciting moments of danger and drama. Tragically, however, the young men in question are not just killing time; they are killing each other. If, in accord with Dalsgård and Bengtsson, we perceive drugs and violence as methods of escapism vis-à-vis the crushing boredom of poverty, then we must also realize that these forms of behavior, while not laudable, constitute variations on the theme of temporal agency.

What of affluent and educated youth who live in comfortable circumstances? We must not overlook the undeniable continuity between their time work and that of impoverished peers. Krøijer's youthful activists court violent (and exciting) clashes with the Danish police by participating in the squatters' movement and by cutting down the fence around a refugee retention center. Nicolescu's Romanian students interrupt the monotony of their lives by engaging in illegal (and exciting) underage gambling. Clearly, time work among these youth diverges from that of their impoverished peers, but cosmetic differences should not blind us to underlying commonalities that suggest the operation of generic temporal processes.

Drugs and violence are not the cardinal forms of time work in this edited collection, despite the frustrating and frequently desperate circumstances that youth confront around the world. Instead, we see them helping each other modify their mutual experience of time. Put differently, the predominant strategies for temporal agency entail often-ingenious efforts at social interaction—efforts that rely on interpersonal relationships of one kind or another. Pablo Picasso's 1905 painting *Family of Saltimbanques* provides haunting insight on the poignant and essentially social nature of human existence. His painting depicts itinerant circus performers in a nearly featureless landscape. The bleak environment offers few, if any, resources beyond their own attributes, yet they must do what they can to distract us (and each other) from dreary chores and looming mortality. The people with whom we associate are the *saltimbanques* in our own lives; we look to them for the stimulation with which to stave off boredom and despair.

To grasp the essence of religious experience, Emile Durkheim ([1915] 1965) distinguishes between the sacred and the profane. The sacred concerns participation in collective rituals and extraordinary social gatherings, while the profane concerns the individualized and routine work of making a living. Urban gangs are considered criminal rather than religious, but we must concede that they transcend individual existence with thrilling collective action, thereby transfiguring a blighted neighborhood into a glorious battlefield on which one can display courage, gallantry, and other virtues (Katz 1988). Gangs are thought to provide the individual with protection in a predatory environment, but through solidarity and pageantry, participation also protects the individual from empty and meaningless intervals of time. Jensen's research in Manila shows us how young unemployed men create fraternal organizations as a collective response to time objectified. With their initiation rituals, special costumes, secrecy, and illegality, they come to each other's assistance in averting the monotony and ennui of their impoverished lives.

Our relationships with others facilitate our time work. Every chapter in this edited collection describes young people striving to redress problematic temporal experience through innovative and consistently interpersonal processes. Seeking the solace of companionship, the young men of Georgia visit each other and establish brotherhoods in a joint effort to dispel their temporally induced misery. Youthful political activists in Denmark do not think of themselves as religious, yet "dead time" consists of individualistic and therefore profane intervals of futility and fatalism, whereas "active time" occurs during sacred and exciting moments during which they coalesce into an awe-inspiring collective entity. Through friendships in a social network, the young women studied by Johnson-Hanks find temporary positions in the corporate world with which to bide their time. Friends serve as role models and inspiration for how to spend one's own time in Brazil. The young men of Uganda need an audience that appreciates their music. In Denmark, Nepalese husbands and wives take turns going to work and school, which enables them to prolong their youthful status. And Romanian students who go online while peers are in school discover that, when their electronic devices cannot connect them with other students, these shiny machines deliver only a disappointing level of distraction. It is, after all, the *social* construction of reality (Berger and Luckmann 1966).

Human experience is characterized by self-consciousness. Unlike other creatures, we know our days are numbered. It follows that we care about our fate. The subjects in these studies are no different from the rest of us in that they are not rational actors. Their emotions shape the way they experience time, and knowing this, they manage their emotions with an eye toward temporal agency. Time work can be primarily cognitive or behavioral, but we frequently alter our temporal experience by changing our emotional experience (Lois 2010). Temporal agency demands effort (which is why we call it time work), and the outcome is uncertain. Hope and confidence, therefore, are prerequisites for taking the initiative to modify one's trajectory. These emotionally tinged feelings may seem insubstantial, but they can help one find a way out of the slums of Recife. Fraternal organizations in Manila manufacture a basis for masculinity out of whole cloth. In so doing, however, they substitute the pride and exhilaration of secret brotherhood for the despair of unemployment and poverty. Three Romanian girls, a clique of *saltimbanques*, gather in a park. Ordinarily, time is not under their control, and it weighs heavily on them. But they conjure joy by improvising a game from discarded trash, and with these moments of fun, alter their experience of time through the re-enchantment of the world. To be sure, the spirit they summon is only temporary, but that is true of every human endeavor.

As with other types of self-determination, temporal agency demands a mindful readiness to take advantage of any opportunity that presents itself. A necessary ingredient, then, is self-confidence concerning one's capacity to produce the desired effect. An orientation toward a possible or imagined future is as crucial as self-discipline and persistence. With a sense of self-efficacy, one chooses not to succumb to one's social location; one refuses to be a victim of circumstances. Doing so, however, often requires distancing oneself from that restrictive location—physically or mentally. One seeks a future elsewhere. In short, time work may be manifested as variations on a theme of migration. The obvious examples, of course, include those who leave Nepal and Mexico for Denmark and the United States. Less obvious but equally important are instances of mental migration, where individuals and groups distance themselves cognitively and emotionally from the here and now of local conditions in order to achieve personal transformations of one kind or another. In the way they think, how they feel, what they do, Cesar and Evinha have already left the *bairro*. For the young men of Manila, time spent with their fraternal organizations is a brief but sacred excursion from the profane facts of life. And self-naming practices among the young musicians of Uganda can be viewed as something akin to identity migration.

Caring about the outcome does not guarantee success. Temporal agency is typically interstitial, in that it transpires within the parameters of existing social structure without challenging or changing the status quo. From this standpoint, success is always temporary, and failure is not uncommon. Time work is, nonetheless, compensatory because it brings about the transient cessation of temporally induced anguish. For now at least, we hope to be pop stars, we cut down the fence, we take steps toward transcendent masculinity, we get away with exciting and illegal activity. In these studies, we repeatedly witness youth assuming a self-determined stance toward the temporal dictates of their social context, but success is usually ephemeral. Instead of structural change, there is individual adaptation. We return from the temporality created during time work as from an excursion, but the structural facts of life have not altered in the interim. The relief time work offers is typically fleeting, but to refrain from it would mean resigning ourselves to repugnant temporal experiences. Ultimately, the empirical dynamics of temporal agency confirm Erving Goffman's view of the human being as "a stance-taking entity . . . something that takes up a position somewhere between identification with an organization and opposition to it, and is ready at the slightest pressure to regain its balance by shifting its involvement in either direction" (1961: 320). Our ongoing efforts to maintain and resist social structure reflect the dialectical tension that is distinctive to human existence. We resist temporal structure but rarely change it.

REFERENCES

Anderson, Elijah. 1999. *Code of the Street: Decency, Violence, and the Moral Life of the Inner City.* New York: Norton.

Auyero, Javier. 2012. *Patients of the State: The Politics of Waiting in Argentina.* Durham, NC: Duke University Press.

Bell, Daniel. 1976. *The Cultural Contradictions of Capitalism.* New York: Basic Books.

Bengtsson, Tea Torbenfeldt. 2012. "Boredom and Action—Experiences from Youth Confinement." *Journal of Contemporary Ethnography* 41:526–553.

Berger, Peter L., and Thomas Luckmann. 1966. *The Social Construction of Reality.* New York: Doubleday.

Dalsgård, Anne Line, and Martin Demant Frederiksen. 2013. "Out of Conclusion: On Recurrence and Open-Endedness in Life and Analysis." *Social Analysis* 57 (1): 50–63.

Durkheim, Emile. (1895) 1966. *The Rules of Sociological Method.* New York: Free Press.

———. (1915) 1965. *The Elementary Forms of the Religious Life.* New York: Free Press.

Flaherty, Michael G. 1999. *A Watched Pot: How We Experience Time.* New York: New York University Press.

———. 2011. *The Textures of Time: Agency and Temporal Experience.* Philadelphia: Temple University Press.

Giddens, Anthony. 1979. *Central Problems in Social Theory: Action, Structure, and Contradiction in Social Analysis.* Berkeley: University of California Press.

Goffman, Erving. 1961. *Asylums: Essays on the Social Situation of Mental Patients and Other Inmates.* Garden City, NY: Anchor.

———. 1969. *Strategic Interaction*. Philadelphia: University of Pennsylvania Press.
Henson, Kevin D. 1996. *Just a Temp*. Philadelphia: Temple University Press.
Hochschild, Arlie Russell. 1983. *The Managed Heart: Commercialization of Human Feeling*. Berkeley: University of California Press.
Katz, Jack. 1988. *Seductions of Crime: Moral and Sensual Attractions in Doing Evil*. New York: Basic Books.
Levine, Robert. 1997. *A Geography of Time*. New York: Basic Books.
Lois, Jennifer. 2010. "The Temporal Emotion Work of Motherhood." *Gender and Society* 24:421–446.
Mannheim, Karl. (1927) 1952. "The Problem of Generations." In *Essays on the Sociology of Knowledge*, 276–321. London: Routledge and Kegan Paul.
Mead, George Herbert. 1934. *Mind, Self, and Society*. Chicago: University of Chicago Press.
O'Rand, Angela, and Robert A. Ellis. 1974. "Social Class and Social Time Perspective." *Social Forces* 53:53–62.
Rogge, Benedikt. 2011. "Boredom, the Life Course, and Late Modernity: Understanding Subjectivity and Sociality of 'Dead Time' Experiences." *BIOS* 24:284–299.
Scheler, Max. (1912) 1961. *Ressentiment*. New York: Free Press of Glencoe.
Schutz, Alfred. 1964. "Tiresias, or Our Knowledge of Future Events." In *Collected Papers*. Vol. 2, *Studies in Social Theory*, edited by Arvid Brodersen, 277–293. The Hague: Martinus Nijhoff.
Schwartz, Barry. 1973. "Waiting, Exchange, and Power: The Distribution of Time in Social Systems." *American Journal of Sociology* 79:841–870.
Swidler, Ann. 1986. "Culture in Action: Symbols and Strategies." *American Sociological Review* 51:273–286.
TenHouten, Warren D. 1999. "Text and Temporality: Patterned-Cyclical and Ordinary-Linear Forms of Time Consciousness, Inferred from a Corpus of Australian Aboriginal and Euro-Australian Life-Historical Interviews." *Symbolic Interaction* 22:121–137.
Thompson, E. P. 1967. "Time, Work-Discipline, and Industrial Capitalism." *Past and Present* 38:56–97.
Turner, Victor W. 1969. *The Ritual Process: Structure and Anti-structure*. New York: Aldine.

Contributors

Anne Line Dalsgård is an associate professor in the Department of Culture and Society at Aarhus University, Denmark. She has conducted long-term fieldwork in Brazil and published on issues such as motherhood, poverty, youth, temporality, and ethnographic writing. She is the author of the book *Matters of Life and Longing: Female Sterilisation in Northeast Brazil* (Museum Tusculanum Press, 2004).

Michael G. Flaherty is professor of sociology at Eckerd College. He is the author of *The Textures of Time: Agency and Temporal Experience* (Temple University Press, 2011) and *A Watched Pot: How We Experience Time* (New York University Press, 1999). His current research concerns the experience of time and temporal strategies in prison and other forms of confinement.

Martin Demant Frederiksen holds a doctorate in anthropology and is assistant professor in the Department of Cross-Cultural and Regional Studies, University of Copenhagen. He has conducted long-term fieldwork in the Republic of Georgia and published on issues such as urban planning, hope, crime, temporality and ethnographic writing. He is author of *Young Men, Time, and Boredom in the Republic of Georgia* (Temple University Press, 2013).

Susanne Højlund is an associate professor in the Department of Culture and Society at Aarhus University and author of *Childhood Constructions* (Barndomskonstruktioner: På feltarbejde i skole, SFO og på sygehus; Gyldendal, 2002). She has conducted fieldwork in Denmark and Cuba and published on issues such as institutional ethnography, home and homeliness, the anthropology of welfare, and food pedagogies and taste.

Steffen Jensen is a senior researcher at DIGNITY—Danish Institute against Torture in Copenhagen and associated with the University of the Philippines. He has published on issues of violence, gangs, vigilante groups, human rights, and urban and rural politics and on the relationship between security and development in rural and urban South Africa and in the Philippines. He is the author of *Gangs, Politics and Dignity in Cape Town* (University of Chicago Press, 2008) and editor of volumes on victimhood, policing, human rights, and security.

Jennifer Johnson-Hanks is associate professor of sociology and demography at the University of California at Berkeley. Her research interests include gender and life course; uncertainty, intentions, and action; and the relationship between culturally mediated experience and statistically identifiable patterns of behavior. Her most recent book, coauthored with S. P. Morgan, C. Bachrach, and H.-P. Kohler, is *Understanding Family Change and Variation: Toward a Theory of Conjunctural Action* (Springer, 2011).

Stine Krøijer holds a doctorate in anthropology and is an assistant professor at the Institute of Anthropology, University of Copenhagen. She specializes in activism, time, and performative politics and has conducted fieldwork among left-radical groups in northern Europe and indigenous peoples in the Ecuadorian Amazon. She is working on a monograph, *Figurations of the Future: Forms and Temporalities of Left Radical Politics* (Berghahn Books, forthcoming).

Lotte Meinert is professor of anthropology in the Department of Culture and Society at Aarhus University. She has carried out fieldwork and worked in Uganda since 1993. Her main fields of research include medical anthropology, education, human security, and temporality. She is the author of *Hopes in Friction: Schooling, Health and Everyday Life in Uganda* (Information Age, 2008).

Răzvan Nicolescu is a postdoctoral research fellow in anthropology at University College London. He obtained his doctorate from UCL in 2013 with a dissertation on boredom and social alignment in rural southeast Romania. Trained in both telecommunication and anthropology, he is interested in material and visual culture, consumption, media, and digital anthropology, especially in relation to emotions, subjectivity, and modernity. He is also interested in the Balkanic and southeast European spaces.

Nanna Schneidermann is a doctoral student in anthropology in the Department of Culture and Society at Aarhus University. Since 2003 she has worked with youth, social mobility, and generational mobility in Uganda. Her current research explores fame and the generative potentials of informal urban networks and economies among young people in the Ugandan music industry.

Karen Valentin holds a doctorate in anthropology and is an associate professor in the Danish School of Education at Aarhus University. She has conducted research in Nepal, India, Vietnam, and Denmark in the fields of education, migration, youth, and planned development.

Index

Absence, 8, 46, 65, 74, 93, 147, 177
Acholi names, 158, 161, 165, 171
Activism, 38, 58–59, 64–67, 71–75, 179
Affect, 9, 11, 14, 58, 70–72, 82, 92–94, 98, 113; economies of, 91; "swamp of," 105; transmission of, 100–101, 111
Affection. *See* Affect
Africa, 24–25, 37, 39, 93, 155, 165, 167
Agency, 3, 7, 9, 14, 18, 108, 110, 132, 165, 176, 182–188; and micromanagement, 100
Alcohol, 185. *See also* Drinking
Ambitions, 53, 134, 141
Anderson, Ben, 93–94, 99, 111
Anderson, Elijah, 179
Anxiety: compared to boredom, 8; as an effect of affection, 111, 113–114; as an effect of boredom, 142, 144, 146, 148, 181; about the future, 175; about young people, 156
Apathy, 6, 58, 60, 63–65, 67, 70–73, 75, 180
Architecture, 87–88
Artist names, 12, 16, 153–154, 157–159, 161, 163–164, 167–171
Atmosphere, 11, 82, 87, 91–94, 103, 166. *See also* Heterochronia
Auyero, Javier, 179

Batumi, Georgia, 15, 81–86, 90–95
Biochemistry, 11, 113
Bloch, Maurice, 49

Bodily function, 2, 144
Boredom: in Batumi, 82–83, 92–93; in Brazil, 101–102; in Denmark, 58, 76; in Manila, 42–43; negative effects of, 180–181, 184; in Nepal, 124; as objectified relation to time, 4–8; in Romania, 139–150; in Uganda, 156. *See also Buryong*; Inactivity; Waiting
Bourdieu, Pierre, 5–6, 41–43, 45, 50–51, 54–55, 141, 163
Bourgois, Philippe, 7–8
Brazil, 11, 15, 97, 100–102, 110, 178–180, 182, 186
Brennan, Teresa, 101, 111, 113
Buryong, 10–11, 15, 42–47, 50–55

CDs, 153–155, 157, 159, 167–171
Cole, Jennifer, 4
Communication, 12, 29, 142, 177; and technology, 140, 142, 149–151
Comparison, 4, 23
Condensing time, 12, 165, 167
Conrad, Peter, 7–8
Construction projects, 84, 86, 88, 90–91, 94, 178
Consumption, 8, 142, 148, 154, 177
Convergence, 10, 23–25, 29–30, 37, 39
Copenhagen, Denmark, 57, 59–60, 62, 66–68, 73, 75, 119

Creative strategies, 156
Creativity, 6, 18, 38, 170
Cultural schema, 25, 37–39

Dalsgård, Anne Line, 169
Dead time, 11, 15, 58, 60, 64–65, 67, 70–76, 186
Decay, 89–90, 110
Denmark, 58–59, 72, 118–135, 177–181, 183–184, 186
Depraz, Natalie, 98, 111
Depression, 1, 180–181; in Batumi, 11, 14, 81–83, 86–87, 91–92, 94; in Brazil, 16, 97, 99, 111, 113; in Denmark, 74–75
Dewey, John, 1
Disappointment, 8, 111, 181
Discernment, 113–114
Discontinuity, 2, 58, 65, 71, 75, 92
Documents, 1, 12, 120, 123–124, 133, 135
Dreaming, 164
Drinking, 48, 51, 61, 74, 82
Drugs, 83, 86, 97, 101, 107, 185
Durham, Deborah, 4
Durkheim, Emile, 140, 186
Dynamic nominalism, 154, 164

Economic change, 3, 30–31, 36–39, 121, 122, 125, 135, 177, 179
Education: and career, 37, 52, 156, 178, 180; cross-national similarities in, 23; homogamy of, 31; investments in, 117, 119, 130–131, 135, 141; marketization of, 122–123; and migration, 118–120, 125–127, 128–135, 177; opportunity for, 97, 155
Eisenstadt, Shmuel, 23
Elite, 10, 25, 46, 50, 167
Emotion: boredom as, 8, 44, 139–140, 142, 144, 146–147; and groups, 91; negative, 105–106, 114; and time, 2, 17, 98–100, 175, 181, 186–187. *See also* Feelings
Ethics, 16, 141
Ethnography, 16, 147
European Union, 59, 68, 122
Evans-Pritchard, Edward, 165
Excitement, 3, 7, 142–143, 146–148, 180
Expectations, 13; of artists, 171; of education, 120, 126, 131, 135; of excitement, 3, 145, 147–151, 180; of the future, 41; realignment of, 38; of young people, 175

Falseness, 105
Family: economic independence from, 156; economic status of, 2, 85–86, 101, 125, 128, 130–133, 142, 160; expectations of, 26, 51, 73, 119, 126, 131, 135, 155–156, 171, 179; and identity, 159, 170; migration and, 120, 125–126; size and composition of, 23; support of, 106–108, 114, 145, 158; values of, 63, 182
Fashion, 156, 168
Favela, 103–104, 108, 111–113
Fear, 42, 45, 51, 81, 105, 119, 143
Feelings, 99, 140, 143–144, 187. *See also* Emotion
Flaherty, Michael, 9, 43, 98, 114
Flexibility, 10, 13–14, 16, 26–27, 29–33, 35–36, 38–39, 183
Foucault, Michel, 87, 89, 146
Fraternity, 45–48, 50–51, 54
Frederiksen, Martin Demant, 8, 14, 25, 169, 183
Friendship, 107, 169, 186
Frykman, Jonas, 75
Future, 1–4, 10–12, 17, 28, 37, 39, 98–100, 154, 156, 175; and agency, 9–10, 43, 182–184; alternative futures, 27, 65, 124, 127; and control, 26, 84–85, 93, 164, 187; multiple futures, 25, 46, 94; and uncertainty, 2, 24, 30–31, 71, 76. *See also* Expectations

Gadamer, Hans-Georg, 7
Gaylin, Willard, 144
G8 protests, 64, 67, 70
Generations, 12, 14, 33, 85, 125, 155, 156, 176
Georgia, Republic of, 8, 11, 13, 15, 81–85, 87, 90, 93, 196, 178–180, 183, 185–186
Germany, 64
Giddens, Anthony, 176
Globalization, 3, 24, 37, 175, 177–178
Goffman, Erving, 188
Goody, Jack, 24
Granovetter, Mark, 34
Great Recession, 31, 36
Guyer, Jane, 28, 66–67

Habitus, 150
Hacking, Ian, 154, 164
Hage, Ghassan, 43, 103
Harvey, David, 15

Heterochronia, 87, 90, 92, 94
Hodges, Matt, 5
Holbraad, Martin, 9
Hope: and agency, 182–183, 187–188; for future self, 153–154, 164, 166–167; lack of, 11, 53, 87, 93–94, 110–111, 178; as linked to youth, 119; as material reality, 71, 169; and possibility, 41, 97–100, 155, 169; as prospective or deceptive, 10; rhetoric of, 13; and schooling, 117, 124, 126, 129; "spaces of," 15
Horizon, 7, 9, 32, 66–67, 92, 100, 134
Humphrey, Caroline, 88, 94

Identity, 37–38, 43, 50–51, 106, 126, 146, 163–164, 183, 187
Illegality, 48, 123, 186
Imagination, 9, 28, 84, 94, 100, 118, 123
Impatience, 5, 17, 175, 180
Imprisonment, 10, 15, 44
Inactivity, 4, 6, 17, 43, 156, 159, 180
Indeterminacy, 10, 17, 71–72, 76, 150
India, 11, 43, 120–121, 124–125, 127–130
Infrastructure, 33, 88–89, 94, 103, 111
Initiation, 3, 47–49, 51, 54, 186
Innovation, 2, 33, 146, 155, 182, 186
Internet, 9, 16, 29, 35, 64, 132, 142–143, 145–147
Intersubjectivity, 7, 101
Intimacy, 65, 150

Jackson, Michael (anthropologist), 6, 16, 164
Jackson, Michael (singer), 167
Jail, 45. *See also* Prison
James, William, 2, 5
Jeffrey, Craig, 43, 124
Judicious opportunism, 29–30, 35–36

Liechty, Mark, 118
Life course, 25, 120, 123, 127, 144, 179
Lifestyle, 3, 31, 36, 156, 171, 179
Lord's Resistance Army, 155, 160
Louw, Maria, 5
Love, 65, 67, 106

Maira, Sunaina, 123–124
Manila, Philippines, 42, 50, 52–53, 178, 180, 186–187
Mannheim, Karl, 14, 176

Marginalization, 11, 42–43, 45, 54. *See also* Temporal marginality
Marxist movement, 60, 65, 66
Masculinity, 49–50, 187–188
Massumi, Brian, 58, 70
Materiality, 2, 91–92, 94
Merlau-Ponty, Maurice, 14
Migration, 11, 23, 117–127, 132–135, 177, 179, 187
Mische, Ann, 98
Mistrust, 104–105, 113
Mobility, 4, 31, 102, 117–120, 126–127, 129, 132, 134. *See also* Migration
Modernity: and economy, 177; and education, 118, 178; and flexibility, 36; multiple temporalities of, 13, 15, 24, 28, 89, 92, 180; narratives of, 38; and regulations of the self, 150
Modernization, 117–118, 123, 129
Money: from connections, 105, 106; and crime, 104; for education, 129–133; and employment, 26, 52–53, 103, 156–157, 169; lack of, 82, 86, 130; promises of, 50
Music: and activism, 60, 68; as employment, 16, 86, 155–171, 178, 180, 183, 186; finding new, 34; as way to avoid depression or boredom, 83, 99, 143, 148
Music videos, 153, 155–158, 162

Navaro-Yashin, Yael, 93
Nepal, 11–12, 117–135; armed conflict in, 121–122, 131, 179; postconflict, 122–123
Normativity, 139, 143, 147, 149–150
Northern Uganda, 153–155, 158, 161–162, 167–168, 171

Objectified time. *See* Time: objectified
Open-endedness, 10, 17
Opportunity: and boredom, 7, 141, 143; for education, 118–119, 124, 126–127, 130, 177; for employment, 34, 38, 170–171; lack of, 83, 97, 122, 134, 178; and social change, 140; and urban space, 15

Parent-child relationships, 85, 106, 110, 149, 180
Pedersen, Morten Axel, 9
Peer group, 42, 47, 98, 143–144, 146–150
Philippines, 10, 15, 42, 46–47, 49, 54

Place: of action, 71; and affect, 113; character of, 108–111; and potential space, 144; in society, 63; and time, 87–89, 94, 98, 120; and violence, 104, 106; workplace, 155, 159
Police: in Brazil, 15, 102–103, 106, 114; in Denmark, 10, 57, 59, 62, 64–65, 67–71, 74, 185
Politics, 58, 62–63, 67, 73, 75, 179
Popular music. *See* Music
Postconflict areas: Nepal, 122–123; Uganda, 155
Potentiality, 71, 146
Poverty, 42–43, 45, 101–102, 179, 185, 187
Povinelli, Elisabeth, 63–64
Power, 50, 54, 67–70, 123, 179; political, 46, 65
Powerlessness, 65, 180–181
Prison, 10–11, 15, 17, 43–45, 54, 86, 145–146, 180
Projectivity, 98

Racism, 60, 74
Rationality, 2, 9, 13, 30, 39, 129
Recife, Brazil, 3, 101, 179, 185, 187
Recognition, 17, 50, 54, 101, 148, 161, 169–170, 183
Reflection, 1, 6, 36, 57, 59, 113, 140
Reich, Robert, 31
Resettlement site, 42–44, 47, 53–54
Responsibility, individual, 4, 54, 106, 110, 131
Revolutionary movements, 46, 59, 66
Ritual, 46–47, 49–51, 54, 163, 165, 186
Rogge, Benedikt, 180
Romania, 9, 12, 17, 140–142, 177, 179–181, 185, 187
Routine, 6–7, 13, 45, 62, 66, 103, 186

Sacrifice, 49
Scandinavia, 11, 58
Scheler, Max, 181
Schonberg, Jeff, 7
Schooling. *See* Education
Secrecy, 48, 186
Self-consciousness, 144, 180, 186
Self-esteem, 183
Self-naming, 153–154, 157, 163–166, 171, 183, 187
Seremetakis, Nadia, 89, 92
Sex, 61, 111
Slums, 187

Sneath, David, 9
Social adulthood, 3, 12, 14, 25, 125–126, 169. *See also* Transition
Social change, 3, 5, 73, 84
Social interaction, 119, 176–177, 185
Social media, 140, 142, 145–150
Social networks, 35, 73, 148, 186
Social relations, 17, 67, 119, 139, 141, 147–150, 154, 166, 171, 176
Social structure, 42, 177, 183, 187–188
Space. *See* Place
Ssorin-Chaikov, Nikolai, 89
Students, 27, 29, 59, 72, 118–119, 122, 130, 133, 181, 186; category of, 123–126
Subjectivity, 11, 111, 120–121, 127, 142, 144, 181
Subjunctivity, 4, 29–30, 32, 34, 39, 154, 166, 169, 171
Svendsen, Lars, 17, 148

Taussig, Michael, 13
Technology, 34–35, 118, 132, 140–143, 147, 151, 158
Teenagers, 10, 12, 16–17, 140–150, 177
Temporal desires, 11, 177–178, 180–181
Temporal distress, 92, 181
Temporal experience, 1–3, 5–6, 9–16, 167, 176, 178–179, 181–182, 185–188; of activists, 75; and affect, 98–100; of fraternity, 50; of migrants, 124
Temporal figure, 2, 4, 6, 72, 76
Temporality, 15, 30, 32, 42, 49–50, 67, 98–100, 118, 120, 134–135. *See also* Temporal experience
Temporal marginality, 8
Temporary lives, 25, 124, 133–134, 178, 183
Thrift, Nigel, 93
Time: being outside of, 15; biographical, 120, 125, 135; bureaucratic, 123–124, 132–133; historical; 14, 87–89, 120–121, 123, 135, 166; objectified, 1–2, 4–6, 8, 12, 17, 24, 54, 76, 81, 88, 98, 171, 181–182, 186; politics of, 179; wasted, 129
Timelessness, 89, 92
Time work, 1, 9, 176, 182–187; avoiding negative surroundings as, 114; involvement in fraternity as, 43; as relational, 12, 16–17, 154; self-naming as, 163–165, 167, 169–171
Timing, 3, 31, 36, 120, 167

Tradition, 5, 33, 36, 46, 75, 110, 166, 175, 183
Transition: to adulthood, 3, 12, 25, 102, 175; and migration, 125; and modernity, 177
Transnationalism, 23, 118–119, 123, 125–126

Uganda. *See* Northern Uganda
Uncertainty: as causing "fatalism of the present," 102; and distrust of others, 106; about the future, 1–3, 54, 114; as linked to youth, 119, 181; as normal, 10, 29–39; writing about, 17
Underemployment, 44
Unemployment: in Batumi, 81, 85, 91, 178, 179, 180; in Brazil, 101, 110, 112, 179; in Cameroon, 37; in the ghetto or barrio, 184; in Manila, 41–43, 54, 180, 186, 187; in the United States, 37, 183
United States, 10, 23–26, 30–31, 33, 35–38, 178
Urban space, 15, 46, 81, 92–94, 156

Varela, Francisco, 98, 111
Verdery, Katherine, 88
Violence, 44, 48–49, 70, 102, 104, 113, 179, 182, 184–185
Vom Bruck, Gabriele, 163, 166

Waiting, 4–5, 17–18, 175, 179–181; in Cameroon, 10, 24, 27–28, 36, 38–39, 178; in Denmark, 11, 58, 63–64, 73, 75–76; in Manila, 42–43, 45, 50, 53–54; in Nepal, 123–124, 132–133; as normalized, 35–36; in Romania, 9, 143; types of, 15; in Uganda, 156, 158; in the United States, 10, 24, 26–27, 30, 35–36, 38–39, 178. *See also* Boredom; Inactivity

Yaoundé, Cameroon, 25, 28, 34, 36
Youth: negative categorization of, 58; and organizations, 60–61; studies of, 2–4, 10, 14, 175–177, 180, 182. *See also* Students; Teenagers